Australia: The Last Frontier

Australia:
The Last Frontier

JOHN GREENWAY

Dodd, Mead & Company
New York

994
G816a
1973

This book was originally published in Great Britain
under the title of: *The Last Frontier*

First published in the United States 1973
ISBN: 0-396-06535-X
Library of Congress Catalog Card Number: 72-12440
Printed in the United States of America

TO SUSAN,
WHO WAS A PIONEER ON BOTH FRONTIERS

Contents

Australia: The Last Frontier

ONE

Yankee-Land Down Under

Go into the Australian West and you go into the past. Yet wherever you go, however remote in distance or in time, America and its own West intrude. About five years ago, during the second of my five expeditionary visits to the continent beneath the Southern Cross, I went to the edge of the Old Stone Age with a party of Australian scientists to study the water metabolism of the aboriginal natives in the hope of determining how these most primitive of people had adapted their bodies to survive in conditions of extreme heat and aridity. One particularly hard day, when the temperature stood at 120° in the waterbag, I sat in the red dust of the dead heartland trying desperately to convince myself that I was in the same world as my university halfway around the earth and that my unrequired presence there was not in itself sufficient grounds for certifiable insanity. Except for the main body of natives nomadically camped near the half-dozen tin-and-transite shacks of the government station twenty-five miles away, our party of seven white men and two dozen natives was the largest group of human beings in two hundred thousand square miles of desert so barren that, as the Australians say, you could flog a flea across the plain and see him every time he jumped.

The adult natives were asleep in the sand, unmindful of the bush flies and the red iron dust settling in their eyes and ears, but a handful of children played in our waterhole and hunted for gecko lizards to trade for hard candy from the 'lolly jar'. I had recorded some of the strange mythic songs from their parents earlier in the day, and since the tape recorder was still set up, I asked the children to sing some of their songs for me – *Tjitji inka!* They gathered around the microphone, naked except for the bush flies, knowing no word of English except 'lolly', never having heard a radio or seen a movie or television; yet after a moment of conspiratorial giggling, they sang out, loud and confidently:

> Daby, Daby Crocka,
> Kingada wile frontee.

This was the second time that 'Davy Crockett, King of the Wild Frontier' had impressed upon me the fact that Australia and America had been following a parallel course of cultural evolution for nearly two centuries. Ten years earlier in a more civilized part of the country I had found a remarkable example of independent invention – white Australian schoolchildren composing parodies of Tom Blackburn's great frontier song, just as American children were doing ten thousand miles away:

> Born on a tabletop in Joe's Cafe,
> Dirtiest place in the USA;
> Killed his mother with a poisoned cup of tea
> And shot his pa with a .303.

Sometimes it takes more than coincidence to explain the parallels in the cultural development of the two countries. While my Pitjandjara children were singing 'Daby Crocka' in the central Australian desert, American movie-goers were laughing at *The Russians Are Coming*, a comedy about the hilariously absurd heroics of a small American coastal town seized by the pretentious illusion that it had been selected by a Russian naval force for invasion. At the same time, in the South Australian city of Adelaide theatre audiences were reliving with the same enjoyment Ralph Petersen's play, *The Night of the Ding-Dong*. Quite independently conceived, researched, and written, *The Night of the Ding-Dong* dealt in the same way with the same theme – except that in Australia's case, the incident was real.

In 1839 one of those heroes unaccountably forgotten by history, Charles Wilkes, eased his American warship silently through the Heads into Sydney Harbour while the young city was asleep. A notorious thumper (later, in the Civil War, his piratical capture of the Confederate emissaries Mason and Slidell brought England within a Lincolnian apology to invasion of America), Wilkes put the question direct to the Australians the next morning when the residents of the nation's tiny chief city awoke to find themselves defenseless under the guns of a foreign power: 'What if I had been a hostile instead of a friend?' The Sydneysiders began almost immediately to throw up a fantastic network of fortifications around their Harbour. It took them a while, of course, because Australians proceed carefully in construction projects, but they finished quickly enough when the Crimean War made it seem more than a possibility that the Russians were coming. Every visitor to that beautiful bay has seen the most unlikely of those installations, Fort Denison, rising out of the middle of the harbour like a great stone warship. Until the Russian scare, it used to be Pinchgut Island, the Australian Alcatraz, where the worst of the early convicts were deposited until the blazing antipodean sun had burned their mischievousness away.

In Adelaide, the locale of Petersen's comedy, the reaction was delayed until solid rumour had assured the South Australians that a Russian naval squadron was indeed prowling the Indian Ocean. With magnificent arrogance, the defenders of Adelaide built Fort Glanville around two 20-ton cannons that could pulverize anything that might venture into their three-mile range. Fort Glanville today is buried up to its parapets by the sands of the Gulf of St Vincent and its two cannons lie impotently on the roof. Nothing is visible of the fort from the beach it once protected, but it is still there – a landmark in the strange history of America's influence on its great neighbour in the South Pacific. As for Captain Wilkes, having terrified Sydney, he sailed away to the south and discovered 53 degrees of Antarctic territory. Properly named Wilkes Land, it eventually was given to the Australians by the Americans, a gift of more than a million square miles that amply expiated whatever debt Wilkes and his countrymen felt for scaring the Sydney settlers. This was a small enough affair, little known to Australians and less known to others, but it does serve to illustrate what Mark Twain said about Australian history – 'It does not read like history, but like the most beautiful lies'.

Australia was both an invention and a discovery. Of the two processes, the discovery was the lesser, of no more moment than Wilkes's butting through the Antarctic fog. Many men stumbled upon the country in the two centuries preceding its invention, but all ignored it in their search for something better. But one of the several unpleasant consequences of the American colonists' filial tantrum in 1776 was their obstinate refusal to accept any more convict migrants from the mother country, and England had to find some other hellhole as a dumping ground for the criminals who had piled up in English jails and prison hulks by tens of thousands during the Revolution. Australia came quickly to mind. Its very name, 'New South Wales', was a recommendation, for was not Wales the land of thieves?

From the time of its first contact by English mariners, the southern continent was unanimously condemned as being good for nothing, and so it seemed an ideal dumping-ground. In 1787, when British hope of regaining its American trash-heap was abandoned, the Australian *Mayflower*, the 'First Fleet' of eleven small ships, sailed off with a cargo of convicts 'totally abandoned and calloused to all sense of shame and even common decency' to establish an impudent new world.

After the establishment of the penal colony, England decorously withdrew, like an accidental mother depositing an unwanted baby on someone else's doorstep. The first criminals sent to America in the days of Sir Walter Raleigh had vanished; 746 felons transported to Africa in the early years of the American Revolution had entirely disappeared; so why should not the Australian transportees shuffle off in the same considerate manner? They would have done so, certainly, had it not been for American whalers, sealers, and other maritime merchants who supplied the colony in its first two decades of struggle.

This is not to say that the American merchantmen worked the South Pacific for love of people who but for the grace of George III would have been Americans. Altruism is like gold: much valued but little found. Help was just something to fill the holds on the outward voyage. Once the American saviours arrived at the new sealing grounds it was every nation for itself. The Sydney *Gazette* of New Year's Day, 1804, recounted the 'unexampled inhumanity' of the American Captain Percival toward an Australian crew impudent enough to set foot upon his island. Percival was followed in that year by Captain Amasa Delano, who clubbed Australians as eagerly as he clubbed seals; there are some who think that Delano's peremptory enterprise was passed unaffected to one of his posterity – Franklin Delano Roosevelt. But perhaps the worst of these freebooters was William Henry Hayes, affectionately known as 'Bully' Hayes, a late comer to Australian exploit and therefore a marginal operator in whatever enterprise seemed profitable, legal or illegal. He came to Australia in a stolen ship in 1857, ill trained to the sea by his father, a Cleveland saloon keeper, but well trained to punch and grab. Though his most notorious professional occupation was 'blackbirding' – the kidnapping of Polynesian men for slavery in Queensland – he also was a pirate at times, and when business was slow, he trouped with a Christy Minstrel show. A practicer of sequential polygyny whose wives mysteriously and conveniently disappeared, Hayes was ultimately killed in a fight, to go down in history as the staid *Sydney Morning*

Herald judged him, 'one of the greatest scoundrels that ever went unhung'.

Americans continued to befriend Australians nevertheless, just enough to keep the friendship strong but never so much as to incur the perverse resentment of debtors that marred later adventures in foreign aid. It helped, too, that the American interference was often displeasing to the British government. One of the first governors of the new colony, Sir Philip Gidley King, complained to England, 'I am sorry to say that if the most decided Checks are not given to the Introduction of Americans and American vessels, any benefit this Colony may possess would become the property of Americans at the expense of England.' It was an accurate prophecy, but not to be fulfilled for a century and a half. More immediate was the American intrusion into political matters – specifically, rescue of Irish and Scottish rebels now known in romantic history as 'martyrs'. Four of the seven Irish Potato Martyrs (to give them a name less pretentious but more accurate than that by which they are usually known) got out of their Australian exile one way or another and settled in the United States. They did not all prosper in Yankee-Land, but it was better than being hanged, drawn, and quartered. One of them, John Mitchel, persisted in political mischief after making his escape to America by supporting the Confederacy and giving two sons to the South. Playing his cards rather better was Thomas Francis Meagher, who organized 'Meagher's Irish Brigade' for the North and was promoted to brigadier general in a year. After the war he was appointed Acting Governor of the Montana Territory by President Johnson, but with traditional Irish perversity found some way to get himself drowned during the journey to the mountains.

Far more famous in a country that for its own reasons admires Scots more than Irishmen were the five Scottish Martyrs, whose rebellious thinking was fired by reading Thomas Paine's *Rights of Man*. Their leader, Thomas Muir, escaped from his Australian captivity in the American ship *Otter*, reputedly sent for the purpose by General George Washington. British warships prevented the *Otter* from landing Muir in America, and he died in Paris appropriately enough in 1799, the same year of Washington's death.

When astronaut John Glenn saw his path across the night sky blazoned by all the lights of Perth, he could not have known that one reason that lovely western city threw up its bright welcome was the memory of what one American whaler did for their blokes on Regatta Day in April of 1876. On that occasion the *Catalpa*, out of New Bedford, nosed quietly into the harbour south of Perth and took off the colony's six leading Fenian prisoners. Sympathy for the Irishmen and gratitude for the Americans were enormous, as a street ballad of the time declared:

> So come all of you crew warders and gaolers,
> Remember Perth Regatta Day;
> Take care of the rest of your Fenians
> Or the Yankees will steal them away!

These things were important to Australians establishing the emotional basis of their history, and so they were remembered: to the Americans they were trivial adventures, and so they were forgotten. At the beginning of the nineteenth century Captain Edward Riou was a hero in war second only to Nelson and in peace second to none; his heroism in the tragedy of the Australian convict transport *Guardian* put his name in folksong – 'Riou was a gallant man; heigh-ho, Riou'; but by the middle of the century American sailormen had persuaded themselves the song had something to do with the Rio Grande, up whose turbulent currents no capstan ships plied:

> Away you Rio! Way, you Rio!
> Sing fare you well, my pretty young girls,
> For we're bound for the Rio Grande!

This historical friendship between Australians and Americans helped smooth the course of environmental determinism, a process having much to do with the parallel development of the two frontiers. When other factors are equal, similar organisms will behave in similar environments in similar ways. The history of America and Australia is a chronicle of frontier conquest, carried on by largely British migrants and their descendants across largely similar environments; and though there were permutations of numerous differences, these basic similarities produced similar histories. As with any valid principle of biological, physical, or cultural movement, what is true for the whole is true for any of its parts. With the Rio Grande in mind, we can look into so small a matter as attitudes to inland sailors. The first American West was opened by the Erie Canal – a great accomplishment, surely, but not one to submerge its navigators with either water or glory. Dozens of satirical folksongs were composed to ridicule the fresh-water sailors who manned mule-powered canal boats at the breakneck speed of four miles an hour:

> Ten miles out of Syracuse
> The vessel struck a shoal,
> And we like to all been foundered on
> A chunk of Lackawanna coal.

The only inland waterway to the Australian West was – and is – the Murray-Darling river system, and there, too, men took a similar view of the achievement. One of these Murray River folksongs tells of the intrepid Captain Bill Jinks, who defied fate and the elements by hurtling his ship through the stormy night, heedless of his crew's pleas:

> 'Goodbye to our maidens, the girls we adore;
> Goodbye to our friends, we shall see them no more!'
> The crew shrieked with terror and the captain he swore;
> We had stuck on a sandbank, so the crew walked ashore.

Gold, greed, and far more competent mariners than Captain Bill Jinks brought the two countries together in a reciprocal migration never again equalled. When gold was discovered in California in 1848, Australia received the news before some parts of the United States, because Australia was closer to California than New York if distance is measurable by time of travel. The first gold-rush vessel into San Francisco from Sydney made the run in just over two months, bringing many Australian prospectors into the goldfields before most Americans had arrived from the eastern United States.

By the end of 1850 more than ten per cent of Sydney's population of 60,000 were digging in the California mines – a circumstance that caused great anxiety among Australian officials already worried about the precarious state of the colony. Newspapers dutifully printed rhymed admonitions:

> Then pause, ye heedless voyagers
> and shun the golden snare;
> Oh, listen to the warning voice
> that cries beware! beware!

And the 'whingers', as Australians term their chronic complainers, sent back a more compelling dissuasion:

> When you start for San Francisco
> They treat you like a dog;
> The victuals you're compelled to eat
> Ain't fit to feed a hog.

But easy wealth still attracted Australians and soon there was a substantial colony of emigrants in San Francisco, concentrated in 'Sydney Town'. These were the more practical-minded of the Australians, who stayed in that booming port to ply the trade for which they were best suited – robbery – while the majority of their fellows went out to the Mother Lode to dig honestly and uncertainly for gold. Though Australians generally have had little impact on American history, the 'Sydney Ducks' made 'Sydney Town' into the Barbary Coast, the most notorious criminal district in the history of the United States. As the introspective, guilt-prone

Puritans set the ethos for American civilization generally, the Sydney Ducks set the style for early San Francisco and the goldfields. They were criminal autocrats, absolute masters of their district. Police approached the area with trepidation. However, a few arrests were recorded; of the first sixteen men arrested in San Francisco by the end of 1849, twelve of them were from Sydney. But for the first hundred murders there was not a single execution.

The Ducks imported an idea probably learned from the Australian natives – the device of burning down an area to be exploited. The aborigines set fire to an area to collect the rats and lizards thereby revealed and immobilized; the Sydney Ducks set fire to San Francisco for more sophisticated scavenging.

It is a principle of social organization that the amount of civil disorder permitted will be maximal in a stable society; on the other hand the tendency to maximal disorganization in man the animal inevitably pushes him to the limit of his society's tolerance – which limit of course cannot be determined until it is exceeded. Then the disorder is stopped, along with the luxury of law with which society amuses itself in times of tranquillity. So it was for the Sydney Ducks. Five devastating fires spread across the city from the Australian district, all at times when the wind was blowing away from Sydney Town; outrages occurred until, ironically enough, two Australians were accused in one of the most remarkable cases of mistaken identity in American criminal history. Their trial for murder triggered among the town's substantial citizens a response to the printed appeal of the influential Samuel Brannan:

> Law, it appears, is but a nonentity to be scoffed at; redress can be had for aggression but through the never failing remedy laid down in the code of Judge Lynch. Not that we should admire this process for redress, but that it seems to be inevitably necessary.

A Committee of Vigilance was formed and took its first action by arresting one of the most notorious of the Ducks, John Jenkins. Though Jenkins's reputation was entirely adequate to justify hanging in their time of civil disorder, Brannan's vigilantes put themselves to considerable effort to ascertain that Jenkins was guilty of robbery. Jenkins and the evidence were examined on the evening of 10 June 1851, his conviction and imminent execution were announced at midnight, and two hours later he became the first Australian to be lynched in the United States. Both the distinction and the lesson were wasted on him, however, for he hanged still expecting the whole of Sydney Town to march out and rescue him. The Sydney Ducks did indeed retaliate by setting San Francisco afire once more, to which the Committee of Vigilance reacted by hanging three more Ducks. This convinced the Australians that the Committee's intentions were serious, and Sydney Town was for practical criminal purposes evacuated, becoming thereafter merely a district of colourful vice.

Among the thousands of honest but poor Australian migrants was a man whom history chose in its mindless arbitrariness to be great – Edward Hammond Hargraves. Though his story will be told in another place, he must be mentioned here as the man who turned the tide of gold migration back to Australia, a tide that carried with it a great flotsam of American prospectors. According to the tale he told later while recollecting in tranquillity, it was his perspicacity in noticing that the Mother Lode country looked strikingly like the land around Bathurst in his own country that took him back to Australia to discover its gold. Dull fact suggests instead that his disheartening failure to find gold in California set him complaining that there was probably more gold back home. By 1850 he had convinced himself that it was true, and he returned to prove it.

Dull fact records also that Hargraves found no more than tuppence worth of gold in Australia either – and even that was found by someone else – but the time was right for an Australian gold rush, and like other discoverers and inventors who cannot sustain the most elementary scrutiny, he was given credit for an inevitability to save profitless argument about precedence.

In any event, it was American gold that took Australians to California in 1849, and in 1851 Australian gold took Americans to Victoria, where they behaved about as loathsomely as everyone expected. Hundreds of books had by that time been written by English visitors to America about the odious habits to be found in that benighted country – principally, judging by the regularity of complaint, the filthy custom of chewing and spitting. The American in Australia packed his vices with him:

> He lounged at billiard tables, tenpin alleys, and hotels,
> And smoked cigars six inches long with other white-
>   washed swells,
> Or chewed his cake tobacco, and by General Jackson
>   swore,
> Expectorating on the furniture, but seldom on the
>   floor.

American equipment came in with the ten thousand Americans digging Australian gold by 1853. Thousands of Australian miners worked in California shirts and California hats, dug with California shovels and sluiced gold in California cradles. And they carried California pistols in their belts to spread the sort of behavior that George Horatio Derby observed in a Californian camp:

> All night long in this sweet little village
> You hear the soft note of the pistol
> With the pleasant screak of the victim
> Who's been shot pre-haps in his gizzard.

The authorities tried to curb what they maintained was American-exported lawlessness by declaring all gold the property of the Queen, and decreeing that it could only be mined by those who had bought a license. They also brought in London bobbies (called 'traps') to enforce both the licensing act and a preposterous law against liquor in the goldfields. The evidence bears out the authorities' fear of the Americans' generosity in exporting rebellion and inciting action to make the world safe for mobocracy. Even Mark Twain during his visit to Australia later in the century violated the rules of proper response to hospitality by condemning the licensing act as a tax 'in its worst form . . . for it was not a tax upon what the miner had taken out, but upon what he was *going* to take out – if he could find it'. No doubt that thought had come to the minds of other men who remembered a war fought ostensibly on the issue of unfair taxation. A folksong still remembered and sung in Australia, 'The Maryborough Miner', has an American feel about it:

> Oh, yes, the traps have trailed me
> and been frightened out of their stripes;
> They never could have caught me,
> for they feared my cure for gripes;
> And well they knew I carried it,
> for they had often seen
> It glistening in my flipper, chaps,
> my patent pill machine.

Eventually the simmering protest of the miners exploded in the only political insurrection in Australian history – an event comparable to the Boston Massacre and, like that spark in the gunpowder of revolution, a disorder that should have been put down with a fire hose. As the Boston Massacre began with idle louts throwing snowballs and stones at the British soldiers, the Battle of the Eureka Stockade began in a drunken brawl outside the Eureka Hotel in Ballarat. Around this nucleus the miners gathered by hundreds and finally by thousands as the police encouraged excesses by restraint. The miners' 'rollup' was directed principally by an Irishman, Peter Lalor, brother to one of the 1848 Irish Potato Martyrs and an educated nuisance. Doubtless he believed in whatever liberating purpose the Eureka assembly had – though the fact that his father had been a member of the British Parliament and three of his brothers emigrated to America to fight on different sides of the Civil War makes one doubt the profundity of his commitment – but the rebellion was an aimless exercise in gratuitous violence. A stockade was built to shouts of 'Taxation without representation is robbery' and other American revolutionary slogans altered with an Australian twist. The barrier was manned by as many as a thousand men whenever weekends and other inducements to drink took the Australians away from their work. Two hundred of the thousand were members of the Independent California Rangers' Revolver Brigade, the worthies who were on sentry duty and who fired the first shots heard round the barricade when the government troops moved in to clear out the place on the first weekend of December, 1854. Like the affray at the Alamo, the fighting was over in a few minutes, the barricade was broken down, and the rebels were apprehended. But the facts of history have little to do with the truths of history, and the Battle of the Eureka Stockade became in those few minutes an immortal part of the glory of the Australian past. The American consul, James M. Tarleton, purified the incident for the Australians by inducing the authorities to release all the involved Americans except the negro, John Joseph, who was thereby allowed to reincarnate the figure of the Boston Massacre's Crispus Attucks. Joseph came out of the affair better in the short run at least than Attucks; he was the first of the Eureka rebels to be tried for treason, and by playing Stepin Fetchit to the court he inspired someone to remark that it was a sad day for Australian liberty when its defence had to be put into such hands. Joseph was acquitted and so were the next ten to follow him into the dock. At that point the government abandoned further efforts to hang someone for the bloody insurrection. Australian romantic historians still make as much of the episode as Americans make of Lexington, though few sully its nativistic purity by noting that 'Eureka', like 'Jim Crow', 'California Gulley', 'Yankee Hill', and similar diggings, imported its name from California.

Although he was far too astute to yield to heady temptation when the risk of failure was so nearly certain, it is very likely that the fabulous George Francis Train momentarily considered the offer made to him by the American leader of the Eureka rebellion; that for supplying $80,000 worth of revolvers to the embattled miners he would be declared President of the new Australian republic they planned on setting up. Even if the scheme had been feasible, it is doubtful that so varied an entrepreneur as Train would have imprisoned his energies and imagination within so restricted a position as a national presidency.

George Francis Train, born in Boston on the 24th of March, 1829, introduced ten-pin bowling and its associated evils to Australia when he arrived in Melbourne as a business agent in 1853. He also introduced the first Concord coaches; American buggies, shovels, hoes, and 'tinned' (canned) foods; organized the first Melbourne fire company, with two fire engines from Boston; built the first important building (across the street from the Flinders Street Railway Station, which presently is being restored at a cost of $112,000,000); imported an entire six-storey warehouse from America; opened a tea trade in Sydney; started forty clipper ships to California; smuggled $2,000,000 worth of gold out of Australia; sold anything anybody wanted and a great deal they didn't want; talked Freeman Cobb into beginning Australia's most famous coach line and lent him the money to get it going; and made a legitimate net income of $100,000, in his first year. 'The country was so full of chances,' he said later, 'and I should have been stupid, indeed, not to have availed myself of them as far as possible.' After exhausting the Australians and their enterprises by 1855, Train went on to build the first street railways in England and the United States, to help organize the notorious *Crédit Mobilier* and the Union Pacific Railroad, to write a dozen books, to run for President of the United States, to grab $30,000,000 worth of lots in Omaha, and to go around the world in eighty days two years before Jules Verne wrote up the accomplishment in his novel. In 1902 he dictated his autobiography in a New York flophouse, promising therein to double his age through 'psychic telepathy'. He gave up the effort two years later, and died certified as a lunatic. Vernon Parrington certainly underestimated the man when he dismissed Train as a mere 'crank'.

With such energetic neo-colonialists as Train running loose across Australia, it is not difficult to see why the young nation became a Yankee-Land under the thin façade of British government. To have even a defeated candidate for the American Presidency working in an emerging nation is risky enough for native integrity, but to have a successful one is dangerous indeed. Train ran for office on the nut ticket, which only seldom prevails; Herbert Hoover ran as a Republican, which gives its candidates a better chance. But that apotheosis came later in Hoover's career; in 1897 he was in Australia following the western gold as Train a half-century earlier followed the eastern gold. Five years after two prospectors took a tomahawk and hacked out five hundred ounces of gold in one afternoon on the eastern edge of the western Australian desert at a place the aborigines called 'Coolgardie', the London mining firm of Bewick, Moreing, and Co. sent this young mining engineer named Herbert Hoover to inspect their new acquisitions in the district. When Hoover arrived, he found the Coolgardie mines petering out, though his invention of the filter press, which permitted the re-use of water, an extremely expensive commodity, kept his company's operations profitable until the richest field in Australia, the 'Golden Mile' of Boulder-Kalgoorlie, opened new areas for exploitation.

The Boulder-Kalgoorlie vein extended in a ragged line northwest into the heartbreak country of the western desert. Hoover followed it until, at its terminus, he came upon a promising dig called 'The Sons of Gwalia' by its Welsh owners. On Hoover's advice his employers bought it, and he was appointed the mine's manager at a salary of $10,000 a year – with nowhere to spend it. Water was as valuable as gold; Hoover confessed in his *Memoirs* that he grew two cabbages in his tiny garden at a cost of $250 apiece. 'I built a corrugated iron residence under the shadow of Mt Leonora, one of the highest peaks in Western Australia,' Hoover recalled. 'It rose 160 feet above the plain.' When I photographed that house from the dizzying heights of Mt Leonora through a telescopic lens in April of 1966, scavengers were taking the last of the rusted machinery out of the long-abandoned Gwalia mine.

Hoover left Australia in 1899, but his mine went on to produce $55,000,000 before all the mines in the billion-dollar line dried up. The other mines are closed now, and their towns are dead, with only a 'White House Hotel' or 'Denver Hotel' left to recall the days of glory and to sell memory-eroding liquor to the few white inhabitants too apathetic to waltz their matildas to greener pastures. As civilization moves out, nature moves back in, as it has done in the Colorado mining country, and as it always will in untended frontiers. I saw one aborigine chase another with a spear one block from the centre of Kalgoorlie, still Western Australia's second city; and in Leonora grass grows in Hoover Street, as the Democrats warned us in 1932. Hoover's influence on Australia was much less than that of Train, but no invidious comparisons should be made between the two men. Hoover has been maligned quite enough by a needful history as the evil genius who contrived the Great Depression in his own twisted mind. The anthropology of the matter is that frontier development is a complex interaction between the established environment and an intruding culture; in Hoover's case, the technological evolution of mining culture had not progressed sufficiently seventy years ago to extract the incalculable wealth still underground in the western deserts of Australia. Hoover had no more to do with his failure to match Train than he had to do with the Great Depression. Had he come a half century later, Hoover might have been J. F. Thorn, the California mine engineer who introduced startling new methods into gold extraction; three quarters of a century later he might have been Julius Kruttschnitt, Tom Price, or any of a hundred other American mining experts who are rapidly making Australia into an incredibly rich producer of minerals. But then he might have done less in politics, like Walter Rice, the representative in Australia of Reynolds Metals, who was appointed American ambassador to Australia by President Nixon in 1969.

The idea that what diffuses most readily from one culture to another is the spiritual rather than the material, the ideal rather than the real, the worthy rather than the worthless, is an admirable delusion. It would perhaps be pleasant to believe that what America was most anxious to give Australia and what Australia was most anxious to receive from America was philosophy, wisdom, democracy, and elevated ideals of that nature, but what actually filled the bills of lading in both directions across the Pacific were things to gratify the animal instincts and desires of the frontiersmen. Instead of philosophers the lists of passengers outward and inward bound were prospectors and pugilists, entrepreneurs and entertainers.

Since frontiers quickly strip off the unnatural incrustation of civilization, the migrants most beloved in Australian folklore were the boxers, the most elemental practitioners of aggression and greed. Having contributed to the senseless uproar myself, I can affirm the occurrence if not the reason for what was perhaps the most joyously riotous event in American-Australian history – the heavyweight final bout in the 1956 Olympic Games in Melbourne, when the graceless, ham-fisted American Rademacher knocked the favored Russian Moukhine out through the ropes with his first artless punch. Other United States fighters fared less well in Australia; the Negro Jimmy Lawson killed Australian Alick Agar during an exhibition in 1884, an accomplishment that put an end to bare-knuckle fights in Australia and got Lawson six months in prison. Even wearing gloves, the Americans did nearly as well; the California Athletic Club in Castlereagh Street, Sydney, a notorious venue for fistic violence, was closed down in 1893 after the deaths of two boxers.

It would be impracticable to mention all the American boxers who fought in Australia and thereby helped direct the course of Australian sports interest, for when all other worlds were conquered – or when no other worlds could be conquered – an American fighter would tour Australia to make a few quid by thumping the locals. Fairly frequent success by the locals against fading American champions encouraged emigration of Australians to the United States, where victories were harder to obtain. The best of the émigrés was probably Albert Griffiths, 'Young Griffo', unforgettably described by ring historian Nat Fleischer as 'the Fastest Thinking Brainless Boxer in the history of pugilism'. Young Griffo took a record of 82 straight victories from Australia to the United States in 1893 and there won twelve more before losing to Jack McAuliffe, world lightweight champion. Another unbeaten Australian fighter, the heavyweight Bill Squires, shipped for America in 1907 and was knocked out in the first round of his first fight. Paddy Slavin, a Queensland pole-splitter before becoming a professional fighter, was among the best fighters of his weight in the world when he emigrated to America; he wound up as sheriff of Dawson City in the Klondike. Without question the most famous of the Australian pugilistic emigrants was Les Darcy, a Maitland middleweight who knocked down all before him in Sydney until beaten by the visiting American Fritz Holland. Darcy was unprecedented in his popularity until 1917, when, instead of volunteering for military service as every other able-bodied Australian man had done, he stowed away on a ship bound for the United States, hoping for a chance to fight for the world championship. Despite the fact that this made many of his countrymen turn against him he has attained the final accolade of being immortalized in at least a half-dozen folksongs, of which the following, sung with love, anger, and sorrow, is typical:

> In Maitland cemetery lays poor Les Darcy,
> His mother's pride and joy, Australia's bonny boy.
> All we can think of each night
> Is to see Les Darcy fight;
> How he beats 'em, simply eats 'em
> Every Saturday night!
>
> The critics by the score said they had never saw
> A boy like Les before upon the stadium floor.
> Oh, the Yanks called him a skiter
> But he proved himself a fighter,
> So they killed him – yes, they killed him,
> Down in Memphis, Tennessee.

In fact Darcy never fought in America (he was rubbished as a draft-dodger and denied any matches) and he died of *Streptococcus Septicemia, Septic Endocarditis Lobar Pneumonia*, as my certified copy of Darcy's death certificate puts it. Yet Darcy's place in the romantic history of his country is such that criticizing him is the only way an American can goad the ordinary Australian to any expression of feeling against the United States – that and of course any criticism of the great racehorse Phar Lap, which we did poison.

The chronicle of migrating bashers is almost interminable. Even John L. Sullivan toured Australia – but in the safer trade of acting: he played in *Honest Hearts and Willing Hands* as a blacksmith.

Although Americans are not pleased by the fact, no product of the United States can approach its entertainment as a wanted commodity. This is an observation true not only in Australia but over the entire world. While American astronauts walked on the moon Moscow demonstrated its disinterest in accomplishments of capitalism by showing an American motion picture on television. And it is not absence of sophisticated taste that sets Pitjandjara children to singing 'Daby Crocka'; all Australia follows the lead of America in the one thing Americans are superbly good at. That bell-wether of profitable enterprise, George Francis Train, was a more reliable guide to the inevitable direction of Australian cultural development than the intellectuals of either country: he invested in visiting American theatrical shows and cleared his usual large profit.

The great unending wave of American actors and entertainers to Australia came in on the tide of gold. C. B. Thorn and his wife brought a very popular theatrical company to Australia in 1853, and in the following year the American actors Joseph Wyatt and the Wallers, husband and wife, opened the famous Prince of Wales Theatre in Sydney. They were joined by Edwin Booth in the same year, but Booth, peddling cultural theatre, found himself stranded without his return fare. Train gave him a free passage home and remembered years later that this brother of Lincoln's assassin was one of the few ungrateful men he had befriended. Tragedians had their *succès d'estime* then as now, but, it was the minstrels who made the money. For most of the nineteenth century the minstrel show, innocent in the absence of negro minorities, was nearly the only form of musical variety to occupy the Australian stage, challenged in popularity only by circuses and straight comedy.

A comedy purchased from a California gold prospector brought the Americans James Cassius Williamson and his wife Maggie Moore to Australia and began two immensely successful careers. The play, *Struck Oil*, occupied the Australian stage for half a century and elevated Williamson from playing the part of a bloodhound in an Australian production of *Uncle Tom's Cabin* to being the progenitor of the theatrical family that today controls absolutely all stage entertainment in Australia. Maggie Moore had success not only with

31

Williamson, but on her own. Born Margaret Sullivan in San Francisco, she married Williamson in 1873 and shared his stage and his successes until their divorce in 1899. She had a few notable adventures on her own, such as her singing duets with Richard Ashe, subsequently infamous for having murdered three of his fellow prospectors and getting caught trying for a fourth. Maggie Moore toured the world as a nomad of the stage after her divorce from Williamson, but she always regarded Australia as home. In 1924, two years before her death, all Australia celebrated the fiftieth anniversary of her arrival in Melbourne.

There were others: Cora Brown Potter, a New York beauty and society figure, the Marilyn Monroe of the turn of the century; Maud Jeffries, one of the early stage beauties; Joseph Jefferson, who came to Australia with *Our American Cousin* about the time Lincoln was assassinated while watching it; Dion Boucicault, the inspiration of Australian theatrical production; and Hugh Joseph Ward, a minstrel dancer who gave up performing to manage the Williamson organization and who continued to build Australian theatre till his death in Sydney in 1941.

Very little of this activity pleased the Australian upper classes and their own entertainers. The intelligentsia identified worthlessness by the degree of its popularity among the worthless. Popular drama's Yankification was an additional damnification in their view, coloured by acquaintance with such observers of the early American scene as Mrs Frances Trollope, whose memory of the Yankee stage was of men who as a matter of heredity and habit would

> sprawl about the benches, throw their feet up on the seat in front of them, spit, take off their coats, spit, roll up their sleeves, spit, exhale stifling odors of whiskey and onions, spit, and applaud by stamping their feet and yelling and spitting.

The intellectuals saw rightly enough that some of the more uncouth habits of Americans were being transmitted to their own proletariat by the Yankee visitors – even to the spitting. In the bush epic *Our New Selection* those arche-typical Australians Dad and Dave welcome to their new home one Sam Evans, who

> sat down on Sarah's hat that had been left on a chair, and told Dad lies about wheat crops, and chewed tobacco, and spat squares and circles till they evolved into carpet patterns on the cleanly scrubbed floor.

Nevertheless, the intellectuals did not appreciate the extent or importance of this American influence upon their country-men. Though Australian universities still are largely English orientated, whoever would understand Australian attitudes must go beyond these cultural centres to the heart of the nation. And there he will find many similarities with America, some deriving naturally from a resemblance in the environ-ment, and some from the influence of those early American visitors. This American influence has permeated the values and habits of everyday life in Australia. Indeed in the thirteen years since the introduction of television to Australia the Australian language has changed more in vocabulary, intona-tion, and pronunciation than it did in the 168 years preced-ing. Only on the last, hard-core frontier would bush conversation be intelligible to the ordinary Australian citizen, for, despite official partiality to British programming, American productions have inundated television and motion pictures Down Under.

Again and again in all aspects of Australian life we find the American themes repeated: Australia has her swagmen (migratory workers), sundowners (migratory non-workers), and duffers (sedentary non-workers), just as the United States has its hoboes, tramps, and bums. Both countries have songs about these characters; sometimes, as with other folksongs, they share the same compositions (one of the more wide-spread hobo songs in the United States is 'The Great American Bum', found in Australia as 'Hang the Man Who

Works'). The bushman complains about his monotonous diet of 'Tea, Damper, and Mutton', while the American outbacker complains about 'Beans, Bacon, and Gravy'. The Aussie 'free selector' sings of his poor accommodations in songs like 'Free-hold on the Plain'; the American homesteader of his bad housing in songs like 'The Lane County Bachelor'. Where the whole country is poor, songs like 'The Arkansas Traveller' or 'Charlie Brannan' are typical responses in America; comparable areas in Australia produce songs like 'The Cockies of Bungaree'. All down the line the same ideas are reflected, even to children's folklore – American kids play 'cops and robbers' while their antipodean cousins play 'bushies and bobbies'. For likenesses that can be precisely traced, the cultural flow has been steady in one direction – from America to Australia, though Americans have versions of 'The Wild Colonial Boy', 'Bold Jack Donahue', 'Bound for South Australia', 'Botany Bay', and two or three other Australian compositions. 'Click Go the Shears' is sung in Australia to the tune of a song written by Henry Clay Work, the popular post-Civil War American composer whose fame has been unfairly eclipsed by that of Stephen Foster (who is unknown to folk singers, except for the recent Australian plaint 'Pub with No Beer' – a sozzled 'Beautiful Dreamer'); and Work's hand is discernible in other Australian folksongs. The Australian 'Wild Rover No More' is the American 'Strawberry Roan'; that delightful bush character Sam Holt has his ribald adventures sung to the American tune 'Sweet Alice, Ben Bolt'; and 'The Old Bullock Dray' is the American fiddle tune, 'Turkey in the Straw'.

However dubious Turner's thesis may be, there has been no stronger impact on native American folksong than that of the frontier, and since Australia's opening of the West was made under much the same conditions, this is true for its folksongs also. Thus the earliest widely developed native theme in both lands was the bushranger-outlaw motif. It is curious that both peoples tended to make heroes out of criminals; indeed, both Americans and Australians extended this courtesy to juvenile delinquents – the Aussie admires Johnny O'Meally and the American cherishes Billy the Kid. The attitudes are also very much alike; the bushranger-outlaw successfully defies an oppressive law, robs the rich and gives to the poor, speaks courteously to women and small animals. Possibly this is due to the British Robin Hood tradition, and even though, like Robin himself in the extant ballads, none of these alleged re-distributors of wealth can stand even cursory scrutiny, the folksongs make heroes out of nearly all of these romanticized thugs. Down to the present time where poverty in America starts at $4,000 a year, the attitude perpetuates: the Australian song of 'The Ned Kelly Gang' and the American Dust Bowl ballad of 'Pretty Boy Floyd' express nearly identical sentiments – that 'some men will rob you with a six-gun, some with a fountain pen'.

Another no more sensible frontier theme in both American and Australian folksong is the Dying Cowboy-Dying Stockman syndrome. Apparently there was something about the cattle industry that turned its practitioners into sentimental idiots; the American cowboy, as rough-hewn as the Aussie 'stockman' ('cowboy' in Australian lingo is a male milkmaid), sworn to hard liquor and hard living, longed to be buried out on the prairie where the coyotes could not get at him; so also the Australian stockman wants his final repose among the sweet wattles and out of reach of the dingoes.

Another of the curiosities bringing America and Australia closer together is the strange hiatus in folksong composition during the days of gold in the two countries. In each case the lack is attributable to the appearance of an exceptionally gifted music hall singer and songwriter who immediately met the mind and mood of the miners and churned out excellent songs as fast as they were needed. In California he was John A. Stone ('Old Put'); in Australia he was Charles Thatcher. Both gathered their compositions into songbooks that eventually reached the hands and voices of every miner.

It is still possible to go into that Australian past, and in so doing find oneself reviewing American history. If one has an eye and an ear for the essentials of national character, and for any inhabitant of a culture that is moving too fast for either comfort or beauty, it will be a journey to where we

> have asked to be
> Where no storms come,
> Where the green swell is in the havens dumb,
> And out of the swing of the sea.

I was there not too long ago, on the very edge of the last frontier, surveying an archaeological site on the featureless Nullarbor Plain of south-western South Australia. And there, not far from the track of bulldust pretentiously named the 'Eyre Highway', was Shingle Hut as Steele Rudd drew it seventy years ago, and emerging as my companion anthropologist and I approached were Dad and Dave – and Joe, too, looking as if he might well spear mice with a fork behind the wallpaper. Dad had about ten thousand dollars' worth of wool baled for shipment to Adelaide, but living on the Nullarbor had so deeply ingrained a pattern of poverty in him that his woolshed might just as well have been empty. His one-storey house was built of railroad ties, hauled God knows how from the transcontinental railway a hundred miles to the north across waterless and trackless desert. Dave was busy with a pair of tin snips, making roof patches out of a pile of empty five-gallon gasoline cans salvaged from a truck crash a hundred and ninety miles down the track to the east. Dad wore an old army jacket with two buttons remaining at the top and a pair of baggy trousers frayed to threads at the bottoms because they were four inches over the soles of his shoes. Only his ears, apparently designed for that purpose, kept his hat from slipping down over his eyes; and his mouthful of no teeth wizened both his face and his outlook. An aborigine, wearing some of Dad's discarded clothes, knelt in the paddock gutting a wombat. Tied by its long neck to a fence, an emu looking like a very old and dirty floor mop with two inverted handles for legs and another for a neck, watched the proceedings as if there were something to eat in them somewhere. I half expected Dad to turn to Dave and order him to 'get that kangaroo out of the well – I mean *all* of him!'

That night, as my companion and I lay in the bush several dozen miles from Dad's selection, basking in the fragrant warmth of a sandalwood campfire built by our aborigine, Dad and Dave and several other equally lank and gawky sons came bouncing through the night over the saltbush and through the mulga in a one-eyed flivver of indeterminate origin with three kangaroos strapped to its hood. The gangly sons unwound themselves, threw the 'roos to the aborigine (who set promptly to work eviscerating them, a process that overcame the aroma of the sandalwood), and took us back to the American homesteading days of a hundred years ago. One of the boys even knew 'The Old Bark Hut', the Australian equivalent of the American 'Little Old Sod Shanty on the Plain' –

> In the winter time – preserve us all!
>   to live in there's a treat,
> Especially when it's raining hard
>   and blowing wind and sleet.
> The rain comes down the chimney
>   and your meat is black with soot –
> That's a substitute for pepper
>   in the old bark hut.

But their prose conversation drew us again to the Australian pastoral backblocks, for (insulated as it is from television, motion pictures, and American radio programs) Australian bush idiom bears little resemblance to any other form of English on earth. One could identify it as English only by the certainty that it was nothing else:

This bloody Bourke shower blows up, see, and Blue's out past bloody Woop Woop on a cold-bloody-jawed alligator sweating on the tailers of his coaches. He reckons when he finds the bloody mulga scrubbers they'll be bloody wind splitters. It's tucker time and the babbler's ready if he hasn't bloody well mucked around. 'Strike me, Blue'd sooner hump a bloody drum or yabber with an ear-bashing wop wop, but you've got to have a go, my oath. 'Strewth, he's bloody ropable when he blows in. And then he finds the slushy's shickered and it's bloody tin stuff again. He can't keep his bloody shirt on and he goes real crooked on that water burner. He does his bloody Charlie, my flaming colonial he does! I'm giving you the good oil, too bloody right!

If I had wanted to break into that instructive monologue, obviously drawn from stockman experience, I could have had the Nullarbor versions of the great treasury of cattle songs that somehow bring the American West closer to the Australian than any recital of cowboy-stockman ethnography. All the boys around the campfire, for instance, knew 'The Dying Stockman', but none of them knew – any more than an American cowboy would have known, that 'The Dying Stockman' is a colonial relative of 'The Unfortunate Rake', that eighteenth-century Irish street ballad about a soldier succumbing melodiously to a social disease. The song came to America with the Irish migrants and metamorphosed successively in the different American folk cultures into 'The Bad Girl's Lament' (Appalachian Mountains), 'St James' Infirmary' (Southern negro), and 'Streets of Laredo' (cowboy). The genealogical line is not pure (who would expect strict legitimacy from such a wastrel?), for also in the eighteenth-century background is a British sea ballad, 'The Tarpaulin Jacket'. The Australian song cleaves closest to 'The Streets of Laredo', as one would expect.

Not a word of any of this to Dave and his brothers, of course. Our rapport as Americans and Australians was not to be made by communicating to them the information that those big cockroaches in their woolshed were members of the species *Blattus americanus*. I knew a better way to reach them. I dug my guitar out of the Land Cruiser and sang

'Pub with No Beer' and a few compositions by those great Australian cowboy singers Smoky Dawson and Tex Morton, and the two Wests met in true harmony under the unifying Big Sky that could have been looming over Wyoming as well as the Nullarbor Plain – except that Orion was upside down.

TWO

The Hostile Land

Australia has always been a country of delusion, illusion and strangeness. It is not surprising, therefore, that attempts by man to equate what he saw in this new land with past experience sometimes led not only to his discomfort but also to his death. Nowhere has Nature more often imposed the harsh lesson that analogues can kill than in Australia. No one in command of his senses would go into the Australian bush today without the best maps available – ordinarily the aeronautical charts supplied by the Division of National Mapping, but even these are sometimes subject to cartographic illusion. This series of maps, like all other polychromatic charts, show areas called 'lakes', coloured blue for water since 'lake' does suggest water. But God help the explorer who relies upon drinking any of the water thus connoted. Not one of them can be relied upon at any time to have even a drop of moisture in its bed, not even the great Lake Eyre, for all its three thousand square miles of cartographic azure. But what else were the map-makers to call these sandy beds and salty shallows? One must always work from the known to the unknown, and if one does not get all the way to the end of the logical process – well, that is the disadvantage of being no more than human. If a man has never before seen a wallaby in nature, prose, or art, how else could he describe this unprecedented animal than the way the Dutch explorer Pelsaert did when in 1629 he became the first white man to see one? It was, he noted in his diary, a species of cats . . . about the size of a hare . . . their head resembling that of a civet-cat; the forepaws are very short . . . resembling those of a monkey's forepaw. Its two hindlegs, on the contrary, are upwards of half an ell in length, and it walks on these only, on the flat of the heavy part of the leg, so that it does not run fast. Its tail is very long, like that of a long tailed monkey; if it eats, it sits on its hind legs, and clutches its food with his forepaws, just like a squirrel . . .

Too great a biogeographical shock makes a man sound not merely confused, but mad. More than two centuries later a competent observer and writer warned English immigrants to Australia that they should expect to find that:

The swans are black, the eagles white; cherries grow with the stones outside, and delicious-looking pears are solid wood; bees have no sting; flowers, for the most part, no smell; birds do not sing; the greater portion of the trees have no shade, whilst, instead of turning the broad part of the leaf to the sun, they turn its edge, giving an idea of a forest in rags; for a great portion of the year the trees are destitute of bark, shewing only their naked stems; animals have pockets, in which they stow away their young; some quadrupeds have ducks' bills, and lay eggs; birds carry brooms in their mouth in place of tongues; owls screech in the daytime, and cuckoos sing at night – with a variety of other contradictions, which convey the idea of nature turned topsyturvy.

The shock of the unfamiliar had much to do with the late occupation and later consolidation of Australian settlement, for it is in man's nature as a creature of his learned comforts to abhor the unusual. Land beyond the frontier of any animal's range is unused because it is unusual; and for any animal, it becomes occupied only through desperate necessity, the action of outside circumstances, or, in the case of man, the drive of greed. Pelsaert, who saw the wallaby as a kind of monkey or civet cat or hare or squirrel; Dampier, who saw it as a kind of raccoon; and Earp, who saw the whole biotic complex as nature upside down, were men conditioned to surprises. Their followers, who came to stay, were less strongly motivated, and if they had been struck with the shock of incomparably more traumatic surprises – like the fact that Australia has a hundred different kinds of carnivorous plants – it is improbable that there would have been any Australian immigrants other than the convicts with bayonets in their backs. Even today, when the worst of migratory discomfort is no more than an annoyance, one can listen to the English assisted immigrants complaining 'Oi wants to gaow 'ome' as they walk down the gangplank, just because the sun is shining – which it rarely does at 'ome. If they had been told by some inhospitable native that the very Harbour on which their ship floated was the 'ome of several species of man-eating sharks found nowhere else, their rate of departure might be even greater than it is now.

By colonizing America in the sixteenth century and Australia in the eighteenth, the white race was pushing to the very limit of the range it could reasonably expect to occupy. However lush Virginia seems today, at the time of its first occupation – when it was more fertile still – it was a place where more immigrants died than lived.

Man is controlled generally by his culture and specifically by his language. He can go far toward making a desert bloom if he just calls it a garden. There were no thrushes or pipits or chats in Australia when the first white men debarked, but they made thrushes and pipits and chats out of the native birds that lay easiest to their eyes. In America as long as the land west of the Mississippi was called 'the Great American Desert', it was uninhabitable. The historian Webb reminds us,

> The language of the maps shows that the Great American Desert existed in the records from 1820 until 1858. The popular concept of the desert had existed in the written records for two hundred and eighty years before that time, and in published accounts and in the public mind it continued to live until after the Civil War. The fiction of the Great

American Desert was founded by the first explorers, was confirmed by scientific investigators and military reports, and was popularized by travellers and newspapers.

Not even in California can one sell land among the Joshua trees by calling it desert, but call it Palm Springs and Apple Valley and suddenly the Joshua trees bear roses. Science cannot prevail against religion if religion's myth enriches a palpable desert with milk and honey. True believers can roam for forty years in the wilderness and never see the sand for the roses. It was faith and greed that drove the white man and before him, the Indians, into Oklahoma; it was loss of faith rather than the dust and the caterpillar tractors that drove him into California. As we shall see in a subsequent chapter, faith, hope, and greed are conquering the last habitable frontier of Australia even as ecologists warn the faithful that

> It is silly to add up the number of Australia's square miles without giving any attention to the fact that more than half of them are arid, at the best sparse pastoral country, at the worst a howling desert. It is mischievous to keep on pretending that any people have ever founded thriving settlements or could ever found them in a land so inhospitable as Central Australia. A recent authoritative survey has stated with severe respect for fact and an unfailing mastery of its details the truth about land utilization in Australia. With expert thoroughness the authors examine the conditions of climate and soil, of scientific knowledge and technique, which have fixed the geographical limits of Australia's several rural industries. 'Whatever the standard of living accepted by the inhabitants', they conclude, 'four-fifths of the country could not be settled much more densely because of rainfall deficiency and other factors. When the proportion of barren upland is deducted from the remaining 20 per cent which is *climatically* suitable for more intensive development, the disparity between people and land takes on an altogether different complexion.'

There are, then, two realities of frontier development: its impossibility and its inevitability.

The whole of biological evolution is a process of equating

impossibility and inevitability. Bacteria have even begun to grow in the heart of working nuclear reactors, and in Western Australia roads are crumbling because bugs are eating the bitumen. America's frontier was conquered first because the evolution of its animal life had proceeded further toward what man, aboriginal and civilized, needed for successful occupation. American Indians before the intrusion of the Spaniards and English were building apartment houses of 800 rooms while Australian aborigines, imprisoned behind Wallace's Line, chipped flint in the Old Stone Age. It was not for them a matter of deficient intelligence, but simply the fact that there were no indigenous animals capable of domestication and no indigenous plants capable of cultivation.

While Darwin was studying his notes in England, Alfred Russel Wallace in Malaya was making similar momentous discoveries about the nature of evolution on a spot whose wealth of evolutionary evidence Darwin had literally stood upon and missed. Wallace was able to trace through Borneo and the Celebes a Rubicon of ecology across which neither plants nor animals crossed. This line, refined later by Weber, protected the more primitive forms to its south-east from the highly evolved types in the rest of the world, making Australasia the natural protective zoo for biota that had been exterminated elsewhere. In effect, evolution in New Guinea and Australia stopped in the Cretaceous period. Some later scholars have attacked the biotic line concept as if Wallace had postulated an actual fence instead of an imaginary one. Nevertheless, except for the dingo, which was brought to Australia by the aborigines, and some bats, rats, and mice that either floated in on driftwood or flew in on mammalian wings, all the mammalian fauna of the island continent are marsupials – primitive mammals that the more ferocious placental animals had elsewhere made extinct. However frightening some of them appeared with a few carnivorous exceptions, Australia's animal life is silly at its best. The monotreme platypus, which proceeded along several forks on the evolutionary road: bird, reptile, amphibian, mammal, was a poor jack of all trades, competent at none, whose aimless characteristics guaranteed nothing except extinction. And the list goes on with the platypus' monotrematous companions, the spiny anteater (*Tachyglossus*) and the banded anteater (*Zaglossus*); 119 marsupials ranging in a subjective view from the lovable to the pathetic; 380 sorts of reptiles, 180 freshwater fish, some of which have no more right to exist in a logical world than the giraffe; 120 varieties of frog; 750 molluscs, to which no one properly pays any attention; and 50,000 different kinds of insects, including the extremely destructive but colorful termites and bushflies – bushflies, bushflies. 'No description of the back country of Australia could ever be complete without reference to the flies. They cannot be called a plague, because plagues go away,' wrote roadmaker Len Beadell. Travel agency brochures never mention the bushflies, for their number and ubiquity take all comfort from life in the bush – and even in the smaller cities. There is no use brushing them off once they have formed a solid blanket on your face, for that only makes room for others. In much of Australia, it is only possible to speak with one's teeth closed (perhaps this is the reason for the Australian's accent), for there is nothing in all the happier parts of the world to compare with the experience of swallowing a bushfly. Even the aborigines, who let them crawl over their eyeballs, vomit when one goes down their throat. Mixed with 'March flies' – a viciously aggressive horsefly – the bushflies should by rights have stopped development of the Australian frontier. And then there are the snakes, hiding in the spinifex or down lizard holes. Not docile serpents, like the rattlesnake, but venomous obscenities that will chase and jump at a man. Some innocent visitors wear knee-length boots, but this is useless since one form of the brown snake can hurl himself over your head – and will, with no more provocation than having got up on the wrong side of its hole in the morning. Many of the other 135 or so land and freshwater snakes are quite poisonous;

reckoning lethality as the sheep-killing power of one bite, there is the cobra, worth 31 sheep; the death adder, 84; the tiger snake, 118; and the taipan, 200.

Other antipodean fauna are more lovable: the kangaroo, a ridiculously constructed amiable giant mouse; the budgerigars (parakeets), flying in flashing green clouds; the mangrove fish of the tropical north, which will crawl out of the water and follow you about, gawking with saucer eyes; and the incomparable koala bear, which comes close to refuting the principle of survival of the fittest. Fat, cuddly, absolutely defenseless, sleeping all the day in sparsely leaved gum trees, it should have been exterminated by aborigines and other predators millennia ago.

But one must employ Paley's Principle in a frontier situation: for all their fascination, evolutionary importance, and amiability, Australian animals are not much chop for eating. In large areas of the continent's interior, the main source of the aborigines' protein was the witchetty grub (*bardi* in the western desert), the larva of giant coccid moths, sometimes half the size of a hot dog. Unlike the American frontier, the Australian outback had no bison, whose importance in opening the great plains of the West has never been properly acknowledged, (though Webb does as much to correct this as any man could with one sentence: 'In the plains area lived one animal that came nearer to dominating the life and shaping the institutions of a human race than any other in all the land, if not in the world – the buffalo'). Nor were there any pronghorn antelope, deer, rabbits, hares, elk, wild sheep, or anything except members of the kangaroo family to waste a shot on. But on the other hand, neither were there any carnivores worthy of the taxonomy; there are no tales in that land's legendary like that of Bishop H. B. Bascom of early Virginia, who

> on one occasion was seated at a puncheon dinner table when blood-curdling screams from the yard sent the family rushing out to see what was happening. When they reached the

yard they found a wildcat bearing off the youngest child. Bascom seized a rifle from the pegs over the door and fired at the animal, but he was too late, for already the cat had thrust its teeth through the child and it was dead.

Only botanists tend to find Australian plants fascinating but there is much to be learnt from plant life nevertheless. Darwin put his theory of evolutionary change together partly if not largely on the speciation of thirteen deviants of a finch genus on the Galapagos Islands; if he had not restricted his activity in Australia to that of an unusually observant sightseer, he could have gathered data to propound his theory of natural selection on Australian flora alone. To mention only two such genera, the eucalypts and acacias have adapted themselves so alertly into otherwise empty econiches that there are now approximately 650 species of each. The eucalyptus varies in height from the dwarf forms of the Australian Alps and the ten-foot mallee (most common in the marginally habitable outback) to the huge mountain ash, as tall as the California redwoods. In shape, colour, and form, there is no way to enumerate the eucalypt variety.

Much of the Australian biota are living fossils. In one small pocket of the MacDonnell Range, for example, one can find *Livistona* palms that could tell tales about dinosaurs. The termite genus *Mastotermes* disappeared in all other parts of the world thirty million years ago but it exists in Australia still. In the rivers of the east one can fish for lungfish (*Neoceratodus*), burramundi (*Scleropages*), and blackfish (*Gadopsis*), which are presumably still trying to crawl out of the water and reach for higher goals. And no one can stand in a grove of blackboys (*Xanthorrhoea*) and not feel somehow that he is in a Cretaceous swamp. But did even a Cretaceous swamp contain anything so unlikely as the Gippsland earthworm (*Megascolides gippslandicus*), fully ten feet long?

Many life forms in Australia have their closest or only relatives in South America. The one rabbit form that established itself so devastatingly in Australia and the virus that nearly killed it off, both derived from South America; the Argentine ant, a serious pest in Western Australia; several species of freshwater fish; Amazonian psittacosis; a number of molluscs and crayfish; and the prickly pear cactus and its lethal parasite, *Cactoblastis cactorum* – not to mention entire families of insects that the entomologist Paramonov calls 'paleoantarcts' – bind South America and Australia together in bonds almost as tight as the imposing geological evidence of affinity. The geological argument for an ancient connection of the Australian, Antarctic, and South American continents – a whole called 'Gondwanaland' from a series of rocks called the Gondwana System – has passed from what was once a lunatic suggestion into something close to orthodoxy.

Such ancient survivals in Australia's ecology bear directly upon the country's frontier and the people who are presently intruding upon it, for any environment comfortable to life forms unchanged since the Devonian epoch 350,000,000 years ago obviously cannot be entirely friendly to an upstart who cannot convincingly trace his ancestry back more than a mere million years. To survive at all, he must remain encapsulated in his culture, and stay as close to his fellows as possible. Western Australia is about as large as the United States east of the Mississippi, but of its 900,000 population, 600,000 live in Perth – and the rest are not far away. In the north central interior, there is nobody. For perhaps as much as a million square miles centering on the South Australia-Northern Territory-Western Australian border intersection, the land is so thinly populated by whites that everyone knows everyone else – by the party-line transceiver radio service of the Flying Doctor network, and everyone thinks (perhaps with good reason) that everyone else is 'bloody crackers' for living out there. The Northern Territory comprises 520,280 square miles (about the size of Texas, California, and Colorado put together) and is certainly no poorer in land or prospects than other allegedly habitable parts of the world like west Texas, but its 1968-1969 telephone directory lists fewer than 1,500 numbers—and nearly all of those are in Darwin and Alice Springs.

Unlike the American frontier, the Australian last lands retreat from all sides toward the centre. By any ecological means, be it rainfall, human occupation, mineral discoveries, reliable surface water, fauna, or flora – one can define zones of concentric ellipses around the uninhabitable dead heart of the country – Take flora as an example. Impose upon the three million square mile buck-backed rectangle of the Australian continent roughly concentric bands of dominant vegetation: around the north, east, and south coasts eucalypt forests are typical (with a few negligible patches of Malayan heavy forest in the east, northeast, and the extreme southwestern tip), joining the slightly less fertile savanna-mallee-saltbush outer band of the west and south coasts; the next interior band is generally savanna, Mitchell grass, mulga, and saltbush; and in the dead heart centering on the tri-state border intersection, the spinifex. This is, of course, a simplification, since even the spinifex has some intruders like ironwood, desert oak, desert willow, and desert holly (all of them poor mimics of their fertile counterparts).

The exploited but unconquered deserts are probably the most inhospitable regions in the habitable world. The dangers are innumerable. There is the chance that spinifex seeds may find their way into the radiator of one's vehicle, causing it to boil over every three or four miles with the loss of its extremely precious water. And if this is somehow avoided, the vehicle itself may actually begin to disintegrate, torn apart by the very high temperature. Nor is it only transport that suffers. Weakness, or even starvation, may be induced in man by a strange reluctance to eat caused by hyperaridity. Diseases are rife; ophthalmia (inflammation of the eyes) and that strange ailment 'barcoo rot' are two of the most common afflictions. One explorer vividly described the perils of barcoo rot. 'It is', he wrote,

. . . very common in the bush, where no vegetables or change of food can be obtained, and must be something akin to scurvy. It is usually accompanied by retching and vomiting following every attempt to eat. The sufferer invariably has a voracious appetite, but what he eats is of little benefit to him. The skin becomes very tender and soft, and the slightest knock or scratch, even a touch sometimes, causes a wound which gradually spreads in all directions. The back of the hand is the usual spot to be first affected, then the arms, and in a bad case the legs also, which become puffy at the joints, and before long the wretched victim will be covered with sores and abrasions. No external application of ointment or anything of that nature seems to do any good, though the wounds are not deep and leave but little scar. After a month or two in the bush one is pretty sure to develop this complaint, which in the dusty, hot weather is further aggravated by the swarms of flies, whose poisonous nature is made evident to anyone who has killed them. . . . Nothing but an entire change of diet and way of living can cure the 'barcoo'; constant washing, an impossibility 'out-back', being essential.

Disease aside, the heat and very high rate of evaporation pose almost insuperable problems for man. Len Beadell, who pushed a 'road' through part of the Gibson Desert a few years ago, summed up the climate succinctly enough:

From November to March it is searingly hot and dry; April, June, and July have ideal temperatures but it is dry; August and September are dry with seemingly never-ending winds, and it appears to be fairly dry in October. It might be a little unjust to say it is all that dry, because for some years we have had up to two inches of rain. After a cycle of about twelve years, six inches can be expected. But clear skies will be seen for most of the year. To quote one small boy's answer to an examination question, 'The climate of Central Australia in summer is such that its inhabitants have to live elsewhere'.

Conceive of Australia as the entire United States with a topography like that of Kansas, with no mountains or lakes except those that cartographers for the sake of decoration draw on their maps; a few coastal creeks, some with running water, and one O-Gauge river system flowing sluggishly from Augusta to Houston, and a national weather forecast predicting continuous high temperatures with only a one per cent chance of rainfall; there you have the last frontier of Australia. Looking at the matter with the unimaginative tool of statistics, one can note that 39 per cent of Australia has less than ten inches rain a year and 63 per cent is either desert or semi-desert. These figures, however, refer to areal water; if the aqueous regions of the tropical north were let in upon the central part and all available standing or running water were entropically distributed over the continent, the entire country would qualify as semi-desert; so much for piping water down through 'the Alice'. Speaking of the Alice – Alice Springs, the town without a function in the center of the continent – there are two 'rivers' which meet in the settlement itself: the Todd and the Charles. Each year on the Todd River a *regatta* is held; the boats have their bottoms knocked out and the crews, holding their boats up like skirts, run a hundred yards up the river bed. As one American visitor observed, 'Old Man River is not a conceivable figure in Australian folklore'.

The one reliable stream, the Murray, is worth looking into, if only to see what is on the bottom. When in full flow, it carries ten million gallons of water, compared to 146 million for the Columbia. For all its songs and romantic legends that make it seem imposing as a waterway, one can jump across the Rio Grande in places, yet it still has three times as much land under irrigation as the Murray. Join to the Murray all other Australian rivers, and you have a water volume only two thirds that of the St Lawrence. Even in the eastern half of the country it takes two rivers, the Barcoo and the Thomson, to make one dry creek (Cooper Creek).

Admittedly there is rain, even on the frontier, but it is little and unreliable. Widespread droughts in Australia since the beginning of this century, occurred in the years 1902, 1914, 1919, 1927, 1940, 1944, 1951, 1952 and 1963. There are more

51

localized periods of aridity every year. A child born in Alice Springs in 1956 did not see any rain until he was eight years old.

Any irregularity in the delicate balance of nature, such as prolonged droughts, sets in motion other imbalances whose effects may seriously be felt long before the processes themselves are understood or even noticed. Dry years make the 'desert pavement' – the thin crust of poorly consolidated surface earth familiar on California's dry lakes – especially vulnerable to damage; one sheep foraging in such country will break the surface, and wind will certainly follow to cause dust erosion. With the surface broken, nitrogen loss occurs, rendering infertile soil still more sterile, and the removal of the pavement permits surface salt to get underground to cause tunnel erosion. Even rain can cause long-term harm: in natural depressions like dry lakes, it has been estimated that even infrequent rain will deposit as much as thirty pounds of salt per acre in a year. So long as the dry lake surface is undisturbed, only an infinitesimal amount of soil is removed from potential farmland, but once the pavement is broken insidious tunnel erosion will drill its network of sterility sometimes to immense lengths. Any rain is quite useless, since there is no feasible way of making any use of it without importing uneconomical condensers and other machinery, and anyway the rate of evaporation that always accompanies rainfall is incredibly high. What the nineteenth-century botanist MacDougal wrote about the western deserts of the United States is today only too accurate for the Australian inland:

> The relative humidity often falls to 5 per cent in the South-western deserts, and in a temperature of over 100° the evaporation from a vessel of water standing in the open may be as much as an inch a day. The amount thrown off by the skin is correspondingly great, and if the loss is not made good, thirst ensues, and ten hours' lack of water may thicken the tongue so that speech is impossible.

Statistics cannot convey what great aridity can mean to

man, physically and psychologically. Anyone who has read Arthur Upfield's Australian murder mystery *Death of a Lake* is not likely to forget what happens to life in those parts of Australia which are desperate for water, where a temporary lake will dry up at the rate of an inch a day.

The Western Australian gold prospectors in the 1890s had no time for the luxury of sentimentality, nor was David Carnegie the kind of man to indulge in it if they had. Yet even he was moved to an exclamation mark or two in recalling those dry times:

> The first aim of a party of Western Australian prospectors is to find not gold, but water. Having found this they make camp, and from it start short excursions in all directions towards any hills that may be in sight. Arrived at the hills, which, though bare of undergrowth, are usually covered with low scrub, they can soon determine from the nature of the rock whether further search is likely to have good results. Should they see hills of ironstone and diorite, or blows and outcrops of quartz, they will certainly revisit the locality. In what manner, will depend upon the distance from water . . .
>
> As lack of water made washing or panning impossible there, the process known as 'dry-blowing' was carried on. I watched the men patiently holding flat tin dishes one above the other, hoping that as the dirt fell from the top to the bottom dish the dust would be blown away. If there was no breeze they blew themselves, repeating the process until only the speck or small nuggets remained in the dishes.
>
> The miners usually worked in pairs, one scouting for water – always their main need – while the other worked the claim. . . .
>
> What scenes of bitter quarrels these watering-places have witnessed! The selfish striving, each to help himself, the awful sufferings of man and beast, horses and camels mad with thirst, and men cursing the country and themselves, for wasting their lives and strength in it. . . .
>
> It was a cruel sight in those thirsty days to see the poor horses wandering about, mere walking skeletons, deserted by

their owners, for strangers were unable to give them water, and afraid to put them out of their misery lest damages should be claimed against them.

The Australian environment always has been hostile but the arrival of man made it worse. Since the aborigines themselves have suffered grievously by what may most objectively be called the ecological imbalances occasioned by the white settlers, it has not been considered charitable to speak of their contribution to the destruction of plant and animal life in Australia. But the aborigines have helped to upset the indigenous balance of nature not only by the indiscriminate killing of animals but also by the gross destruction of the floral cover by burning. Anyone who goes into the Australian interior can see the result of hunting fires – charred spikes of mulga ten and more years dead, with no sign of revival. It has been argued that sporadic burning actually improves the land and its products, but it is not so very long since physicians tried to cure desperately ill patients by draining their blood. When missionaries or government native welfare agents bring water to a band of aborigines, they trade a little comfort for a large measure of biotic destruction. Three weeks around a water tank for a few dozen natives means at least three years of despoliation of several square miles.

Moreover, immeasurable damage has been caused in Australia by the introduction of the dingo or wild dog by the aborigines. It has been argued that the wild dog was useful to the natives and no more than a mild annoyance for Australia's marsupials. While it is true that the half-wild dogs that come six to a person in aboriginal Australia will join their masters in beating a rat out of a bush – co-operation ends there and it is even chances who gets the rat. At its best the dingo is a last resort for a hungry man when no other game can be found.

The wild dog still does incalculable harm to animal life. Farmers have had impressed upon the rest of the country what this uncontrolled carnivore can do to a flock of sheep, and to try to prevent the appalling sheep casualties, the government has helped to build dingo fences across the whole continent. South Australia has a dog fence 1,350 miles long. Queensland has the largest in the world – 3,500 miles of fence six feet high, enclosing 135,000,000 acres. It is fairly effective in keeping Northern Territory dogs in the Northern Territory, and Queensland dogs in Queensland. Bounties have for years been offered to both aboriginal and whites for dingo scalps, with the predictable result that a new profession of 'dogging' was created. The professional native dogger actually breeds dogs for the bounty business. In the early days, the government paid bounty on dingo tails, so as to avoid the messiness of bloody scalps. Presently what waggish bushmen called 'Manx dogs' began to appear in native camps. The mutation was simple; when an aborigine wanted to buy something, *flick!* and another tailless dog joined the new breed.

But a dog is a dog for all that, and whosoever would live in peace with his fellow man must not undertake extended criticism of the one animal created by Providence for his comfort in trouble and pain. So let the dog go in peace. But what of the Scotch thistle? How can the deliberate, calculated introduction of this noxious nuisance be vindicated by any conceivable recourse to human reason? Yet it was brought in, presumably by Scotsmen, may God in His infinite mercy forgive them, as He may yet forgive those who attempted to introduce poisonous snakes into Polynesia. Yet to some Australians, there have been worse things than the thistle brought to that new land where, as Alan Moorehead said, 'humanity had a chance to make a fresh start'. Let 'Tom Collins' (Joseph Furphy), that greatest of all Australian bush philosophers, make the complaint:

> When Australia was first colonized, any sensible man might have foreboded sorrel, cockspur, Scotch thistle etc., as unwelcome, but unavoidable, adjuncts of settlement. A many-wintered sage might have predicted that some colonist, in a fit of criminal folly, would scourge the country with a legacy of

foxes, rabbits, sparrows, etc. But a second and clearer-sighted Jeremiah could never have prophesied the deliberate introduction of hydrophobia for dogs, glanders for horses, or Orangeism for men. Yet the latter enterprise has been carried out.

Every man to his own distaste. Few of us in Australia or out have been offended by Orangemen – possibly because few of us contend with them for the same socioreligious econiche – and fewer still are offended by horses, regardless of how silly we believe horses or their owners to be. Wherever man and his dog have gone during the last four thousand years, the horse has been close ahead – or beneath. Six of them debarked from the First Fleet. Long, long after they were proved to be worse than worthless in desert country, explorers burdened themselves with this beast of burden. Read the journal of any explorer and share with him vicariously the bracing experience of searching the wilderness for the horses every morning. Inevitably some of these horses escaped and some of the escaped horses lived to establish 'mobs' of 'brumbies' – on the American frontier 'mustangs'. Some are descendants of cavalry horses released after the first World War. In any event, large numbers of these wild horses established themselves, and since they, like other immigrant plants and animals, had no natural enemies in the Cretaceous environment, they became vermin to the pastoralists. In grazing country where 640 acres of winter range are needed to support one steer (as against 75 in the United States), it is easy to understand the pastoralists' feelings. On one station (ranch) in Queensland 4,000 horses were shot; and on one South Australian station the same number fell to the rifles of bounty hunters; on five adjoining stations in Queensland 9,000 more wild horses were killed, some return being made on them by selling them as pet food.

Without doubt, of all the animals that were introduced the one that most upset Australian natural ecology was and still is the rabbit. The story of rabbits in Australia has become the world's classic example of what can happen when an organism with no effective natural enemies and a great propensity for reproduction intrudes upon an innocent environment. For theoreticians of youth's rebellion the Australian rabbit establishes the demographic significance of making love, not war. Like horses, convicts, and a few other equivocal contributions to the settlement of Australia, rabbits came over on the First Fleet. Neither these nor subsequent introductions of the familiar European field rabbit 'took'; and the few that did survive failed to make any impact on the new environment. In 1859, however, the year Darwin published his book *The Origin of Species by Means of Natural Selection, or the Preservation of Favoured Races in the Struggle for Life*, Thomas Austin of Barwon Park, Geelong, Victoria, brought in several pairs of wild rabbits, congeners of South American wild rabbits, and released them on his property. By the year 1880 they had crossed the Murray River and moved into the interior, reproducing all the way. Within sixteen years they were at Fowler's Bay on the western half of the desolate South Australian coast, more than a thousand miles from Mr Austin's property. With equal or greater speed they migrated through the northern part of Australia. In 1894 the Western Australian government exhibited apprehension to an extent one would not readily credit in politicians whose own life-preservation system requires studied lethargy in critical matters. Rewards were offered for schemes to put things as they were before 1859; one otherwise sensible man, the working explorer H. S. Trotman, suggested the importation of cats, which is rather like bringing Bengal tigers into your house to catch mice. Some cats were in fact released in Western Australia, and that is one reason a number of the smaller marsupials in that state have vanished. Money was also spent on erecting fences for rabbits to burrow their way beneath.

Finally – to use that word rhetorically – the authorities accepted the suggestion of a South American zoologist, H. B.

Aragao, that they should introduce the highly lethal viral disease carried by South American rabbits called myxomatosis. Aragao's recommendation was made in the 1920s; in 1950 myxomatosis was officially released upon the susceptible Australian rabbit population. The death rate was astronomical – close to one hundred per cent. But not *quite* one hundred per cent – and those rabbits in which an apparently natural immunisation against myxomatosis had occurred found each other in the reduced population that would ordinarily have swamped them out. They met and bred, as rabbits will do, and so now the rabbit population is as numerous as it ever was, and myxomatosis only accounts now for a few rabbits each year. Many observers of reference works tell us that the rabbit in Australia now has achieved an ecological accommodation with the environment and other herbivores. These people have not visited central and Western Australia recently. Those who have been in the deepest bush are generally the kind of men whose best talents are not literary, and therefore the comfortable delusion that rabbits are no longer a problem is firm in the minds of people who wish it to be so. Let it be affirmed here that there are no numerical superlatives to communicate how many rabbits infest the Australian frontier, unless some mathematician has devised a term beyond the googol.

At almost the same time as the rabbit was brought in to make Australia look a bit more like 'ome, someone – an American perhaps, in whom it aroused the same nostalgic delight that the thistle works for Scotsmen – introduced several species of the prickly pear cactus. There was some sense in the idea, as there is in Five Year Plans and other utopian notions of socioeconomic improvement, but like these things, no one anticipated the whole of what happens when a balance, ecological or economic, is upset. *Opuntia inermis* and *Opuntia stricta* are excellent substitutes for split rail fences in wood-poor country and fine anticipations of the barbed-wire fence. Moreover, argued the proponents of prickly pear, they make excellent fodder (though one might well doubt the value of an edible fence).

The only circumstance that prevented Australia from becoming a solid mass of prickly pear was this plant's limitation to regions of little rainfall. In 1900, it was estimated, ten million acres of Queensland were completely covered by the cactus. In 1920, 58 million acres. By this time the authorities had become aware of the danger and, it must be conceded, approached the situation with more care than the rabbit men, possibly because the cactus was spreading at the rate of three acres an hour. About sixty species of cactus predators were tested before *Cactoblastis cactorum*, a South American moth, was found to be capable of destroying *Opuntia* without any assistance from other insects. *Cactoblastis* reproduces at a rate to shame the rabbit – the first introduction of 2,750 eggs in 1925 produced a *Cactoblastis* population laying 2,540,000 eggs within a year. By the early 1930s cactus was hard to find even in central Queensland. Since then the subject of the *Opuntia-Cactoblastis* complex has become a fascinating academic study – with the cactus a stealthy arsonist and the moth an alert fireman. Today, the cactus is no longer a problem for pastoralists and farmers, who have turned the land over to that most noisome of all quadrupeds, sheep. An amusing if not important parallel in the story of introduced pests is that in the Queensland agricultural town of Boonarga there is a memorial hall dedicated to the *Cactoblastis*, as in Richmond, Virginia, there is a statue erected to the boll weevil, which in that area forced the cotton farmers to diversify and prosper. Today the government might well be advised to keep an eye on the American mesquite, introduced into the north-west of Western Australia in 1930 as a natural fence, but which since has gone beyond its purpose.

In one way or other man is the ravager; he brought the rabbit in, and rabbits have to eat. They do not ponder Malthusian significances. And in one way or other, he has done as much as he humanly could to destroy many species of indigenous Australian life forms. Forty-four per cent of an originally noted 52 species of marsupials are now extinct, and many plants have suffered the same fate; eaten by the animals he brought with him. Near the point of no return are the Mountain Ash (*Eucalyptus regnana*), the Anemone buttercup (*Ranunculus anemoneus*), the Giant Wallaby grass (*Danthonia frigida*), the waratah (*Telopea speciosissima*), the platypus (*Ornithorhynchus anatinus*, whose skin was used for rugs), the koala (*Phascolarctus cinereus*, two million of which supplied skins for trappers in 1924, and which were nearly extinct in 1930), the Australian gannet (*Sula serrator*, down to fifty pairs in 1952), the bustard (*Ardeotis australis*), the wedgetailed eagle (*Aquila audax*), the cassowary (*Casuarius casuarius*), and the emu (*Dromaius novae-hollandiae*) – to list only those plants and animals most commonly associated with Australia in popular tradition.

In America the biotic complex of buffalo (bison) and buffalo grass was destroyed almost at once when the white man changed his 'Great American Desert' to his 'Great Plains'. The bison at the coming of the hunters and settlers constituted perhaps the largest assemblage of wild animals seen by man, and it fed on what several observers independently called 'a sea of grass'. But within fifty years both the bison and the grass were gone – the one killed for meat, hide, rugs, bones, souvenirs, and trophies by Buffalo Bill and other scourges of the West, the other displaced by eastern grasses. It is futile to apportion blame for most ecological change, unless there is an ulterior purpose in blame-placing. If wise men see a need for radical economic change in the United States when an inevitable Depression has begun, they make a monster out of Herbert Hoover. Doubtless the man who introduced the Scottish thistle to Australia was an unmitigated villain, but for most of the vast changes wrought by man in his ineluctable pursuit of the final entropy, there are simply not enough villains to go around. Thomas Austin meant only to make his property a bit more like the green fields of his motherland when he brought in his rabbits. The French physician who destroyed most of the rabbits in Europe less than twenty years ago meant only to clear these vermin out of his garden with a little myxomatosis. Vito Marcantonio intended only to assure a voting base for his position on the New York city council when he devised the mass immigration of Puerto Ricans to that city. Hindsight in these things is as worthless as it is cheap.

How did the American grasslands that fed the bison become grasslands in the first place? This was no special act of providence but merely another example of change brought about by imbalance induced by man. Botanists Schantz and Zon blame no one when they explain the creation of grasslands:

> Grasslands characterize areas in which trees have failed to develop, either because of unfavorable soil conditions, poor drainage and aeration, intense cold and wind, deficient moisture supply, or repeated fires. Grasses of one kind or another are admirably suited to withstand conditions of excess moisture, excess drought, and fires which would destroy tree growth.

Occasional fires do occur naturally, caused by lightning or some similar phenomenon; frequent fires have only one cause: the arsonist man. For the Great Plains, he was the Indian; for the Australian interior, the aborigine; for the karri forests of south-western Australia, the white farmers. And let not the myth of accidental fires through carelessly discarded matches or cigarettes be allowed to explain away bushfires and forest fires. These conflagrations are set alight deliberately. In March 1966, the visitor to south-western Australia could drive through two hundred miles of nearly continuous forest fires and actually see farmers setting fire to more, for the conditions were excellent for 'a bit of a burn'. All along the highway from Albany to Perth the visible bush abounded with signs exhorting drivers to be careful with cigarettes and avoid forest fires. But the farmers were not smoking; they were only burning off the scrub.

Forests will fight fires with reproduction if conditions for their propagation are good and the fires are not too persistent; but repeated fires discourage tree growth and the grass takes over, for better or worse. This is what happened long before the arrival of white man on the Great Plains of America. In aboriginal Australia, areas comparable to the American prairie plains were at the time of white settlement seas of grass. James Backhouse visited the Adelaide plains in 1837 and marvelled at the promised fertility:

> Some of the Kangaroo grass was up to our elbows and resembled two years seed meadows in England in thickness; in many places three tons of hay per acre might be mown off it.

But the promise was unfulfilled. Kangaroo grass and other tall summer perennials were, under the imbalance of grazing, displaced by other native, but short, grasses; these in turn were displaced by dwarf species – all leading to an eventual loss of cover. In more arid regions where the aborigines unwittingly assist the sheep, the benign saltbush has died after grazing and burning, and has been for the most part replaced by spinifex.

If grass and soil conducive to its growth are in fact the desiderata for human settlement and prosperity, then the inescapable necessity for exploitation of the last frontiers in America and Australia is water. A single faucet protruding from the earth in the Amata aboriginal reserve in the far north-west of South Australia, left dripping by the improvident natives and with no introduced seed whatever, accumulated around it for some ten square yards a knee-deep, tropically rich growth of native grass not seen in that country for generations. But where is the water to come from for the withered wilderness?

Webb in his classic work on the Great Plains looked into

the problem for America's dry land and concluded lugubriously,

It has been customary for enthusiasts to compare the possibilities of the arid region of the West, the Great Plains, with what has been accomplished by irrigation in the Nile Valley of Egypt and in the Tigris-Euphrates valley of Mesopotamia. The analogy is misleading and will not hold. Wherever a flourishing and populous civilization has been built up on the basis of irrigation, it has been done by rivers flowing from areas of heavy rain fall and bringing enormous quantities of water into arid lands. The Nile flows from a region where rain fall is from forty to sixty inches; and the Tigris-Euphrates from the mountains of Armenia. For example, if the Mississipi, draining into the humid eastern country, could be induced to flow into the arid West, it would be impossible to imagine the possibilities of irrigation. But what we have is a series of rivers flowing from an arid mountainous region into a more arid plain, with the result that the water problem in the Great Plains has ever been the paramount problem and will no doubt long remain so.

Australians like the Americans, are still trying – to make rain by both magical and scientific means. The first experiments in the United States with rain cloud seeding after the Second World War were taken up quickly in Australia – and, indeed, it was the Australians who first made rain to fall upon the ground by artificial stimulation. But the conditions that keep rain from falling also keep rain clouds from being made, so not finding succour above their heads, the Australians have looked under their feet – to the great artesian basins that underlie one third of their continent. The first of these resources was discovered in 1878, and immediately bores were sunk all along what then was the frontier, mainly the line of pastoral claims running north-south east of Lake Eyre. At the turn of the century other marginal areas were drilled for water – the Perth-Coolgardie track, for example, and along Canning's stock route from Wiluna to Hall's Creek, some of the most hostile country on this earth. But even while these ambitious wells were being bored, the others were drying up. Even in the main underground reservoir, the Great Artesian Basin centering upon south-western Queensland, two thousand wells dried up shortly after 1900. It is possible, with proper equipment, to travel along the line of eastern Lake Eyre – and see the ruins of ambitious stations, all abandoned.

Reference works even now being published refer to such things as the 'Eucla Basin' lying under the Nullarbor Plain, as if by drilling into it resourceful men could draw up water to make that particular desert bloom. Water is being drawn up, no doubt of it. But on the Yalata Mission, an aboriginal reserve in the center of the southern edge of the Nullarbor, the bore water is used only for hosing down the dust. Clothes washed with it become so heavily mineralized that they seem as stiffly frozen as if they had been hung out wet in Tabernash, Colorado, in midwinter. Aboriginal children who insist on learning by experience sometimes wash their hair in the bore water, and promptly grow hairy stalagmites on their heads. All of this water is heavily impregnated with salines. The Yirrkla aborigines, who used to inhabit this part of Australia, subsisted on water drained out of the roots of certain types of mallee; the indigenous fauna (like the wombat, whose last range this is) normally obtain water from the vegetation, and when they drink water laid down by infrequent rains, sometimes literally burst.

The Australian artesianists have been encouraged by the apparent success of bore irrigation in El Paso, Texas. This city of one-half million people is situated in a region where rainfall is an irregular 8.65 inches a year and the evaporation rate 108 inches for the same period, and yet it thrives mainly on what it draws from the Hueco Bolson artesian basin just north of the city. The people of El Paso talk – as they must – with the same surety against natural calamity as the people of Pompeii probably did in AD 78. They do not heed the warning given in the *Twenty-Second Annual Report of the United States Geological Survey* in 1902:

> . . . to withdraw even so little as 3 or 4 inches for application in surface irrigation would leave the ground water unreplenished and result in increase of the pumping lift by a foot in a single year. Even on the assumption that lifting from the present depths would be economically practicable, the withdrawal of an amount sufficient for irrigation would rapidly result in exhaustion of the stored supply.

Twenty per cent of Australian sheep depend on artesian water supplies. Australian farmers draw up some 350 million gallons of artesian water each day. One thousand head of cattle require a supply of one million gallons.

And while the sheep and cattle drink, they also eat. In South Australia grazing country, stock have destroyed up to ninety per cent of the earth-holding vegetation. With the destruction of the cover and the pulverizing of the desert pavement by the ungulates, the earth has begun to blow away, as it did in the American Dustbowl in the 1930s. The situation is worse in Australia than it was in Oklahoma during the red-sky years, for the disturbed salt-heavy dust beds are not drained by rivers and must therefore deposit the lethal salinity over more and more land. Not all of America's great technological and scientific knowledge in land utilization could do anything with the Dustbowl except allow natural economic pressures to drive the people out. Only then could work begin to restore the cover artificially – an enormous reclamation project proceeding at this present time.

In May 1969, the Australian Office for National Development reported that the arid land problem was becoming serious, that aridity was increasing, and that many grazing properties were being abandoned. As Americans would say, official notice has been taken, and action is expected. We can expect a comfortable length of time to elapse that probably will last to the end of this century before anything effective is done – the government is leaving the problem to the states, who are leaving it to the graziers, who are leaving it to itself. As rhetorical tradition compels us to say, the frontier will inevitably be conquered; but we must remind ourselves that 'conquest' is a word out of the vocabulary of violence and destruction. We conquer our frontiers only by destroying them.

THREE

A Wicked Way to Found a Nation

Francis Bacon, counselor to the first Elizabeth and Lord Chancellor to the first James, esteemed in his own lifetime as the new Aristotle and in later ages as the father of modern science for his serious endeavors and as the true author of Shakespeare's plays for his frivolity, once advised his peers on the establishment of foreign colonies that 'It is a shameful and unblessed thing to take the scum of people and wicked condemned men, to be the people with whom you plant'.

Mindful of the First Fleet and its cargo of 729 criminal settlers and forgetful of chronology, casual Australian readers of Bacon might infer from his remarks another criticism of their founding fathers. In fact, of course, he was not writing about Australia; he was writing about America, the 'brave new world' that Shakespeare had just used as the setting for his play *The Tempest*.

But only the time was out of joint, for there was not much difference between the Virginians, Puritans, and incipient Australians beyond the fact that criminals of the Puritan specialization (subversive smuggling) are best dumped in a colony that cannot become an economic threat to the motherland. Lord Egremont, British Secretary of State, argued prophetically that American colonists be prevented legally from moving to

> the Heart of America out of reach of Government where from the great difficulty of procuring European commodities, they would be compelled to commerce and manufactures to the infinite prejudice of Britain. . . .

67

But Lord Egremont was writing in 1763, long after the American mistake had been irrevocably made. In any case, had it been possible to transfer either group of convicts across the two centuries, Lord Bacon's stricture would have applied equally well. America's bunyip aristocracy, the upper class Southerners, trace their New World origin to what is pleasantly known as the First Families of Virginia. In fact, their real progenitors were the Second Families of Virginia—the First Families were abandoned felons who did their nominal posterity a service by dying off promptly without leaving issue. These sacrificial pioneers are entirely forgotten by the generality of Americans who have enough to do as it is to make their history palatable.

At the other end of the stick the character of the planters themselves – whom at this safe distance in time we can call the uncaught criminals – also applies in the case of either colony; it was well said more than a century ago by Sidney that in its dealings with criminals 'the commercial spirit of Britain was displayed; while the Italian stabbed or poisoned his enemy, the Englishman sold him for a soldier, a sailor, or a slave.' And why not? Dubious compassion aside, slavery after all is no more than the logical extension of the Neolithic discovery that like all domesticable animals (except the cat, created solely to confound indubitable theory), man is gregarious, normally docile, stupid, and leader-following, and is paradoxically enough happiest in that state so long as he is given a lot more of the stick than the carrot.

A further stimulus to treating convicted criminals as slaves was the initial profit. Just before the American Revolution an English convict was worth about £25 to the master of a convict ship. The first women sent to Virginia were sold by the English authorities for 120 pounds of tobacco each. So everyone profited: the government by avoiding costs of execution or imprisonment of its various nuisances, the transporters by the transaction, and the colonists by escaping the rope on one hand and by the possibility of prospering in a new environment on the other.

The character of those who left the mother country free and those who left it slaved was by the force of circumstances the proper one to conquer a wilderness, Bacon notwithstanding. All were tough-minded men and women, eager to work for their own pockets, and differing mainly in how good they were at it. Earp, writing about the same time as Sidney, correctly estimated that

> In America, as in Australia, [the convict system] laid the foundation of an enterprising nation; for, whatever may be his other faults, the thief is invariably a more enterprising man than the generality of his more honest neighbours, when he is placed in a position in which he needs not, or dares not, steal any more.

Earp is lacking an important concluding phrase: 'and under the administration of governors who are placed in a position to steal even more.' Both colonies had that; the American leaders were more successful than the Australian partly because of the better physical and economic environment, but also because their motivation in exploit was greed spurred by fanaticism, a duple prime mover that cannot be withstood. Because what should have been is so much more simple and satisfying than what was, ordinary Americans believe that the Puritan settlers who made their nation's ethos were men of God who turned their backs against the material world when they sailed westward. They are able to sustain this illusion because they do not go to original sources for their historial information. If they read the *History of Plimmoth Plantation* by William Bradford, the colony's second governor and one of its most worthy men, they would find therein a depressing story of selfishness, greed, and vicious competition. In his annal for 1623, to choose one example, Bradford laments the human weakness that caused the disintegration of godly communality:

The experience that was had in this common course and condition, tried sundry years and that amongst godly and sober men, may well evince the vanity of that conceit of Plato's and other ancients applauded by some to later times; that the taking away of property and bringing in community into a commonwealth would make them happy and flourishing; as if they were wiser than God. For this community (so far as it was) was found to breed much confusion and discontent and retard much employment that would have been to their benefit and comfort.

From the time of their landing in 1620 until 1641 (when the English partners gave up) the history of the first of the two Puritan plantations is a tedious journal of trouble with the English capitalists who financed the venture, men who in the words of historian James Truslow Adams were 'not subscribing to foreign missions'. The main Puritan settlement was founded at Boston in 1630, and contention between the two colonies soon began. By 1634 they were murdering one another. Bradford's counterpart in Boston, Governor John Winthrop, sadly acknowledged the irony in his Journal, writing that the murder of a Plymouth man and a Massachusetts Bay man 'had brought us all and the gospel under a common reproach of cutting one another's throats for beaver'. Nor was all their fighting internecine – witness for example the shameful business of the outsider Thomas Morton, whom the Puritans framed for murder to stop his successful relations with Indian trappers. Up to the Revolution as subjects and ever after as citizens Americans have cut one another's throats for beaver and other negotiables. Possibly the rebellion itself might not have occurred if Boston's political leaders had not been heavily committed to tea smuggling when the British government saved the defeated holders of the legitimate tea trade monopoly, the East India Company, with a remission of their annual £400,000 profit-sharing payment and a subvening loan of £4,000,000.

In both the American and Australian colonies, rum led to

rebellion – in America by its practical destruction of the Navigation Acts and in Australia by the less subtle but more exciting Rum Rebellion. In the latter affair, the rapacious and unloved William Bligh, having come to the governorship fairly fresh from the *Bounty* mutiny, was defeated by a man even more grasping than he – John Macarthur, the wool pioneer. After going to the trouble of stocking his own plantation by such winsome devices as borrowing pregnant cows from the Crown and returning them after they had dropped calves, Bligh was deposed by Macarthur, Johnston, and the New South Wales Corps, and run off back to England, there again to be promoted in accordance with the Crown's policy of demonstrating confidence in officers who had lost the confidence of everyone else. Had he lived long enough, Bligh might have become King.

The resourcefulness of their predaceous leaders was often mirror-imaged by the lesser colonists. Bligh again provides an illustration. When he was deposed as captain of the *Bounty* by Fletcher Christian and put in a longboat in the Tonga Islands, Bligh proceeded to accomplish one of the greatest feats in the annals of navigation: he took his tiny boat 3,618 miles to the island of Timor. But the voyage of William and Mary Bryant, two First Fleet transported convicts, in a stolen fishing boat three years later, again to Timor, for them 3,254 miles distant, ought to be better known to Australians at least. Ironically the Bryants and their companions were arrested and turned over to Captain Edward Edwards, who was then prowling the South Seas in a futile search for the *Bounty* mutineers.

'How do you start a nation?' the Australian historian Donald Horne asked rhetorically, and answered his own question:

> In this case the answer was to take 729 men and women convicts out of the British prisons, combine them with 19 officers, 24 NCO's, 8 drummers, 160 troops, 30 women and 12 children, add food, tools, seed, pigs, poultry, 4 head of

cattle, 6 horses, 44 sheep, and the other minimum requirements of nation-building, put the convicts into six transports, the equipment into three store ships, add two naval vessels as a convoy and send the lot on an eight months' voyage out to Botany Bay, then establish a prison farm – without any farmers.

The foundations that underlay this Australian colonization were the same on which the American settlements were based: a letter converted by King James from the Act 39 Elizabeth c.4 and addressed to the council of the colony of Virginia, authorizing the shipment of 'a hundred dissolute persons to Virginia, that the Knight-Marshal would deliver to them for that purpose'. The alleged inhumanity of transportation is one of the most tiresome themes of those most tiresome people, the professional humanitarians. It must be remembered – if it is known at all – that these convicts were criminals caught without benefit of police in a frighteningly criminal age, when every man's hand was at the throat or in the pocket of another man. Who would question that transportation put them to better use? It has been regretted – for it is regrettable – that by our standards of transportational safety many of the exiled convicts died on the long voyages – 267 on the Second Fleet by one count, 199 on the Third. But there has been far too much notice paid for the worth of their insight to complaints like that of Captain Hill and the Reverend Mr Richard Johnson. Hill is often quoted to the effect that compared to the conditions on the Second Fleet the slave traffic was merciful, and that masters encouraged the convicts to die early so that their uneaten food could be sold. Mr Johnson was a craftsman with gloomy prose and is quoted as often as Captain Hill. There is always a Captain Hill and a Mr Johnson to provide tears and flapdoodle for the obfuscation of a serious question in history unto the seventh generation. Usually they are found upon investigation to be like the real Captain Hill, officer in the notorious Rum Corps and duellist off his own bat, and the real Mr Johnson, Australia's first great whinger (he complained that there was no place on earth worse 'than this poor wretched country, where scarcely anything is to be seen but Rocks, or eaten but Rats' – though he made rather a good thing of his stock-raising and wheat-growing), who made the gray hell of New South Wales black with his officious virtue.

Deaths there were in the Australian colony among vicious criminals left to the dubious mercy of vicious masters. But there were deaths in the American colonies, where both land and masters were kinder. Whole colonies vanished in the green lands of Virginia, and in New England, half of the *Mayflower*'s passengers died before the first summer came. Who remembers the prisoners sent to make colonies in Africa, colonies that utterly disappeared, thus removing their inhabitants from history and sympathy? And what of England itself – what of London, the capital of the world, the center of civilization? Those who did not live on oatmeal lived on gin and found their entertainment in public executions of people no worse perhaps than themselves and whose deaths at least were dramatic, not a whimpering out of life in conditions of indescribable dirt, squalor, deprivation, and immorality at the rate of fifty per thousand each year. To differentiate between the vicious and the virtuous in eighteenth-century England is an exercise in arbitrary absurdity. As one of the first Australians put the difference with great good humor within the first few weeks of settlement, those who came in the First Fleet were

> True patriots all, for, be it understood,
> We left our country for our country's good.

Prime Minister Menzies expressed it well when he delivered the Jefferson Oration at Charlottesville, Virginia, on the Fourth of July, 1963:

> When people in England jest to me about the lowly origins of our now thriving and law-abiding Commonwealth, I make the good-natured retort that, though many thousands of con-

73

victed persons were sent to America and many thousands to Australia, the records show that the great majority of persons convicted in England during the transportation era remained in England.

When we think too long in an orientation of social history our minds are in danger of being trapped in narrow corridors. The whole question of criminals and what to do with them is a distraction from the real cause of England's drive to make extensions of itself in empty lands. Like the matter of slavery in the American Civil War, transportation for crime was a manageable symbol of causes invisible to those whom they moved to action. The act of colonization for all organisms is an effect of redundant population. Looking at the phenomenon from an ecological point of view, we recall that within a decade of the Australian settlement Malthus wrote his *Essay on Population*. Even so, Malthus was making a theoretical expression of a hard fact of nature that soon or late all successful biota must face. Man faces it differently from his unique situation; for him, it is not simply a matter of proxemics, of optimum population density or even of maximum population density; his habits of economics drive him afield long before the question of actual survival obtains. Europe started to move at the end of the fifteenth century, for economic reasons, though no one knew enough about these pressures until much later. The American Revolution was an economic revolution, not a political one; Thomas Jefferson and his fellow conspirators were probably no more conscious of their credibility gap than those who really believed that the United States moved against the expansion from the north for the purpose of assisting the people of South Vietnam. The second important colonization from England – the Australian settlement – was an economic, political, and ecological phenomenon.

Economically, it was a continuation and expansion of the drive that settled the New World. Ecologically it was Malthusian, though once again the facts were not known for a long time – that about the time Malthus wrote his important paper, England lost the ability to feed itself. Politically, the redundant population was one that meant little to Australia and has been conveniently ignored by patriotic Americans who like to see their Revolution as a wholly good political alteration that injured no one but a few mercenary Hessians. But with the facts of the American Revolution in hand and with a knowledge of the character of the Revolution's engineers – Samuel Adams, as the archetypical example – many of us would not have joined the rabble had we been there. We would have consequently been in the same crowded boat with James Matra and other Loyalists, deprived of land and livelihood by the victors who made these things their spoils.

The American James Matra had however a different plan. His thesis, *A Proposal for Establishing a Settlement in New South Wales*, was that an Australian colony should be founded primarily for those Americans who remained loyal to Britain during the War of Independence. Recognizing the urgency of the problem of convicts awaiting transportation, he was willing to allow these unfortunates to emigrate with his own people, but as free men with equal rights as subjects and tenants of the new land. An enlightened man was Matra, and so far as his character can be assessed at this distance, well elevated above the morality so gratuitously awarded by history to the American revolutionaries. Still, the ancient truth obtains: reason and enlightenment have almost nothing to do with human behaviour. New South Wales could have been established as Matra (and others) recommended – the settlement of South Australia a short fifty years later proved the theoretical point – but the Home Secretary, Lord Sydney, wanted a penal colony, so a penal colony it became. As for what the colony was to be once it was proclaimed, no one in government seemed to know. When Arthur Phillip, Captain General of the First Fleet, landed his horses, sheep, poultry, drummers, cows, and convicts, he had no instructions what to do with them. The few honest trades represented among the various skills of his colonists were not the most useful occupations one could hope for in the situation. A drum has its place, but its place is not in a wilderness. Phillip had his one farmer, so he began farming, combining what was practical in the parable of the buried talents and what was hopeful in the parable of the loaves and fishes. Those who were redundant in the farming enterprise he put to work constructing buildings and bridges while he set to work constructing a viable socioeconomic system. After an initial period of unavoidable egalitarianism (like the Plymouth Plantation), the two-class division of society was established for all time – contemporary Australian opinion to the contrary notwithstanding. Convicts were let out to free settlers to work for their subsistence – a social device eminently just and logical from the settlers' point of view, but rather lacking in opportunities to satisfy the convicts, and ultimately a system of emancipation and free employment with an end reward of a land grant was inaugurated. But in the United States later, the promise that the meek will inherit the earth was soon revealed to be a wicked deception. The small farmers tilled the soil and became, by reason of their occupation and their disposition, herbivores. The rapacious and the rich came in and devoured them, for it is in the nature of carnivores to eat herbivores and in the nature of herbivores to be eaten. The Decalogue is as irrelevant as the Sermon on the Mount.

Of course the process was more complex and complicated than this generalization allows. For one thing, the land around Sydney was hopelessly poor; farmers dug the earth right down to Parramatta, fifteen miles from Sydney Cove, before the soil returned profitable crops. And some of the herbivores escaped their predators for a while; as an extreme example of how such beasts react, there is the case in 1791 of the group of Irishmen who began walking to China. A few herbivores mutated into predators themselves and lived as bushrangers until they became sufficiently annoying to the genuine carnivores to justify the bother of exterminating them.

And always in Australian history, the Yankees, seeking whom they would devour. At the time of Sydney's settlement, their appearance was, for once at least, a blessing. As she was to do again a century and a half later, Mother England abandoned her unwanted child, and America, as she was to do again a century and a half later, saved it. For the first two decades of the young colony's life, the 'wooden ships and iron men' out of Boston and New Bedford were nearly the only traders Australians were to see. No more than in World War II was American motivation altruistic in its aid to Australia, but though the American eye was on the Orient on both occasions, the incidental assistance to Australia was as real as if it were primary, and the Australians were generous enough to judge the act by its effect and not its intent. On this generosity reposes the friendship between the two countries that has withstood such irritations as the early American mariners brought along with their help.

Australia's first exportable commodities were seals and their oil; since American ships had been stopping at Sydney on their way to China for some years before the discovery of seals in Bass Strait in 1800, American sealers were working some parts of the area before the Australians. Far to the west, Captain Joseph Pendleton, master of the *Union*, opened Kangaroo Island to sealing and even built there a second ship, the *Independence*, commemorating the spot by naming it American River. With sealers as industrious as Pendleton, who took 14,000 seals in the 1803-1804 season, working the southern coasts, the industry collapsed quickly for the Australians. The Americans expanded their hunting far beyond New Zealand; Captain Folger of the *Topaz* out of Boston managed to find Pitcairn Island and the one white man still alive of the *Bounty* mutineers.

England still ruled the waves, however, and succeeded in

driving some of the American sea merchants away from sealing into a trade they had had some success with before the Revolution – rum-running. But even though the War of 1812 stopped American sea trade with Australia, it was resumed at a greater level than ever after 1815.

The Americans' exploitation of Australian sealing grounds was an adjunct to their exploitation of Australian whaling areas, which began shortly after the landing at Port Jackson. At the time of the Bass Strait seal discovery, even registered English whaling ships for the greater part were commanded and manned by Americans. Again the war interrupted exploit and trade in the South Pacific, but with peace came resumption and expansion, so that by 1840 several hundred whaling ships from the United States were hunting off Australian coasts. Trade thereafter diminished only according to the dictates of political events like the American Civil War, and, as competition and opportunities grew, trading diversified. All ice imported to Australia between 1839 and 1860, for instance, came in American ships.

According to those gifted people who are able to reduce events so vast in their complexity to simple questions of what is right and what is wrong, the wickedest phase of colonization in America and Australia was the displacement of the native peoples. Except for the staggering differential in intelligence, professional humanitarians are like the masters of multiple simultaneous blindfold chess play. Without ever seeing what is going on, they are able to keep several completely different mental processes going at the same time, with neither confusion nor contradiction intruding into their minds. Simultaneously they can weep for the victim and abominate the oppressor, whether they be English master and Australian convict, Australian convict and Australian aborigine, English master and American settler, or American settler and American Indian. Subleties like the sequence of displacement and extermination that gave rise to the various Australian aboriginal races – the Murrayians, Barrineans, Tasmanians, Wadjeri, and Carpentarians – or the successive occupation by force and violence of England by the Bell Beaker folk, the Picts, the Celts, the Romans, the Anglo-Saxons, and the Normans, are irrelevant to the main point, which is to expiate by weeping over a hapless surrogate some sin in themselves unrecognized and unrepented. The humanitarianism is commendable enough, but it gets in the way of historical fact, and with fact gone or distorted, understanding and the whole purpose of scholarship vanish.

If we are to understand the inevitable displacement of a hunter-gatherer of the Old Stone Age or a primitive farmer of the New by advanced civilization driven to inexorable expansion by the circumstances of its own ecological efficiency, we must do two things: first, keep emotion out of the equation, and second, see events in the light of their own times. Abraham Lincoln expressed in public discourse views on the American negro that even Governor George Wallace would not dare repeat now – views that absolutely denied the equality of black and white, the right of negroes to vote or to become equal in society, or even to be free in States adhering to the Union. In this enlightened age, the United Nations agency UNESCO has commanded anthropologists and other agents of neo-colonial imperialism to stop using opprobrious and invidious words like 'race', 'tribe', 'kaffir', 'primitive', 'native', 'jungle', 'vernacular', 'underdeveloped', 'savage', 'backward', 'colored', and 'pagan'. In the old days observers described people as they saw them, with no regard for propriety. In 1688 William Dampier, whom we can describe as a pirate, discovered the Bard tribe of Australia's north-western coast:

> The inhabitants of this Country are the miserablest People in the world. The *Hodmadods* of *Monomatapa*, though a nasty People, yet for Wealth are Gentlemen to these. . . . Setting aside their Humane Shape, they differ but little from Brutes. . . .
>
> They all of them have the most unpleasant Looks and the worst Features of any People that ever I saw, though I have seen great variety of Savages.

The Australian natives evidently had not appreciably improved in appearance in the 164 years that passed before Butler Earp gave his opinion of them:

In appearance they are in many cases revolting – reminding the European of the link between himself and the baboon, whose cunning they emulate, without any of the higher attributes which distinguish even savages in other parts of the Southern Hemisphere. To a European a more disgusting sight can scarcely be encountered than these people present: their black skin, covered with all kinds of greasy abominations; long coarse hair matted with gum, after the fashion of a thrum mop, and frequently stuck with kangaroos' or human teeth; the roof shape of their heads, with the sensual formation of the hinder part of it; the mouth of the men, minus the front tooth, etc. etc., combine to impress the beholder, the new comer especially, with anything but the philanthropic idea – "Am I not a man and a brother?" a sentiment which till of late years the stockmen repudiated by shooting all they came across, or, as was often the case, poisoning them by wholesale. . . . Their other qualities are not worth enumerating.

Such verbal abuse was translated by imagination if not by fact into physical abuse and murder in the writings of modern commentators, all of them well removed in time and place from the subject. Quite typical is the following summary of white and aboriginal relations written in 1961:

The process of settling Australia was accompanied by acts of incredible cruelty committed against the native occupiers of the soil. Courageous as were so many of the pioneering families who went out into the wilderness, the courage of those they sought to dispossess was often even greater. Disposed to be friendly to the white invaders, the Aborigines found their overtures answered with treachery and murder. Most reports of early relationships between settlers and natives suggest that it was the whites who were first responsible for hostile acts.

This opinion is completely dominant today, and anyone

who ventures to suggest even so much as its moderation becomes a poisoner of wells and a strangler of dogs. Yet contemporary diaries, journals, and other writings by persons in actual contact with the Australian natives at the time of settlement, persons who do not otherwise seem to be monsters, confute the popular notion that the main amusement of the colonists was Sunday excursions to hunt natives for dog meat. That wholly admirable charter colonist of South Australia, John Wrathall Bull, recalled in his memoirs of the first years of Adelaide the massacre of the crew and passengers of the brig *Maria* in 1840, when seventeen men, women, and children were hacked to death by aborigines. Governor Gawler, hoping to prevent further incidents of the sort, had the murderers captured and brought to trial, and after hearing not only the circumstantial evidence but aboriginal witnesses as well, had two of them hanged. The effect, wrote pioneer John Wrathall Bull, was otherwise than Gawler expected:

> . . . severe censure was visited upon the Governor by a certain party at home, and by a small section in the colony in opposition to Colonel Gawler, who made this a handle against him, but were not in the habit of exposing their own precious bodies to dangers in the bush of any kind.

This 'handle' was certainly used against Gawler later when, in order to keep the colony alive, he wrote government drafts that the Crown repudiated, bringing economic disaster to the whole community.

Bull's remarks on the reluctance of armchair humanitarians to expose their own precious bodies to bush dangers recall the poetic justice of the time when Bull and the military police forced the Missionary Protector to accompany them on a patrol to apprehend some forty or fifty aborigines who had attacked the homestead of an aged couple named Stubbs, smashing the faces of the 69-year-old woman and a young shepherd into a bloody paste and missing the old man because he was so drenched with the blood of his wife that he seemed as dead as she. The Protector was frightened into a palsy when Major O'Halloran informed him that the outnumbered soldiers would scrupulously obey the standing orders of the government, recommended by the Protector, that a white man was not to raise a firearm against the aborigines until a spear thrown at him was actually in the air.

This particular piece of humanitarian irresponsibility had caused the death of one Master Frank Hawson earlier in the same year. Frank Hawson, a twelve-year-old boy, was alone in the house on his parents' station seven miles from Port Lincoln early in March of 1840. Ordinarily he would not have been left unprotected in a district that had experienced a number of aboriginal depredations, but at this time assurances of eternal friendship had been given by the natives, and settlers gave them yet once more a chance to prove their better natures. The hut was attacked suddenly by a mob of 22 aboriginal men and boys, surrounded, breached, and entered; the young Frank Hawson was pierced through by one of the spears. Then and then only he seized a heavy rifle and fired upon his attackers, wounding one, whereupon they fled, leaving the boy to die.

It would be tedious to recount all the cases of wanton slaughter of whites by aborigines, just as it is to read the cases of slaughter of aborigines by whites with which other books on this profitless question are filled. It is enough to know that in the process of colonization, desperation on both sides leads to death. David Carnegie, the explorer of the frightful central wilderness of Western Australia, was as humane a man as one can find in frontier history, yet he was censured for capturing and chaining aborigines several times on his difficult journey through the spinifex and sand. A decade later A. W. Canning labored through the same deserts in a chimerical search for a practicable stock route; he also captured and chained aborigines. So did Peter Egerton Warburton when he crossed the worst of the northern deserts. So too did other explorers. The need to detain natives forcibly was not understood in the cities, and the compassionate ignorance of city people was exploited by the various enemies that every expeditionary leader incurred by exercising necessary discipline. Chaining and mistreating aborigines by feeding them salt meat and denying them water seems a clear enough crime to anyone who has not been through the western deserts, but let the man who would automatically condemn Carnegie, Canning, and the others for such conduct enter this country and follow their path with the supplies and equipment to which they were limited and he will surely die. The few waterholes that do exist in this lunar wilderness are so difficult to see that one can pass within yards of them and miss them altogether – and one missed waterhole means death, as it did for the Wells party in the same year David Carnegie made his north-south penetration.

Canning's opponents charged him with cruelty and he was brought before a Royal Commission, with attendant adverse publicity in the newspapers. Though such attacks did not usually succeed, the explorer's bewilderment at them often led to an inarticulateness in defense which still besmirches their memory. Giles and Carnegie almost alone had the forensic skill to reply to their calumniators. Carnegie put it bluntly: that in the 3,000-mile journey he undertook from Wiluna to Hall's Creek and back again he never once found water by chance. His practice therefore was to surprise and capture a native, rope and chain him, feed him on salty food until he abandoned his determination not to lead the exploring party to water.

Neither the explorer nor the aborigine behaved during this test of wills in a charitable – one hesitates to say 'Christian' – manner, for each was motivated by the need to continue his own life. For Carnegie, it was the problem of immediate relief from thirst; for the native, the problem of future supply. 'We could hardly blame him', Carnegie admitted in speaking of one recalcitrant native, 'for leading us away from his own supply, which he rightly judged we and our camels would exhaust.'

We in our turn must admit that the white men were taking land already occupied by natives. Simplistic morality again clouds rather than clears the picture. The white men were driven by their manifest destiny of moving into new territory. Other expanding peoples in the history and prehistory of the world – Mongoloids and Negroids as well as Caucasoids, though their sin is little known and less proclaimed – walked the same path of ecological original sin, since there is no other. Even Australoids: after the disastrous drought of 1916 the Pitjandjara pushed east and displaced the Jangkundjara and Antakarinja who in turn moved south and drove out other tribes in a great arc of nearly 2,000 miles until the empty country once held by the Mirning absorbed the refugees. In most of the non-white cases of forced population movement the process of displacement was simply one of extermination, with the intruders troubling neither their own minds nor their posterity's conscience with guilt and the consequent need to repair the irreparable. Anglo-Saxons are almost alone in the history of imperialism in scourging themselves for the imagined sins of their remote forefathers. Anyone who does not share the guilt is thought to have no conscience, for indeed he has no conscience. But he may have what is more useful to him if he hopes to arrive at an understanding of how these things happen – a sense of the inevitable and its methods – and an accommodation with life. Several of the early writers in both Australia and America understood the motivation, and history has not thanked them for making our assumption of guilt more difficult. One of the bluntest and least equivocal of the Australian realists, Alexander Harris, concluded, after describing the enormous injury to the aborigines caused by the state's hanging of seven white men for the Myall Creek killings,

> The matter fell into its true and old form, from which it should never have been disturbed; a simple question of *intimidation* (nothing more) between the musket and the spear. And every black's common sense solves this question so readily

and correctly and uniformly, that the simple consciousness of its being the true and only question is sufficient at any time to bring them into a state of submission. And if we want more than that, if we want a league of peace on equal grounds, really there is no road to it but that we give up their land and forsake their country; for this and this only is of the old axiom – that men should be just before they are generous. The blacks cannot be conciliated unless by giving up their country. If they are to be intimidated, it must be by something that is more prompt and effective than their own spear, and less dilatory than our law.

Most of those who experienced the psychological and physical hardships of making the frontiers safe for posterity, and who were strong-minded enough to accept truth without the amelioration of a falsifying conscience, agreed with Harris. The government, however, in both America and Australia did not, continuing a policy of what one antipodean colonist called a 'bastard sentimentality' that has perpetuated friction, hatred, and social instability to this day. In Australia the official policy that the aborigine was to be protected no matter what became of the settlers encouraged needless aggressiveness in the natives. There are still at least a half dozen places in Australia today where aborigines will spear white men without more than the briefest hesitation – and if there is any response by the authorities, the victim is more likely to be punished than the native. In the United States too Indians can assault white men with little danger of punishment.

In both America and Australia the practice followed during the initial occupation, of buying land from tribesmen who had no understanding of land ownership, purchase, wealth, its symbols, or contractual transactions, was a concession only to the consciences of those who engaged in it. In many cases history has ridiculed these tradesmen in aboriginal real estate, and properly so; in too few instances did they live long enough to read of the derision their sanctimonious dishonesty deserved. John Batman, co-founder of Melbourne, was one who did; he survived to see in a contemporary newspaper this account of his 'purchase' of two million acres from a man named Fudgaree,

> rather an advantageous bargain, having purchased the whole for a dozen pair of blankets, six dozen tobacco pipes, 150 figs of tobacco, and two bottles of rum; a glass of the latter exhilarated Fudgaree so much that he embraced Mr B., and called him his PICKANINNY.

In order to make the transaction impressively official, ink was smeared on Fudgaree's hand and rubbed over the document to validate the sealskin-and-kangaroo-sinew seal, but in delimiting the extent of the new land of Batmania,

> Some difficulty occurred in endeavouring to explain to the native what an acre of land meant, and he seemed to have no idea of millions, being ignorant of numbers, never having counted over ten; but this obstacle was got over, by shewing him the stars on a fine night, and explaining that the number of acres to be granted were as numerous as the stars, to which he agreed with the greatest complacency, but seemed to have a better idea of the use of a fig of tobacco.

On American shores the first real estate swindle was the notorious conveyance of Manhattan Island to Dutchman Peter Minuit by the Indians, but in this case the swindle set the pattern for subsequent sales of the Brooklyn Bridge – the salesmen did not own the property. They were Canarsie Indians visiting the island for the day in the absence of the occupant Scaticook tribe.

Some white men appreciated the absurdity of purchasers in the European sense imposed upon an impecunious culture and wrote about it with sardonic humour little appreciated by those who take the matter of land purchases, deprivation, and the force of Calvinistic conscience, seriously. Having received grudging guidance from a band of aborigines who then decided to tag along beyond their usefulness, David Carnegie paid them to go their own way:

> . . . and they made tracks for the glen, bearing with them many rich gifts. An empty meat tin and a few nails does not sound a very great reward for their enforced services, and yet they would have been far less pleased with a handful of sovereigns; they could put these to no use whatever, whereas the tins will make small "coolimans", and the nails, set in spinifex gum at the end of a waddy, will find their way into a neighbour's head.

The Australian settlers had one psychological advantage over their American counterparts in this area at least: they were not driven by Puritan guilt in their dealings with the natives. In assessing the historical factors of England's colonial policies, one should not forget that the emigrants who established the successful northern colonies of America and who consequently established the American ethos were the Puritans, discredited before and ever after their brief possession of English government in the middle of the seventeenth century; Australians to the contrary were in the mainstream of English culture, upper and lower class, and while they partook of the Calvinist legacy, it was attenuated to a propensity for doing penance, not a compulsion. The upper-class public officials suffered to some degree from *noblesse oblige*, whose encumbrances they imposed upon the lower-class settlers in their relations with the aborigines. From this conflict derived the sharply differing views of the problem as expressed by Alexander Harris and the Missionary Protectors. But in neither case was their conscience so strong as to warrant the intervention of political nations among the aborigines, dealing with them on a state diplomatic level, encouraging them to sue for enormous damages in compensatory cases, and buying land – the same land – many times over, as the Americans have been doing since the foundation of the United States.

Jefferson paid Napoleon $15,000,000 for the Louisiana

Territory, considered a great bargain at the time by people who were not told that a further $300,000,000 was paid under the blanket to the Indians. Some Indians were paid as many as six times for the same landhold without accepting dispossession. Indians have been suing whites for land compensation and other alleged deprivations for more than a century, but until an enabling act was passed by the Congress in 1946 suits against the government had to be approved by the government before proceeding to actual litigation. In 1946 an attempt was made to obtain overall absolution for the crime of entering the American continent, with penitence expressed in enormous compensations. The incidental injustices of the concept are epitomized by the award of nearly $32,000,000 to the Utes of the Four Corners region of the South-western United States for land which the Utes forcibly appropriated from the moribund Pueblos. American Indians have traditionally been disunified and independent in a strangely enthusiastic way that strikes white Americans as foolishly self-defeating.

Even at this most favorable time to take advantage of American affluent compassion, they seem to delight in betraying leaders who need only a little intertribal support to force some state or federal concession. In another direction the ulterior intent of the enabling legislation – to allow Americans to achieve peace of mind – is illustrated by the inequity of granting large sums to negligibly small tribes (some $55,000,000 is being claimed for 600 Quapaws), of recognizing factitious tribes (the historical Seneca are unrecognizable in a troika comprising the Seneca Nation, the Seneca Republic, and the Seneca tribe of the Iroquois Nation), and certifying claims to authority by 'chiefs' who are almost complete fabrications.

In suits alone the United States may have to pay out ten billion dollars to a half million Indians. How much money is being paid in various other guises is impossible to calculate, but there are nearly four hundred reservations, most of which are actually as well as potentially rich in natural resources (in 1965 Indians received $70,000,000 in rentals alone) on which no taxes are paid; and hundreds of millions are paid through such agencies as the Bureau of Indian Affairs. As the Australian aborigines were encouraged by official laxness in asserting social and legal order, the American Indians have been emboldened by governmental largesse to claim the return of seventy per cent of the United States. The Seminole, who have no historical right to any Florida land, were confirmed in their claim to the entire state by the Indian Claims Commission, which offered the customary multi-million-dollar payment – but the Seminole declined the cash and demanded the state instead. No special experience, education, or intelligence is required to infer from this debauch of conscience on the part of white Americans that the last state of both Indians and Americans will at its conclusion be worse than the first. The Indian himself is in a serious state of anomie by having been turned from a proud, fierce, aggressive, merciless, and always dignified warrior into the self-fulfilling stereotype of a drunken, stupid, downtrodden, oppressed, helpless, pitiful object of charity, nothing more than an artifact created by the white man with which to whip himself.

The irresistible centrifugality of American culture, which is engulfing the distinctiveness of most of the remainder of the world's nations, is especially influential in changing the traditional attitudes of Australians in matters thought to be beyond infection. So it is that as the last Australian frontier goes under civilized exploitation, the American policy toward its aboriginal natives is reflected in the uncritical acceptance of American emotional conduct as if it were the product of both reason and experience. The notion that there are such things as inalienable civil rights, monetary equivalents of land usufruct, equality (of the sexes, of individuals, of social and racial groups), and hereditary compensation for imaginary ancient evils, is beginning to dominate Australian official thinking. Worse than the new attitudes are the new actions, applied without serious thought about what their ultimate effects might be. Even so holy and wholesome a thought as the decision to grant aborigines full citizenship rights has resulted in rapid disintegration of cohesiveness among tribal aborigines for whom only cohesiveness can assure survival.

There is neither blessedness nor benignity in conscience money; it corrupts both donor and recipient. Aborigines who pluck at one's sleeve and beg 'gibbit tikpense' may at least appreciate the position of degradation that charity imposes, but the native that demands sixpence – or nowadays a dollar – is a lost soul; nothing is left him but dishonour. And what is just for the white may be unjust for the native, Indian or aboriginal. Unearned income for oil rights never suspected or understood by Indians made them literally good for nothing. An aborigine who was proud with a spear on land found to be nearly pure manganese beneath the topsoil may indeed by our concepts be entitled to a fair share of the exploitation of the mysterious black resource, but in fact and effect such payments are unearned income, unavoidably corruptive. He puts down the spear and takes up the cash and his hands are idle, thereafter – and even the atheist understands that there is a devil that finds work for idle hands. One can see the process on nearly every aboriginal mission in Australia, though on so small a scale that nowhere is it more than a model of what is to come. In the last three or four years Australians have willingly if unwittingly gone further in pursuit of their own immolation by following the American example – they have in the face of all reason and reality imported the American racial problem, together with its foredoomed solutions. One hears now the same factitious cries for aboriginal rights among university students who have never seen a fullblood aborigine, but who nevertheless affect to know what he wants and how he thinks. One sees Freedom Busses, and perhaps there will be a Resurrection City thrown up in Sydney's

Domain. If the movement is permitted to continue in Australia simply because of what is happening in the United States, we may live to see cities burn like the *karri* forests. At the moment there are not enough aborigines to bring about the race risks seen in present-day America imported from the American civil righteousness; but factitious minority groups may well cause such things to occur.

It was only five years ago that Americans laughed at the suggestion that since Indians were being paid for all that land taken from them a century ago negroes should sue for wages for all that free labour during slavery days. Now it seems more than possible that they will not even have to sue. What then will the descendants of the First, Second, Third, and succeeding convict fleets do? If one can measure a field in bushels as well as in acres, one can conceive of a new frontier in economics as well as in land. Wealth lies easier to hand in banks than in mountains of ore.

When Sir Francis Bacon advised against founding a colony with wicked condemned men, his conception of evil was limited by the inexperience of his time. He thought there was no good in the people who were being sent to inhabit the New World; he would have found less to commend in the cargo of the First Fleet. But the petty iniquities of the condemned and indentured settlers were the product of an energy that was to build two great nations. Ironically, as England declines, the countries established as sinkholes for her moral castaways appear now to be her greatest achievements. But that will be so only so long as they preserve the strength that constructed them, however badly it seemed to be used in the first days of settlement and in the years immediately before. Morality does not consist of adherence to arbitrary Decalogues of specified prohibitions, but rather to whatever conduces to the preservation of the group. The troubles of the United States, whose symptoms are already appearing in Australia, are the signs of an unhealthy soul not, as commonly believed, of the body societal; the invention of an unreality as malevolent as the doctrine of original sin. Were he to return, Bacon might appreciate the paradox - that there is more wickedness in virtue than in vice.

FOUR

What Manner of Men?

Let an Australian and an American get together over a couple of strong Australian beers and in a few minutes each is likely to decide that the other is bloody mad. And each will probably be right. What other country in the world, for instance, would send men out to carry boats across the desert, and what other men would eagerly do it? Captain Charles Sturt dragged a boat over the bone-dry ghastly blank of central Australia, looking for an inland sea; his second-in-command, James Poole, thought he found it, but died instead of thirst. Lt. W. F. Lynch of the United States hauled two metal boats over the Palestinian desert in 1848 – boats too heavy for horses to pull, so for the first time in the history of their species, camels were used to transport boats. Missing his way on the River Murray during an unprecedented flood, Captain George Ritchie, known ever afterward as the 'Mud Pilot', was steaming confidently toward the Simpson Desert with forty tons of cargo aboard when a wandering aborigine put him right. And those Alice Springs yachtsmen who annually gallop up and down the riverbed carrying their boats in the Henley-on-Todd regatta have little in the way of irrationality on the thousands of American tourists who set powerboats on trailers and tow them back and forth across the southern Mohave Desert each summer.

These are only the acceptably sane Austramericans. Both countries produced certifiable nuts in abundance. In the United States the worst of the maniacs gravitated to Battle Creek, Michigan, and Los Angeles, California. Los Angeles had the greatest quantity and variety, probably because it was the last place these people could go in the compulsive westward march of lunacy without continuing into the sea; but Battle Creek had the purest. At the latter community's Western Health Reform Institute, Corn Flakes were invented to strengthen the teeth (they were supposed to be eaten dry); Shredded Wheat to put some body in soup; Postum to spare the American people diabetes and blindness, both caused by drinking coffee; Graham crackers (best described as vegetable cinders) to scour out the bowels when the ordinary regimen of 15-gallon daily enemas did not return clean results; grape juice and Grape Nuts to assuage the body's longing for tea and its consequent insanity; and sexual continence to escape cholera.

In the associated areas of sex and insanity Australia put forth one W. J. Chidley, a 'three-barrelled crank' inventor of a new method of copulation, 'the strangest method yet propounded' (unfortunately undescribed, since his autobiography has never been published), and advocate of a diet restricted to fruit and, understandably, nuts.

America's utopian communities like Fruitlands, Zoar, Oneida, Brook Farm, New Harmony, and Icaria (in the most unlikely place for an earthly paradise, Texas) had their counterparts in the land Down Under, principally New Australia, carried to Paraguay by William Lane, often mistaken for Ben Turpin. New Australia collapsed within a year from frictions one would suppose to be incompatible with a heavenly community, and Lane went off to establish a better colony which he named Cosmé. Out in Western Australia a visionary utopianist and practical communist, Don McLeod, gathered up a large mob of susceptible aborigines and fled with them into the iron and stone wilderness of the Kimberleys, there to shun white man and his corrupting works and live by scrabbling up tantalite to sell to the white man to make his weapons of total war.

Everyone who goes of his own free will into the centre of

Australia is, like America's Death Valley Scotty and similar internal expatriates, *ipso facto* off his bloody chump. They must be met again and worked with in amity, so they must not be identified even by description, but the extent of their eccentricity can be gauged by those comparatively lucid people running cattle on the fringes of the Center – like the millionaire pastoralist in western Queensland who tore the electric clock out of his car when he discovered that it was running when he wasn't in the automobile.

But what can be expected of the man who goes deliberately

. . . out into the music of the silent bush, with his pick in one hand, his water bag in the other hand, and his life in the other. He goes into the bush, where the hand of man has never set foot, and let me tell you, he don't come back again until he have left his bones to be picked clean by the crows and dingoes!

We have the name of the 'hatter' who wandered about Tasmania at the beginning of the last century christening innocent towns with Bedlamite names like Abyssinia, River Jordan, Jericho, Lake Tiberias, and Bagdad (he was Hugh Germain, a kangaroo hunter), but what madman about the same time inflicted upon outback New York communities such identities as Attica, Babylon, Cairo, Troy, Mount Sinai, Syracuse, and Jericho?

Like the curve in baseball, national character is an intangible and unprovable reality. Australian and American people may be as individually varied as their numbers in the population, but the man at the top of the bell-shaped curve is unmistakable to anyone who has met him and his fellows, whether in the Australian bush or the American bowling alley. Some audacious analysts, heedless or ignorant of the popular statute in contemporary social science that says anything that cannot be replicated does not exist, have made guide lists to the least common denominators of what makes an Australian and what makes an American. For the Australian, a man practical; rough-and-ready; critical of any affectation; improvising and ingenious, but not eager to excel; no lover of work; much giving to swearing, gambling, and drinking; taciturn; anti-intellectual; anti-religious at worst, apathetic at best; noisily independent, an ineffectual hater of authority; hospitable and nearly always genial in his drunkenness; faithful to his 'mate' (not his wife) above all things; insular; gregarious; and with a moral sense arrested at the pubescent level where the worst of sins is 'snitching' – informing on a lawbreaker, no matter how villainous the miscreant may be. For the American, a latter-day Anglo-Saxon: proud, prudish, practical, unimaginative, sentimental, democratic, muddling, acquisitive, bibulous, gullible, credulous, and gloomy. He also spits, buys friendship; hates foreigners; blunders into places where he has no business to be; execrates opera, ballet, piano playing, and other recognized forms of culture; expresses his status competition in monetary success for lack of titles and similar immaterial honorifics; inclines to violence by permitting Communist expatriates and Jordanian visitors to kill his political leaders; distrusts himself inflexibly; preserves his naïveté with fierce determination; forces his negro minority to work for wages higher than only ninety per cent of the rest of the workers of the world (including white Australia); deprives his negro minority of education to the extent that they do not reach quite twice the number of university graduates per capita as white Australia; imposes his neo-colonial capitalistic imperialism in undeveloped countries until they have evolved sufficiently to expropriate his property; feeds the world's mouths that bite him; wins wars but appropriates no territory as spoils; and sends up men to walk on the moon.

Since misfortune helps in a small way to expiate his share of Adam's heinous Original Sin, the American does not usually whine, whinge, or complain. The Australian sees no fault in himself, and consequently does not accept bad luck with good grace. Indeed, if there is any single national characteristic that the Australian has developed from an hereditary instinct into a fine art, it is complaining. The best illustration of this facet of the Aussie's disposition is the recitation known as 'The Greatest Whinger on Earth', known to everyone Down Under, but because of their censorious 'wowserism', heretofore unpublished:

I struck him first on a shearing station in outback Queensland. He was knocking the fleece from a four-year-old wether when I asked him the innocent question, 'How would you be?'

He didn't answer immediately, but waited until he had carved the last bit of wool from the sheep, allowing it to regain its feet, kicking it through the door, dropping the shears, and spitting a stream of what looked like molten metal about three yards. Then he fixed me with a pair of malevolent eyes, in which the fires of a deep hatred seemed to burn, and he pierced me with them as he said, 'HOW WOULD I BE?'

'How would you bloody well expect me to be? Get a load of me, will you? Dags on every square inch of me bloody hide; drinking me own sweat; swallowing dirt with every breath I take; shearing sheep which should have been dogs' meat years ago; workin' for the lousiest bastard in all Australia; and frightened to leave because the old woman has got some bloody hound lookin' for me with a bloody maintenance order.

'How would I BE? I haven't tasted beer for weeks, and the last glass I had was knocked over by some clumsy bastard before I finished it.'

The next time I saw him was in Sydney. He was trying to get into a set of webbing [Army uniform], and almost ruptured himself in the process. I said, 'How would you be?'

'HOW WOULD I BLOODY WELL BE?' he said. 'Take a gander at me! Get a load of this bloody outfit. Look at me bloody hat – size nine-and-a-half and I take six-and-a-half. Get a bloody eyeful of these strides. Why, you could hide a bloody brewery horse in the arse of them and still have room for me. Get on this shirt – just get on the bloody thing, will you? Get on these bloody boots – why, there is enough leather in the bastards to make a full set of harness. And some know-all bastard told me this was a man's outfit. How would I be? How would I bloody well BE?'

I saw him next in Tobruk. He was seated on an upturned box, tin hat over one eye, cigarette butt hanging from his bottom lip, rifle leaning against one knee, and he was engaged in attempting to clean his nails with the tip of his bayonet. I should have known better, but I asked him, 'How would you be, Dig [soldier]?'

He swallowed the butt and fixed me with a really mad look. 'How would I be? HOW WOULD I BLOODY WELL *BE*? How would you expect me to be? Six months in this bloody place; being shot at by every Fritz in Africa; eating bloody sand with every meal; flies in me hair and eyes; frightened to sleep a bloody wink, expecting to die in this bloody place; and copping the crow every time there's a hand-out to anybody. How would I be? How would I bloody well be?'

The last time I saw him was in Heaven, and his answer to my question was, 'How would I be? HOW WOULD I BLOODY WELL BE? Get an eyeful of this bloody night-gown, will you? A man trips over the bloody thing fifty bloody times a day, and it takes a man ten minutes to lift the bloody thing when I want to piss. Get a gander at this bloody right wing – feathers missing all over the bloody thing – a man must be bloody well moulting. Get an eyeful of this bloody halo – only me bloody ears keep the rotten thing on me skull. And look at the bloody dents on the bloody thing. How would I be? Cast your eyes on this bloody harp – six bloody strings missing, and there's band practice in five minutes. "How would you be?" you ask. HOW WOULD YOU EXPECT A MAN TO BLOODY WELL BE?'

The worst and most frequent misfortune suffered by any one class of Australians invariably fell upon the bullockies – the drivers of outback bullock teams whose difficult job it was to haul freight across prohibited properties to distant stations. In the Riverina market town of Gundagai, which has increased its population during the last 130 years to 2,167 souls, there stands a vulgar statue of a dog sitting upon a tuckerbox – a food box sometimes carried by swagmen and other itinerants. The story one will be told about the monument is a heart-warming tale of man's best friend, in this instance a dog left by a swagman to guard his tuckerbox while he was away on other business. He never returned, and the dog, faithful to its trust, pined to death. A beautiful, inspiring story, and wholly false. The story is actually about a bullocky who had an extraordinary run of rotten luck, capped by his dog's 'sitting' in the food box. The point of the following traditional song is obscured by a euphemism: the dog did not *sit* on the box – the verb is missing an aspirate – and he did not perform the act *on* the box, but *in* it.

> I'm used to driving bullock teams
> across the hills and plains,
> I've teamed outback these forty years
> in blazing droughts and rains;
> I've lived a heap of troubles through,
> without a bloomin' lie,
> But I can't forget what happened me
> nine miles from Gundagai.
>
> 'Twas getting dark, the team got bogged,
> the axle snapped in two;
> I lost me matches and me pipe –
> now, what was I to do?
> The rains came down, 'twas bitter cold,
> and hungry too was I –
> And the dog sat in the tuckerbox
> nine miles from Gundagai.
>
> Some blokes I know has all the luck
> no matter how they fall,
> But there was I, Lord love a duck,
> no flamin' luck at all;
> I couldn't make a pot of tea
> nor keep me trousers dry –
> And the dog sat in the tuckerbox
> nine miles from Gundagai.

> I could forgive the blinkin' team,
> I could forgive the rain;
> I could forgive the dark and cold
> and go through it again;
> I could forgive me rotten luck,
> but hang me till I die –
> I won't forgive that bloody dog
> nine miles from Gundagai.

To which another bullocky might well respond, 'Serves you right for not havin' better luck'.

Work, we have been told on good authority, came into the world as an additional punishment for Adam's sin. Since the American eagerly accepts the inherited responsibility, he delights in work; the Australian thinks of work as a bloody nuisance, and he does as little of it as slowly as he can. The International Labour Organization reports that Australians have the shortest working hours in the world – 1,864 as compared to 2,016 in the United States. The figures are impressive, but misleading: they do not include 'smoke-ohs' several times a day, long lunch periods, portal-to-portal time, and the most frequent, longest, and inconsequential strikes since Adam was flung out of the Garden. Even in the arid pastoral runs of outback New South Wales shearers have voted on whether the sheep were wet – from rain or heavy dew, for wet sheep could cause pneumonia, onychogalea, macropus major, coreopsis, and God knows what other frightful diseases. Curiously, wet sheep occurred most often in the same climatic conditions that produced strikes among the wharfies [longshoremen] – warm, dry, pleasant weather.

In those industries managed by Americans and worked by Australians some invidious figures are reluctantly admitted; the Australian worker is paid to labour at a production rate about 30 per cent behind Americans on the same job. The differential is conceded by most Australian managers, but it is attributed to 'the vicious piece-work system used in the US and their system of instantaneous lay-offs whenever demand slackens temporarily'. Russel Ward, whose view of necessitous collectivism may be slightly exaggerated by his early association with agrarian reform, argues still another reason for this phenomenon:

> ... the typical Australian frontiersman in the last century was a wage-worker who did not, usually, expect to become anything else. The loneliness and hardships of outback life, as on the American frontier, taught him the virtues of cooperation, but his economic interests, unlike those of the American frontiersman, reinforced this tendency towards a social, collectivist outlook. By loyal combination with his fellows he might win better conditions from his employer, but the possibility of becoming his own master by individual enterprise was usually but a remote dream. So far from being 'precipitated by the wilderness into a primitive organization based on the family', he was precipitated into an equally primitive organization of 'nomad tribesmen', if one may conceive of a tribe without women and children. Thus it came about that differing frontiers in the United States and Australia produced two different kinds of frontiersmen, with mental attitudes which were very similar in some respects but very different in others.

Urban Australia differs much more from rural and frontier Australia than these areas differ in the United States; but there has always been sufficient interaction to require some compatibility between the attitudes and behaviour of the outback worker and the city laborer. The Australian worker's view of life as sunshine and easy beer delivered him into the hands of the Barefoot Man, when hungrily ambitious Southern European immigrants began pouring off the boats after World War II. In Sydney and to a somewhat lesser degree in other cities the small businesses have been appropriated to nearly the entire exclusion of the born Australian – proving that the opportunity was there all the time, but the first comers' social and psychological inherited prejudices had more to do with their failure to achieve economic independence than unalterable deprivation. Manual workers in Australia's cities are beyond the ability of American visitors to observe; moving at koala speed they are habituated to a dawdle so artful that one has to be trained to stand it, let alone understand it. The Spit Bridge, essential to North Shore Sydney traffic, was planned to be two years in the building; it took six, and the English contractor in charge publicly vowed he would never undertake to build in Australia again. One of the most beautiful buildings in the world to the external eye (inside it is a hopeless mess) is the Sydney Opera House, now in its second decade of construction; the first cost estimate was a barely acceptable $8,500,000; at this moment the cost has gone to $95,200,000 with completion not really expected in our lifetime. One of these days someone is going to notice a resemblance between the Opera House and *Bleak House*.

Russel Ward's theory of collectivism; the history of labor unionism in Australia; the working class ethos, willing mateship and unwilling compulsion to restrain if not eliminate ambition; attitudes toward the economic outcrop; and a submissiveness toward actual authority and noisy defiance of imagined authority – and these and other factors inherent in the history and character of Australia's lower class joined to create in the arid mulga scrub of western New South Wales a small corner of collectivist Paradise: the improbable town of Broken Hill. Since it is a microcosm of what Australia's old-line labor leaders want today for Australia and tomorrow for the world, it is worth an overview.

Seven hundred miles west of Sydney in the eastern edge of the central deserts, Broken Hill enjoys a sun-drenched climate of nine inches annual rainfall and ninety inches evaporation. Waterless itself, it subsists on what comes to it through a pipeline from the Darling River 70 miles away. With its borrowed water Broken Hill is an oasis, like Palm Springs, but there is no other resemblance – and whoever would want to see the difference between Australians and Americans should keep the Palm Springs equivalent running parallel with what is said here of Broken Hill. In 1844 the explorer Charles Sturt in his journey toward the 'gloomy and burning deserts' passed this place, then marked by a curiously shaped hill which he named 'Piesse's Knob', after his storekeeper's head. Piesse's Knob got the attention it deserved for nearly forty years, and then in 1883 a boundary rider, one Charles Rasp, saw a glint in the earth as he passed by. He considered for a moment the bother of taking a closer look, but in a prophetic anticipation of its ultimate residents, he passed on. The next time through, however, his path took him closer to the hill and he 'fossicked' around, concluding that he had struck tin. He formed a syndicate with six friends, each contributing £70 to buy the hill. Persons with more geological acumen than Rasp saw that what he thought was tin was really ironstone, but what they could not see, a hundred feet down, was the extraordinarily rich silver deposits. Within a year the Broken Hill Proprietary Company was capitalized with 2,000 shares of stock offered at £20 each; another year and the 'BHP' was worth £1,500,000. Other claimants came in to work the rich edges of the claim and all prospered mightily until the Amalgamated Miners' Association hit the camp in 1886. A series of bad strikes hit the town in 1892, 1908-1909, 1916, and 1919, after which the power of the union, having conquered the proprieters, burgeoned to the point where, in 1939, BHP withdrew from the area entirely. Wishing to cloud fact with illusion, some apologists explain the BHP abandonment of its original enterprise as a result of its long-planned intention to develop other prospects throughout Australia, but the company took advantage of its freedom – not permitted American companies, strangely enough – to close down operations when union pressures became too oppressive to bear. The wealth continued great (100,000,000 tons of ore by 1966) but the annoyance was greater, and the BHP moved on to new and what proved to be richer pastures. The city continues to prosper with the silver lode still producing at a depth of 2,500 feet, but the social situation is more than any capitalist worthy of the opprobrium can accept. Peter Robinson, writing in the *Australian Financial Review* in July, 1966 put the matter succinctly:

> Broken Hill is not just another mining town. . . . It is a town which has built a unique social structure on the foundations of a unique mineralization. . . .
>
> To the visitor it sometimes seems that Broken Hill regards the line of lode as a piece of community property – to be hoarded and preserved for the sole purpose of maintaining indefinitely the Broken Hill way of life. . . .
>
> The industrial history of Broken Hill has been dominated by the fact that the richness of the lode made it economically possible to accede to pay demands, manning requirements and mining methods which would have been ruinous for poorer mines.

The Barrier Industrial Council – a combination clearing house for unions and dictatorship of the proletariat – is in control of the city and the mines and the residents to such a degree that neither the state of New South Wales nor the Commonwealth government cares to challenge it, preferring to ignore the situation in hope that the lode will run out and destroy the Council and its members. Meanwhile, the Council exercises authority just short of absolute. Private enterprise exists so long as it pleases the Council; if prices of any commodity, even beer, rise beyond what the Council will accept – regardless of what economic pressures bear upon prices – the Council simply declares the commodity 'black', and the storekeeper either gets into line or gets out of town. The Council publishes the newspaper, which every union member – which is to say, every Broken Hill worker, no matter how many may live in one household – must subscribe to. All commercial enterprises in Broken Hill must advertise in the paper, or they are declared 'black'. If for any reason the Council prefers not to disclose, a merchant falls into its disfavour, advertising space in the newspaper is denied him, and thus he becomes a non-advertiser, and 'black'. Henry Lawson, the greatly admired chronicler of life in the bush, once wrote a story called 'A Union Town', in which a new chum [tenderfoot, especially an English immigrant] arrives in a town like Broken Hill and is confronted by what appears to be two hanged men dangling from a tree limb. A townsman assures him that the incident was a minor infraction of the community's rules – the men were non-unionists. The new chum takes the first train out, never learning the 'corpses' were effigies. The fiction is funny, but the reality is sobering; Broken Hill might well hang two men for such a crime.

In 1966 the retiring head of the union, W. S. 'Shorty' O'Neill, was interviewed on the Australian Broadcasting Commission's television network. Shorty is a jolly fellow, rotund and genial as Santa Claus or Nikita Khrushchev. He assured the rest of Australia that Broken Hill was a fine community, greatly maligned by its illiberal critics. Union membership was not, he declared, compulsory. But under the sharp questioning of the interviewer, he admitted that if an unaffiliated worker 'hasn't got a badge on Badge Show Day, he'll find that no one will work with him. . . . If he doesn't join the union, he can't work in Broken Hill; that's an impossibility'. Communists? '. . . only four Communists in union positions . . . I don't think there would be fifty or sixty Communists in Broken Hill.' Australian Labor Party officials either admit to Communist control or declare their opposition to it, but the man is purblind indeed who will deny that it would be hard to find a Labor Party official who could not, if necessary, find the Communist Party platform broad enough to accommodate him.

The Barrier Industrial Council spokesmen will concede some arbitrariness in their governance, but they offer more than mere compensatory balances; crime, for example, does not exist in Broken Hill. Law may not be in clear evidence, but order certainly is. Crime, however, is what government defines crime to be. In probably every other mining camp in the civilized world pilferage of ore is considered stealing, and with rich ores like silver and gold, ingenious methods of detection and rigorous application of punishment for thieves are standard operating procedure. But in Broken Hill the BHP was compelled to allow workmen to keep anything they could carry out in their pockets.

All this is not to imply that the residents of Broken Hill are unhappy or conscious of oppression; they demonstrate Eric Hoffer's thesis that in-group cohesiveness more than offsets the deprivation of 'civil rights', affluence, or any other boon man thinks he wants. Pro Hart, for example, is one of Australia's finest painters – which is to say that he is one of the finest painters in the world – and his works sell for what they are worth, which is a very great deal; but Pro Hart proudly considers himself to be a Broken Hill miner, and his painting is something he does when he is not down in the mine.

As Hoffer and other wise men before him advised those who would be successful in making revolution and establishing their new order, the union leaders of Broken Hill gave their people what they did not know they wanted, but without which nothing else is worth having: comforting, protective, participatory membership in an impregnable group solidly opposed when needed to all others. The ancient failure of Australia and the recent failure of America in this most essential component of political stability are more than sufficient to account for all the overt and covert civil disorder both nations experienced.

Though the governing class of Australia accepted condemned men as settlers against the warning of Bacon, it agreed with his prediction of their behaviour in the new plantation, that they 'will ever live like rogues, and not fall to work, but be lazy, and do mischief, and spend victuals, and be quickly weary'. Such people might be useful, but they were never to sup at the masters' table. Nor in the mind of the upper class were the free proletarians that augmented an inadequate supply of convict labor qualitatively different from the lags – the one group had been caught, the other had not; a distinction not worth considering in making policy of government. William Macarthur, son of the founding father, in arguing for free immigrant labor, blandly wrote,

> I will suppose such a man to be a shepherd and to have several boys of nine or ten upwards. He might, with his boys, undertake the entire duties connected with a sheep station consisting of three or four flocks. It will not surely be contended that such a family would be more expensive to their master, than four or five convict servants. . . . Even the females may with propriety be employed. . . . At Camden my two brothers and myself have about thirty women. . . . We have generally from ten to twenty children, from five and six years old, employed at wages from 3d to 1/- per diem.

Shorty O'Neill would not have spoken this way about his comrades, however much he might have agreed with the implied estimation of their worth.

From any period of recorded Australian history class division can be documented. In Tom Collins's *Such Is Life* a lady of quality chides a free servant whom she has injured so grievously and so unjustly that the girl finally speaks out in protest:

> 'My parents done the best they could to keep theyre home together,' protested the girl, in a choking voice.
> 'Speak grammatically, my dear. No doubt your parents did as you say, but my point is, that they forgot their position. Instead of accepting the fair wages and abundant food which society offers to their class, they joined the hungry horde that has cut up those fine Victorian stations. Part of the retribution justly falls on their children, part, of course, on themselves. Your father, I venture to say, often envied the life of the domestic animals on the station where he had selected. But he aimed at independence – independence! A fine word, Mary, but a poor reality.'

Even Robert Menzies, probably Australia's greatest Prime Minister, could not understand the necessity of giving his constituents the illusion that they were men and brothers. Menzies pinpointed the difference between *hoi polloi* and his own caste when, during a political rally, an unwashed heckler shouted, 'Wotcher gonna do about 'ousing?' Menzies shot back, 'Put an "h" in front of it.' And here is the difference in one aspirate: the unbridgeable distinction between the Brahmin and the Untouchable, denied perhaps by law but confirmed continually by reality. By arrogating this position, Australia's labor leaders have built what amounts to a feudalistic democracy assuring their own perpetuation – so long as they stick to domestic issues and do not venture into things – like the campaign to withdraw from Vietnam – standing outside the ancient relationship between squatter and bushman.

This traditional relationship is a paradoxical thing; on the one hand the working-class Australian hates his nominal oppressors but on the other respects them for the strength that makes them oppressors. Analyze the summary judgment of a Melbourne saloon keeper upon Sir Thomas Bent, Premier of Victoria early in this century:

> Say what you like about Sir Thomas Bent, but he was a man. He mightn't have much honesty if there was money to be got, and he liked his gin and tonic strong and frequent, and he had a rovin' eye for the women, but outside them matters he was as pure as the drivellin' snow.

When there is a paradox irritating the subconscious, the unrecognized but strongly felt irritations must be expended upon a third class, one which implements the upper-class oppression but shares the lower-class social position: in a word, the police. Over the years the Australian opposition to the policeman has become a cherished tradition whose origin, like all ancient customs, has long been forgotten. One hates the police for the same reason one puts up a Christmas tree for the 25th of December, which is no reason at all. Historians can prattle about the legacy of unrequited vengeance for early brutality, such as those 332,810 lashes of the official whip expended on 7,103 backs in 1835, but only historians know about it. The Australian man in the street reacts to the policeman for the same reason a heliotrope keeps its bloom to the sun: it is in his nature to do so. An old Ballarat miner, asked to sing an appropriate song at his daughter's wedding, could think of nothing except this romantic ballad:

> Oh, the traps [goldfield police], the dirty traps!
> Kick the traps whene'er you're able;
> At the traps, the nasty traps;
> Kick the traps right under the table.

That marvelously old-fashioned journal, *The Bulletin*, the 'bushman's bible' around the swing of the last century, was alone in its popularity with men on the frontier because it expressed what they thought better than they could say it. On the announcement in September of 1888 that applications were being processed for additions to Victoria's police force, it contained this observation:

> At the present moment there are 600 young Victorians applying for a possible 100 billets in the police force of the colony. Noble six hundred! Just bursting into vigorous manhood, they have no higher ambition than to loaf around in uniform and order little boys to move out of that. Policemen are necessary evils in a civilised community, but it makes us shudder to think about the 500 unsuccessful candidates who have started life with a determination not to do any work. We suppose they will ultimately be arrested by the 100 lucky enough to get in.

It would be gratifying if a closer parallel could be made between the Australian frontiersman *vis-à-vis* the law's minions and the American pioneer in his relations with authority, but here the two peoples diverge. Once again the causes came in with the first immigrants: the Puritans were ferociously independent rebels who came to the New World to set up a theocracy with no more than nominal allegiance to

England, whereas the Australians debarked from the First Fleet figuratively and sometimes literally in chains. The Bostonians pulled England's nose for the better part of two centuries while the Australian pulled his forelock. For all of their history Australians battered the police with verbal violence leaning over a bar or as part of a large crowd sooling on some drunk flailing against a policeman attempting to arrest him. There is a goldfield song chronicling the Great Riot of 24 March 1898, when most of the city marched out against the police, shouting defiance:

> Where the roofs of Kalgoorlie gleam bright o'er the plain
> They are carefully checking the lists of the slain.
> There's a square yard of glass come to grief in the shops
> And five buttons the less among seventeen cops.

The notable feature of the Great Riot of Kalgoorlie was the extent of police casualties – the loss of five buttons. Usually a single frown from an Australian policeman would have had the same effect as the swagger stick of a British army officer in India – the crowd would grumble ferocious threats as it quickly dispersed. In the American West, things were very much different. Until after the Civil War the United States government left the goldfields to themselves so far as even the simplest exercise of law was concerned, and this policy was continued through much of the conquest of the Land Frontier. In the Indian Territory and contiguous areas of the dry South-west, it was not until 1875 that a really effective jurist appeared with federal authority – the notorious 'Hanging Judge' Isaac Parker. Parker's reputation has suffered grievously at the hands of later moralists, both in folklore (in which he is represented as a man of comic arbitrariness) and in what purports to be history (as a sadist). In fact he was barely able to keep ahead of the opposition. In his tenure of office as Judge of the United States Court for the Western District of Arkansas at Fort Smith, Parker hanged a total of 79 men, but during that time 65 of his deputies were killed. (The latest and one of the very few novels to portray this area and this era accurately is Charles Portis's *True Grit*.) Parker was probably the best qualified and most dignified of the American frontier judges, but even he had adventures that today's jurist could not imagine as falling within his jurisdiction – like catching and wrestling to the floor a prisoner who tried to jump out of a window during his trial. Absolutely scrupulous, trained well to the law, combining common sense and scholarly acumen, he was much closer to the Australian magistrates than to others of his profession who brought order if not law to the American frontier. His decisions when they bore upon the conduct of law in general – as for example his arguments against the United States Supreme Court when it overturned in one way or other all 27 of the capital verdicts referred from his court without considering the circumstances of any case – are prophetic of what happens to social order when technicalities become the only issue in appelate consideration. In his own courtroom he insisted on the high standards of rectitude and dignity; once he fined each of the roomful of observers $50 for applauding a popular verdict. Rarely and only under unbearable provocation did he allow his own feelings to be expressed, as in the case of a negro convicted of rape who, when he was asked the formal question whether he had any comment to make before sentence was passed, said, 'Yes, suh. I wants my case to go to the Supreme Court'. 'I don't blame you,' replied Parker.

But Australian judges do not figure in readable Australian history, for the donning of the wig erased them as personalities and made them into honest, fair, unexceptionable instruments of a mechanical legal system, and, behind that, the aristocratic caste which they represented.

American frontier judges had neither *noblesse* nor *oblige*. Generally coming from the same social stratum as those around whose rough throats they ordered the rope, they had to be as unreasonable, tough, and arbitrary as the men in the dock. Judge Roy Bean, 'the Law West of the Pecos', is very well known, but he was only one among many. There were magistrates by the benchful like R. C. Barry, Justice of the Peace in Sonora, California, in the first years of the gold rush. From his docket for 9 July 1851 we are treated to an example of his nature and his logic:

No. 516. This is a suit for mule steeling, in which Jesus Ramirez is indited for steeling one black mule branded O, with a 5 in it, from Sheriff Work. George swares the mule in question is his'n, and I believe so to on hearing the caze. I found Jesus Ramirez gilty of feloniously, and against the law made and provided, and the dignity of the people of Sonora, steelin the aforesaid mare mule. Sentenced him to pay the cost of court – $10 – and fined him $100 more as a terrour to all evil-doers. Jesus Ramirez not having any munny to pay with, I rooled that George Work should pay the cost of coort, as well as the fine, and in default of payment that the said one mare mule be sold by the constable, John Luvey, or other officer of the court, to meet the expenses of the costs of court, as also of the fine aforesaid.

R. C. Barry, JP

N.B. – Barber, the lawyer for George Work, insolently told me there was no law for me to rool so. I told him I didn't care a damn for his book law; that I was the law myself. He continued to jaw back. I told him to shut up, but he wouldn't. I fined him $50, and committed him to goal for 5 days in contempt of court, in bringing my roolings and dissions into disreputableness, and as a warning to unrooly persons not to contradict this court.

The vocal defiance and physical submissiveness of frontier Australians inevitably eroded their resoluteness toward unconstituted authority as well. On both mining frontiers the absence of machinery of formal justice required the creation of extralegal organizations to assure minimal order. In the American mining towns 'miners' associations' were formed with explicit codes of behaviour, rigorously enforced. And since jails were a luxury in transient communities that moved with each rumour of new strikes, a man who violated the rules was either expelled or hanged (though in both America and Australia the practice of chaining a minor offender to a log for the day was common). When there was any danger of interference by formal law, as in San Francisco during the suppression of the Sydney Ducks, each member of the vigilantes put his hand on the rope to make responsibility too tenuous to fix. Australia's 'kangaroo courts' – or 'roll-ups' – were designed for the same purpose, but the similarity was in the principle rather than the practice. The explorer David Carnegie describes the frequent ineffectiveness of these communal trials by citing the case at Kurnalpi when a man was caught passing counterfeit currency in a two-up game and subsequently given notice to quit the town.

> He refused to budge, and seeing that he was a great giant with the reputation of being the roughest and hardest fighter in the country, the question arose who should 'bell the cat'. The man who had been swindled was a stranger, and unwilling to fight his own battle; who, therefore, would volunteer to get a sound hammering from one of the toughest blackguards in Australia?
>
> The 'roll up' slowly dispersed, every man muttering that it was not his business, and that, after all, passing a 'stiff 'un' to a new chum was no great crime as compared to stealing gold or robbing a camp.

Traditions die hard; the Australian goldfields prohibition law, unthinkable in any American mining community, can be uncovered today by the merest kind of cultural archaeology; in Boulder, Western Australia, heart of the old Golden Mile, the only hotel (saloon) allowed open until midnight is the famous Boulder Block; others must 'chuck out' at 11.00 p.m.

It must not be supposed that Australians on the frontier or anywhere else were not capable of both courage and ferocity. Americans in their systematic conquest of the world have brought back more tales of Australian furious intrepidity than of any other nationalities, friend or enemy. Though it is not bruited about, some of the wildest battles in World War II were fought in Australia between GI's and Diggers over the formers' acquisition of the latters' women. It should also be said that Australia's population of 5,000,000 in World War I gave up as many men killed as the United States with its one hundred million – and all of the Australian servicemen in both wars were volunteers. It is easy for strong men to weep on seeing those pathetic cenotaphs in tiny frontier communities covered with the names of what must have been the majority of their men who did not return.

And they were the honest men, unaccustomed to violence, untrained to ferocity. Those who came from criminal stock and who were trained to no other trade were, pound for pound, head for head, as savage as any of their more infamous counterparts that scourged the American frontier. The Americans were more notorious – in the sense that their reputations were inflated and in some cases wholly fabricated by the popular press, which dug more gold than any mine ever produced from the discovery that hundreds of thousands of people who themselves were not violent liked to read about violence. Among the better known hagiographers were Stuart N. Lake, creator of Wyatt Earp; Prentiss Ingraham (who wrote 200 novels about Buffalo Bill, the bison butcher); E. Z. C. Judson (who assisted in the creation of Buffalo Bill); Charles E. Averill (Kit Carson); Timothy Flint (Daniel Boone); Edward S. Ellis (Seth Jones); Joseph E. Badger, Jr. (Pete Shafer); and Edward L. Wheeler (Deadwood Dick – an entirely fictional personage who now is often identified in the new black history books with a real negro). It is the unhappy way of the world to deny persons best entitled to fame (or infamy) credit (or blame) for their deeds, because of some intangible flaw in their negotiable image. In America, for instance, who has heard of Bully Bill Sedley, the Mississippi riverboat thumper who got drunk one night in New Orleans' French Quarter, broke into a circus managerie, and beat a tiger to death with a club? In Australia, who knows of that most obdurate outlaw, bushranger Morgan? Morgan chose to be handcuffed with his arms around a tree, there knowingly to wait for at least four days without food or water kicking off the wild dingoes come to eat him, rather than give his parole to his police captors. And who later had an arm shattered by bush police, directed a shepherd to cut it off (without anaesthetic), and walked a hundred miles into Melbourne. Captured again by the first party before the stump had healed, Morgan invited the police leader to try handcuffing him around a tree this time. Compared to Sedley and Morgan, Frank James – who dropped from legendry as a shoe salesman in St Louis – is a model of timidity. For sheer effectiveness as killers on the American frontier, there is little to choose between two other generally unknown lethal practitioners: on the wrong side of law, John A. Murrell, whose victims along the Natchez Trace cannot even be estimated; and on the right side of order, Randy Runnels, who took the Wells Fargo commission to clean up the Yankee Strip and in a few weeks with a handful of hired gunmen like himself hanged hundreds of highwaymen. Runnels is never even given the attention of students of criminology compiling evidence on whether or not capital punishment deters criminals. Runnels deterred them, permanently, and discouraged others from filling their vacated econiche.

Unconsciously assisting the deliberate builders of outlaw and bushranger legendry in Australia and America are the folktale-makers, those unidentifiable amanuenses of the common wish and will, who make violent heroes out of even less raw material than God used to create Adam and Eve, when the folk need arises. To the upper classes in both frontier countries the folk are 'a race of boors about as uncouth, mean, and stupid as the hogs they seem chiefly to delight in', and they often in fact are just so – which is all the more reason for them to make heroes out of anyone who succeeds in discomfiting the oppressing upper classes. The need for heroes where few exist has made a symbol of virtue out of an unmitigated ruffian and murderer like Ned Kelly, or a 'civil rights leader' out of a homicidal maniac like Nat Turner.

Australian historians, otherwise apparently rational, see some worth in Ned Kelly. The real Kelly, grandson of one Mary Kelly (*née* Cody, a relative of the brave American buffalo slaughterer, Buffalo Bill Cody) and pig thief John Kelly, grew up in a Tobacco Road household that produced in addition to himself horse-, cattle-, and pig-thieves. Ned began his wild career at the tender age of 14, when he assaulted a Chinaman, and ended it on the gallows. He is said to have *died game*, as if that were a commendable accomplishment on being dropped through a trap with a rope around one's neck. The only hero ever associated with the Kelly clan was the Glenrowan schoolteacher, Tom Curnow, of whom few people have heard and fewer care. In the United States professors of black history are paid up to $35,000 a year for teaching those who want to hear such things that when Nat Turner saw the moon turn green as a signal for him to begin the holy work of beating and hacking 150 persons, negro and white, to death, he was engaging in legitimate protest against his social condition. If any anger is ever aroused by the history of creatures like Ned Kelly and Nat Turner, it falls like Nat Turner's axe on the heads of those who tell the factual truth about them. But, as Ned Kelly said when they put the noose around his neck, 'Such Is Life'.

In any event, discussion of the Australian bushrangers and the American frontier outlaws who fall into the Robin Hood – Robbin' Hoodlum classification is on best advice restricted to drawing attention to such inconsequential oddments about criminal hands across the ocean as the information that the first Australian bushranger was a negro, John Caesar, very popular with the other First Fleet immigrants, and in debt four hangings to the colony by the time its patience and his luck ran out in 1796, when he was shot; that one of the worst of all the Victorian bushrangers was 'Yankee Jack Ellis', an American who did much to make the Melbourne-Bendigo road as unsafe for travellers as his natal land's Natchez Trace; and that the most successful of all major Australian bushrangers, Frank Gardiner (*alias* Francis Christie and 'The Darkie'), escaped hanging to serve eight years of a 32-year sentence, after which he was *de facto* sentenced in commutation to transportation to the United States, setting up as a saloon keeper at the corner of Kearney and Broadway in San Francisco, leaving there to get himself killed in a card game in Colorado around 1895.

The folksongs of crime in frontier Australia continue the parallel lines of cultural history seen in so many other aspects of the two nations; the natural shyness of American prospectors in California that was satirized in songs like

> What was your name in the States?
> Was it Thompson, or Johnson or Bates?
> Did you murder your wife
> And fly for your life?
> Say, what was your name in the States?

brought a blush also to the modest cheeks of the Australian goldfields refugees, who for a bit of a tease were sung to with

> To say they swarmed Coolgardie was to say the very least,
> For they overran the district like rabbits in the East.
> Their name predominated in the underlay and drive,
> The open-cut and costeen seemed to be with Smiths alive;
> And while Jones and Brown were just as thick as herrings
>   in a frith,
> If you threw a stone at random you were sure to hit a
>   Smith.

Though all manner of men swarmed the edges of both frontiers to pursue all manner of careers, the curious parallel of culture and character so striking in the Austramerican West winnows them into categories so similar that they are as nearly interchangeable as men of two nations could possibly be. While the needs of manageability limit the overview to the majority, it is axiomatic that a minority group in one country resembles its counterpart in the other. For example, though the dullness of virtue disqualifies good men on a bad

117

frontier from making any lasting mark in folk legendry, there were brave men and strong in both Wests worth any number of Kellys or Turners. In the United States the Texas Rangers, though adumbrated now into clownish Keystone cops for sociopolitical ends, were in their time – which lasted for more than a century – the most deservedly famous band of lawmen. Songs in their praise exist, but they are not in a number to compare with those memorializing the badmen. For twenty who sing of the juvenile delinquents Billy the Kid in America and Johnny O'Meally in Australia, does even one sing of Ranger Dallas Stoudenmire, who like Rooster Cogburn in Portis's *True Grit*, routed a gang of outlaws by charging at them alone? The song about John Wesley Hardin (revived as 'John Wesley Harding' by the American singer-composer Bob Dylan) claims for him high courage and invincibility, but in point of fact he surrendered meekly to a crippled Texas Ranger who single-handed attacked and shot up his gang as they stepped off a train like the killers in *High Noon*. The motion picture and subsequent folksong *Bonnie and Clyde* affirmed the immortality of two psychotic killers while maligning the character of Ranger Captain Frank A. Hamer, who killed the two of them along with some fifty other desperados in a hundred gunfights. Nor was Hamer only a gun fighter with extraordinary fast reflexes; most of the many prisoners he took were taken senseless after he had knocked them down with his bare hands.

Australia had her Frank Hamers and Dallas Stoudenmires, but one has to go to the original sources to learn of their existence. Sergeant Major Harry Alford will one day make some Australian writer of the non-fiction novel a subject as good as any in this genre, for he combined in one real man the qualities and characters of the fictional Rooster Cogburn and the factual Frank Hamer.

Minorities of race and lawfulness combined in the native police employed on both frontiers, and to draw the parallel lines closer still, both groups produced members who crossed the line of legality freely and dramatically. Bob Dalton, head of the gang that terrorized frontier Kansas, was once chief of the Osage police. In Australia a most notorious turncoat – if one could apply that term to someone who for much of his life wore not so much as a pair of trousers – was the aboriginal Musquito. This famous blacktracker and infamous bushranger is, like Ned Kelly, known for a memorable gallows statement. When asked to make a last observation on his closing life and times, he said, 'Hangin' no bloody good for blackfellow.' The official in charge of the ceremony was intrigued enough to ask, 'Why not as good for blackfellow as for whitefellow?' 'Very good for whitefellow,' replied Musquito. 'He used to it.'

In Australia women are too little regarded to justify a man's praising them in a book designed for general reading; in America, they have had a sufficiency of praise for a nation torn between making itself at once into a matriarchy and a pediocracy. Let two Australian memorials suffice, therefore, to commemorate their place in civilizing the frontier. One is the text graven into the headstone of a woman whose husband handily enough was a stonemason:

IN MEMORY OF
MY DEAR WIFE, MARTHA,
THIS STONE WAS ERECTED
IN RESPECT OF
A GOOD WOMAN
AND ALSO AS A
SPECIMEN OF MY WORK.
THESE MODELS £15.

And finally, one for Caroline Chisholm, Mary Bryant, Margaret Catchpole, Good Old Mother (wife to Dad, mother to Dave and Joe), and for all the wonderful Australian women who waited, unappreciated, until the American soldiers in Australia during the Second World War made their men at last see what they had; the tribute by Dame Mary Gilmore:

Theirs but a grain of wheat,
Theirs but the small frail hand,
But they gave the race to eat,
And they made the land.
For they were women who at need took up
And plied the axe, or bent above the clodded spade;
Who herded sheep; who rode the hills, and brought
The half-wild cattle home – helpmates of men,
Whose children lay within their arms,
Or at the rider's saddle-pommel hung.

FIVE

Greed and Other Theories of the Frontier

The world is experiencing upheavals in human attitudes inconceivable a generation ago; firm traditions are wisping away like fog before a dry wind; monolithic religions old a thousand years ago are crumbling like their ancient cathedrals; the fundamental beliefs of man's purpose on this earth are being reviewed without regard for the opinions of philosophers before or since Aristotle – but not in our lifetime will it be possible for a theoretician of the American frontier to begin his discussion without consideration of the thesis born of pique by Frederick Jackson Turner. One could more easily imagine the blasphemy of a Catholic beginning prayer without making the Sign of the Cross.

Let us therefore with reverence hear once more Turner's rhetorically memorable evocation of the march of American history:

> Stand at Cumberland Gap and watch the procession of civilization, marching single file – the buffalo following the trail to the salt springs, the Indian, the fur-trader and hunter, the cattle-raiser, the pioneer farmer – and the frontier has passed by. Stand at South Pass in the Rockies a century later and see the same procession with wider intervals between.

And let us hear his disciple Hancock communicate the same epistle to the Australians:

> There is a famous gap in the range of the Blue Mountains, that wall of rock and scrub which for a quarter of a century hemmed in this colony of New South Wales within the coastal

plain. Stand at this gap and watch the frontiers following each other westward – the squatters' frontier which filled the western plains with sheep and laid the foundations of Australia's economy, the miners' frontier which brought Australian population and made her a radical democracy, the farmers' frontier which gradually and painfully tested and proved the controls of Australia's soil and climate. Stand a few hundred miles further west on the Darling River, and see what these controls have done to the frontier. The farmers have dropped out of the westward-moving procession, beaten by aridity. Only the pastoralists and prospectors pass on. In the west centre of the continent, aridity has beaten even the pastoralists. On the fringe of a dynamic society there are left only a few straggling prospectors and curious anthropologists, infrequent invaders of the aboriginal reserves.

Ritual completed, let us proceed to exegesis. Turner himself admitted that the pique which led to his revelation was a reaction to the arrogant Germanic chauvinism of one of his professors, Herbert Baxter Adams, who disposed summarily of American national character by attributing its origin to medieval Germany. 'The Frontier theory', Turner said, 'was pretty much a reaction from that day due to my indignation.' Unworthy origins in themselves do not rubbish theories of frontier settlement any more than unworthy origins rubbish frontier settlers; if they did, where would we be, any of us, Australians or Americans? It is, nevertheless, rubbish in this case, but for reason.

Ironically enough, Turner's purpose in following history was Germanic, for if Professor Adams did not succeed in convincing the young man of the specific assertion, he did succeed in establishing a method and a philosophy: to make for America a parthenogenic *Volksgeist* owing parentage to nothing but itself. Although German historical scholarship except in times of patriotic crisis (such as the Roman conquest; the Frankish subjugation; invasion by Magyars, Slavs, and Scandinavians; the Thirty Years War; the Napoleonic conquest; the Austro-Prussian war; the Franco-Prussian war,

World Wars I and II; and a few lesser traumata) is not so blatantly subjective as that of Communist Russia or of those modern emergent nations presently fabricating history, the subsidiary discipline of folklore research in Germany is very nearly as wilfully distorted to a patriotic end as in Finnish and Celtic nativistic endeavor. In less nationality-confident periods of American history the same attitude interrupted objectivity: the notion that a nation simply by taking thought could add a cubit to its stature. That is the message received by sophomores of all ages in all periods by Ralph Waldo Emerson from his famous Phi Beta Kappa address:

> We have listened too long to the courtly muses of Europe. . . .
> We will walk on our own feet, we will work with our own hands; we will speak with our own minds. . . . A nation of men will for the first time exist. . . .

Just like that. For his self-esteem a man does not read books; one bathes in the waters of Walden pond and becomes a new nation was that small boy on that Fourth of July rebelling what above all else was the necessity of self-confidence. The man and a new nation. In 1837 this was needful nonsense, for against the injunction about sucking his thumb – 'It's my thumb, and it's Independence Day, and I'm going to suck hell out of it.'

But intellectual thumb-sucking in 1893 was another matter entirely. As Demeunier said when he first heard of totemism in that appropriate year of 1776, 'It is clear that this is nonsense, and one is not able to give a reason for nonsense.'

It was his rhetoric as much as anything else that caught the minds of his historical colleagues, and influenced by that way of talking, we might say that the literature of the statement whitened the sepulchre of its fallaciousness.

One should not use literal fact to impugn a metaphor, but many people have not seen the thesis as a metaphor, and in his later elaborations Turner himself seemed not to understand he was working in literature, not history. So let it be said for the quotation above that the buffalo had to come East before they went West; the Indian came from the north-west and then east through the gap at Cumberland as well as through other entry lines (though he went West fast enough when the expanding settlers got after him); that the first significant cattle movement came East by way of the north; that the farmer went in all directions, often at the same time; and that the first white man through the Cumberland gap was an English physician, Dr Thomas Walker, and he did not get out of the mountains.

Nor was the procession single file, except for the few eccentrics; people are as gregarious as buffalo despite their paradoxical natures as carnivores, and they settle frontiers in groups, if for no other reason, because true frontiers are too hostile for individuals to penetrate. The projection of the metaphor as his readers piece out his imperfections with their thoughts is that all these marchers kept on to the West, with the procession swelling like a communist parade. In fact immigration to the Kentucky mountains pretty well ceased by 1830 and all those Indians and fur traders and hunters and cattle raisers and pioneer farmers and buffalo became hillbillies.

Stand you then at Raton Pass with the desert on one side and that 'bright green valley with the river running through' on the other during the great migration into California in the late 1930s and early 1940s. You will see farmers driving Fords piled above the roof and bulging at the sides with wives and chickens and dogs and guitars – all people who had their fill of land and pioneering, refugees from the frontier come to pick fruit until they could build airplanes.

In the two generations of elaboration to which Turner was encouraged by admirers and disciples (principally *The Frontier in American History* and *The Significance of Sections in American History*) rhetorical opinion evolves to a theory. American democracy (by which he means not only democracy but American national character) came not from a theorist's dream; it was not carried in the *Sarah Constant* to Virginia, nor in the *Mayflower* to Plymouth. It came out of the American forest, and it gained new strength each time it touched a new frontier.

In order to get to a summary of the thesis to be disposed of, we will not linger to argue matters of mere fact, like democracy after the *Mayflower*, beyond pointing out that the Puritan-Pilgrim immigrants had an inchoate democracy while they were still meeting in the Scrooby congregation, that it was developed in their social isolation during the Amsterdam period, that it was actually put in formal writing with the *Compact* enunciated on the *Mayflower*, and that for the first winter of their democracy these settlers stayed on board their ship without putting down any roots, real or metaphorical, in the American frontier.

However, American character-democracy, according to Turner, was a unique phenomenon, formed on the first frontier and reformed as each succeeding ecological barrier was entered and overcome, until 1890, when the last viable empty spaces were swallowed up. The most important of the frontier factors was the presence of enormous tracts of arable land, free to the taker, but so difficult and demanding that only an independently invented democracy could assure survival and ultimate prosperity.

Turner, having inseparably hitched his star to a covered wagon (as one commentator happily described his predicament), gathered specious proofs for his beliefs from statistics; having made his first suppositions from the census, he made this source his bible. With the infinite ambiguity of statistics and with generalizations about character as flexible as astrological horoscopes, Turner held an impregnable position for forty years, for one cannot easily attack an ectoplasmic bastion. A few tangibles were sifted from the insubstantiality and at once destroyed, but in such cases disciples of the first filial generation argued simply that Turner never meant what he said. In Billington's words,

Attackers and defenders alike squandered their energies on an academic trifle, for the validity of the frontier hypothesis had nothing whatever to do with Turner's *statement* of that hypothesis.

Argument of this sort elevates the question to theology and what semanticists have usefully named a *non-sense* region, an area of the Intensional World for which no sense data can be assembled – and therefore profitless for serious discussion. Keeping the question therefore as far down the Abstraction Ladder as possible, one can find in Turner's own protean essay a source of error which few have thought important enough to consider:

> In an interesting monograph, Victor Hehn has traced the effect of salt upon early European development, and has pointed out how it affected the lines of settlement and the form of administration. A similar study might be made for the salt springs of the United States.

In this suggestion it is not the salt that is important, but the admission that small, unimportant, overlooked, and often purely fortuitous occurrences have paradoxically incalculable results, changing, as rhetorical historians are fond of saying, the whole course of history. Examples come to mind easily – the lead in Roman drinking water conduits, which brought early death to a significant proportion of the patricians, but spared the plebeians who could not afford the luxury of lead poisoning. Or that insignificant sherd of medieval Chinese porcelain found built by accident into the heart of one of the earliest walls of Zimbabwe, the bit of irrefutable evidence that at once destroyed the illusion of an ancient African civilization. Contrariwise, the most influential theories of explaining great cultural developments are often wrong because they ignore the revelations of disciplines ordinarily beyond the curricula of history – ecology, ethnology, anthropology, ethology, biology, bioenergetics, and even Game Theory – and because their general nature forces them to assume that similar phenotypes have identical genotypes. Thus environmental determination, the essence of Turnerism, is unquestionably a factor in every phenomenon – animal, vegetable, and mineral – but it is only one factor among many. It is a disagreeable fact that all or nearly all influential theories are influential for the simple reason that they are simple. A kindergarten ruler graduated in quarter inches is easier to use than a slide rule.

Even the concept of the 'frontier' will bear some revision. What is a frontier? One respected American frontier historian defined the frontier as

> a geographic region adjacent to the unsettled portions of the continent in which a low man-ratio and unusually abundant, unexploited, natural resources provide an exceptional opportunity for social and economic betterment to the small-propertied individual.

Only an American could have devised a definition like that – only a member of a civilization that makes paradisiacal valleys out of Joshua-tree infernos could make history read like a real estate prospectus. Is the moon a frontier? James Boyd, the 1969 president of the American Institute of Mining, Metallurgical, and Petroleum Engineers, thinks so, though he warns against any premature development of that region. So what is the man-ratio of the moon? Are its resources unusually abundant? What opportunities for social and economic betterment does it hold for the small-propertied individual?

It is not necessary to go to the moon to find cause for questioning the applicability of Billington's definition. Australia's outback is a frontier if ever there was one. It is being opened now at a rate unprecedented even in America of the Reconstruction Era. In the last two years more than one and a half billion dollars has been spent in speculative exploration of Australian mineral resources. If he cannot afford to join such enterprise, he can enter the field with a wildcat oil well;

all he needs is $100,000 and the willingness to lay it out on a one-in-fifty chance of making a profitable return. Assuming his success in the venture, he has now to arrange for entering a market which might occasion some difficulty when billion-dollar competitors do not feel very hospitable. Social betterment? One can strike oil, gold, uranium, manganese, or diamonds in the spinifex, and except for the absence of snow and saloons, he would be in the same predicament of the bored American prospector who complained 'There's nothing to do but hang around the saloons, get drunk and fight, and lie out in the snow and die'. At Giles Meteorological Station in Australia's presently uninhabitable Rawlinson Range there are all the amenities possible for the staff except women, but tour of duty is limited to six months, which is about as long as the normal man can stand the solitude emphasized rather than relieved by the other half-dozen or so rusticated companions.

For definition, then, it is better to contrive one of a Least Common Denominator: *A frontier is the unexploited ecological range of any human sociopolitical group.* In the hands of any person with experience and skill in forensics this definition can be topologically manoeuvred to include or exclude any area under consideration. It does not offer any inconvenience in subsuming the moon at one extreme and the tribal boundaries of a named Australian aboriginal band at the other. It allows also subsequent delimitation – in the United States one can divide the same physical frontier by means of the chronological succession of evolving products: the Cotton Frontier, the Wheat Frontier, the Pork Frontier, the Cattle Frontier, the Industrial Frontier, the Technitronic Frontier.

The single-file image of frontier settlement created by Turner fastened tenaciously on the minds of his followers. It is pleasing to the eye, but a wicked delusion to take into a wilderness – this Jed Clampett Syndrome that persuades a man that he can bring up an oil well by shooting his rifle into the ground, and then develop and market his resources without help from anyone. But human beings are not content with their unique taxonomic status as carnivorous sheep. They are willing enough to be carnivores, but the psychological ambivalence of being friendly with those they prey upon is less agreeable. So they imagine themselves to be viable as individuals, and they have the assurance of scholars that this is so. Walter Prescott Webb, whose influence on frontier interpretations is almost as dominant as that of Turner, argued that

> the frontier furnished conditions exceptionally favorable to the emergence of the individual, who has played such an important role in modern history. In the first section [of his first chapter] the idea is developed that the frontier acted as an abrasive on the metropolitan institutions, wearing them down until man stepped forth with old human restraints stripped off, old institutions of aid or hindrance dissolved, leaving him relatively free of man-made masters. The new master he faced was nature, but since nature is passive, man was the only active agent present, and was free to do what he would. It was in the exercise of this freedom that the particular kind of individualism associated with frontier society developed.

Thus the frontier is what one wants to make of it; it can produce for one scholar democracy and for another individualism; and since historical consensus supports both Webb and Turner, the two products are compatible. Anyone's mind is sufficiently ambidextrous to hold a few contradictory ideas without serious inconvenience, but our influential theorists demand too much in the way of mental agility. As a further example take the idea of 'free land'. Turner requires this; so does Webb. Webb is indiscreet enough to specify explicitly that a frontier must be uninhabited, so that settlement is 'an advance against nature rather than against men'. The fact that this requirement eliminates both the American and Australian frontiers from consideration is no embarrassment. That small matter aside, the larger concept of free land is not satisfactorily established. It cannot be established. Always and everywhere it is another of those philosophical bad pennies that persuade people that there is intrinsic value in such things as paintings by Klee, imperfect postage stamps by the post office department of some minor member state in the United Nations, slaves, specie, gold, and greenbacks. Or that one 'buys an automobile' in the sense that the purchase is of an autonomous entity. It is no such thing. When a man buys a car he buys one part of an enormous complex including roads, maintenance, workmen, loafers, tax grifters, road-building machinery; police, courts, judges, laws, and prisons; rubber plantations in Vietnam, chromium mines in Soviet Russia, potash plants in Israel, oil wells in Arabia, and diplomats to maintain international amity in deed if not in word. The automobile purchaser is even deceived into thinking he is buying a means of transportation, though so unsubtle a philosopher as the used car dealer will not try to sell transportation for more than $150. Some men, we are told by motivational researchers, are acquiring a surrogate mistress when they buy a hardtop convertible. That is as may be, but assuredly what most men buy is a measure of status and more importantly than that, mobile territoriality – a shell of protective metal from which they can safely inflict verbal, gestural, and sometimes physical abuse upon all that lovable mass of humanity which they hate. When one considers how many illusions and delusions must be kept in the air at once by jugglers of fact and fancy, it is difficult to see how these most influential theses were accepted in the first place and impossible to understand how they have persisted. One is finally driven to accept the paradoxical truth that the more outrageous a dogma is, the easier it is to believe, for something that does not touch reality cannot be in conflict with reality.

Before the Turner thesis was propounded, historians saw the frontier in the image of primitive genetics, the awkwardly named 'germ cell' theory. As Carl Sauer expressed it later, 'the kind of frontier that develops is determined by the kind of people found on it.' We will take Sauer at his word and not agonize over the incompatibility of this view and the environmental-deterministic 'Culture Worlds' interpretation of ethnogeography he established through his students Russell and Kniffen. We will say simply that culture does not work upon the human *tabula rasa* for the first thirty or so years of a prisoner's life just to have a few months in the bush make a different man of him. Americans can go on thinking that their country is a melting pot to which a hundred nations and more contributed the best of their civilization and their subjects, but Americans will go on behaving pretty much the way their distant Puritan forebears – themselves outnumbered fifteen to one in their own Massachusetts colony in their own century – directed them to. Man is a functionary of his culture; he carries it from generation to generation the way a telephone carries a conversation, and has as little to do with the content. The needs of human culture acted upon natural selection to implant certain drives in man, some of which he acknowledges, more of which he does not, to assure the continuation of culture. Therefore, man achieves no more than a symbiotic relationship with culture; he preserves it as its beast of burden over the centuries, it preserves him by making him do what is best for him until the final entropy takes them both. So when we ask why man goes into the frontier, we are asking a metaphorical question. Culture goes into the wilderness, riding hard on the back of mankind. How little man himself – man the soulful animal – counts in the process is shown by the contemptuous way culture displaces one carrier by another. If it eases Webb's mind to depopulate his frontier before occupying it with his pioneers, so let him be comforted. But where life is possible, life exists; Carnegie found enough aborigines in the Great Sandy Desert to lead him from one water to another. Australia was for centuries worthless to the rest of the world, yet it domiciled 300,000 aborigines, according to the best suppositions.

Equally reliable guesses put the Indian population of what was to become the United States at a million. However baseless these estimates may be, it is certain that both lands were populated – and populated to the extent of the subsistence method to which the natives' cultural evolution had attained. Yet so far as the next stage of subsistence evolution was concerned, each frontier was free and unoccupied.

Demography abhors a vacuum. Culture abhors inefficiency in land use. Consequently, a hunting-gathering people must inevitably be displaced by a people subsisting by primitive agriculture – 'neolithic' groups. Advanced agriculturalists in turn displace the horticulturalists. And advanced farmers are unconquerable, except in a temporary political sense. Thus peoples displace peoples as generations displace generations. It is hard lines for those being dispossessed, but Such Is Life. As long as there is any value to culture in human migration, humans will be made to migrate; if others have to make way for them, way will be made, though the late comers may torment themselves and their posterity for the sin of having been compelled to a necessity.

Still, a natural aggressiveness of this most successful of all large carnivores makes him intractable to peremptory cultural demands, regardless of how good they may be in the long view. Nature therefore has implanted in him a few instinctual propensities to deceive his presumptuous intelligence into doing what is best for his culture and incidentally for his species. Philosophers labour to make the animal sublime by assuring him that man has an instinct to propagate his kind and preserve his life – but these are again comfortable delusions. If man had an instinct for individual survival he would not be so easily persuaded into sacrificing himself for fleeting religious and patriotic beliefs; if he had an urge to reproduce, nature would not have made the initial act so pleasurable. The world would be in no danger of submersion by overpopulation if reproduction were left to reason.

The instincts themselves are generalized, not specialized;

man's physical evolution advanced by means of the flexibility of his biological responses – the hand rather than the hoof, the arm rather than the wing. So in behavioral imperatives a small number of generalized drives encode directions for works of unimaginable complexity, in much the same way that 26 letters can form a half million words in English alone and four nucleotides in DNA can determine whether a fertilized egg becomes a man or a potato. In the most un-emotional view, the greatest work of man so far is his construct of the nation; from it flows everything that makes man into what he best thinks himself to be. Plato thought nations were made by the altruistic realization that each individual must give up a little of his own freedom so that all might prosper; that once more is the philosopher speaking. History sees the reality:

> Likelier the barricades shall blare
> Slaughter below and smoke above,
> And death and hate and hell declare
> That men have found a thing to love.

It is a thrice-told story, yet its truth is not known so well that it may not be told again. Seventeen years after Frederick Jackson Turner closed the frontier the inheritors of the western frontier's wealth gave themselves the pleasure of atoning for their fathers' sins by uncovering 'corruption' in the city that had pioneered California. Lincoln Steffens, a political analyst of far more impressive acumen than Turner, looked in on the matter and then went down to Los Angeles to chide that sanctimonious city for its delusion that it was pure. Steffens easily enough proved his contention to an astonished and shocked group of the city's leaders that 'corruption' was universal. But where, asked the bewildered bishop of the diocese, did this system begin – not just in San Francisco or Los Angeles, but its first appearance? Steffens replied with considerable insight:

Most people, you know, say it was Adam. But Adam, you remember, he said that it was Eve, the woman; she did it. And Eve said no, no, it wasn't she; it was the serpent. And that's where you clergy have stuck ever since. You blame that serpent, Satan. Now I come and I am trying to show you that it was, it is, the apple.

No truth so human and so cynical could have escaped Mark Twain's independent notice. Only three years after Turner's closure of the American frontier Twain observed that Adam was only human; he didn't want the apple for the apple's sake – he wanted it only because it was forbidden. The mistake was in not forbidding the serpent; then he would have eaten the snake.

The truth is, as both these men saw, that it is vices, not virtues, that develop a wilderness, and that the worst – and best – of these is greed. Greed drove man out of his first garden, but it drove him to make all his subsequent gardens. No motivation understood by unsentimental social psychologists is as reliable a prime mover as greed. Fanaticism works more energetically over the short run, but it cannot be depended upon; it is unpredictable in its immediate results and impermanent as a foundation for social change. The son of a True Believer is more likely to become a flim-flam man than a genuine disciple of his father's faith.

The eudemonic function of greed is not popular with humanists or social scientists striving to become social workers, and for their own peace of mind and the reputation of the human race they find it easy to construct worthier motives for human action. Significantly enough these imagined virtues are always high up on the Abstraction Ladder, many rungs above reality. Charity comes to mind as an example of man's putative better qualities, but unless it is part of a reciprocal complex charity has no survival function and therefore does not exist so far as the laws of natural selection are concerned. Visitors who approach the Polar World with a virtuous psychological set admire the Eskimo's great hospitality as charity beyond any measure of our own.

They do not understand that an Eskimo stores his surplus food in another man's stomach. His charity is no more than enlightened self-interest, like our own charity. If our charity is overt, we buy status; if covert, comfort for our souls.

Evolutionary laws require all appetites to be gratifications of the organism for the ultimate purpose of survival. As far back as we can trace man's behaviour he has been gratified by the satisfaction of his instinct of acquisitiveness – the apple, in Steffens's metaphor. Greed is only a bad name for augmented acquisitiveness; if acquisitiveness is good, the more the better.

By ignoring the injunction of the Humanist John Ruskin against the Pathetic Fallacy and agreeing instead with the biochemist J. H. V. Butler that 'in the analysis of living things, if we pursue it far enough, we find everywhere traces of feeling and sensation', we can identify the equivalent of greed in lower organisms. On our American desert greasewood bushes grow in regular distribution, each to its plot of perhaps twenty square yards, in apparent observation of some rule of plant proxemics. In an age of philosophy a meticulous Gardener, assigning territorial imperatives by the careful implantation of his seeds, might have been supposed; in our less sentimental time we learn that the roots of an established greasewood bush secrete a poison lethal to intruding seedlings. When cactus overran the Queensland bush only an extraordinarily acquisitive pastoralist would have bought land at ten shillings an acre – and only so greedy a man would have been able later to sell it for ten pounds an acre. In this context greed is known as foresight or business acumen.

No euphemisms were demanded to obscure the rampaging avarice that brought pioneers into the frontiers of Australia and the United States. Hear Mark Twain:

Bathurst is mad again! The delirium of golden fever has returned with increased intensity. Men meet together, stare stupidly at each other, talk incoherent nonsense, and wonder what will happen next. Everybody had a hundred times seen a hundredweight of flour; a hundredweight of sugar or potatoes is an everyday fact, but a hundredweight of gold is a phrase scarcely known in the English language. It is beyond the range of our ordinary ideas, a sort of physical incomprehensibility, but that it is a material existence our own eyes have borne witness.

Mr Suttor, a few days previously, threw out a few misty hints about the possibility of a single individual digging four thousand pounds' worth of gold in one day, but no one believed him serious. It was thought he was doing a little harmless puffing for his own district and the Turon diggings. On Sunday, it began to be whispered about town that Mr Kerr, Mr Suttor's brother-in-law, had found a hundredweight of gold. . . .

Mark Twain also followed the rush for gold begun when a prospector named Richard Oates dug out of a wagon track at the Ballarat field a nugget of pure gold weighing 142 pounds. When Twain himself visited Ballarat toward the end of the century on a tour to pay off a bankruptcy caused by his own greed, he recalled the wealth of the region that precipitated the madness:

Ballarat was a great region for 'nuggets'. No such nuggets were found in California as Ballarat produced. In fact, the Ballarat region has yielded the largest ones known to history. Two of them weighed about 180 pounds each, and together were worth $90,000. They were offered to any poor person who would shoulder them and carry them away. Gold was so plentiful that it made people liberal like that.

Sam Clemens thought too much to be a successful worker in any field where greed was requisite; he agonized over his own participation in what he conceived to be a uniquely human condition, purged himself of the debts it led him into, and wrote one of the great indictments of greed as a vice in his story 'The Man That Corrupted Hadleysburg'. But Mark Twain was only a writer, and acknowledged himself the clear inferior of the robber barons of his time. Neither he nor any other moralist was able to bring moderation or reason to a goldfield in full riot. How could there be reason when a man could dig out a single lump of gold seven feet long, as Holtermann did at the Hill End field in 1872?

> Where at the present moment is the house, or establishment, that is not turned upside down? Where is the man whose head is not upset, and whose legs are not in the air – and not only his legs, but his whole body and soul busy in building castles? Are not the mice catching the cats?

In a less spectacular but no less convulsing gold rush on the western diggings in Australia, Carnegie described a similar madness:

> The rumours of a new find so long bandied about, at length came true. Billy Frost had found a thousand! two thousand!! three thousand ounces!!! – who knew or cared? – on the margin of a large salt lake some ninety miles north of Coolgardie. Frost has since told me that about twelve ounces of gold was all he found. And, after all, there is not much difference between twelve and three thousand – that is on a mining field. Before long the solitude of our camp was disturbed by the constant passing of travellers to and from this newly discovered 'Ninety Mile' – so named from its distance from Coolgardie.

Carnegie and Twain were conscious only of the absurdity of such behavior and made their share in it bearable by making it humorous. Other men saw in this eagerness to be deceived by greed an opportunity to create wealth beyond the dreams of avarice. The method of raising money to exploit a mining claim known as the assessment system was described by a miner from San Francisco to a fellow miner from Utah, in an anecdote in the Salt Lake City *Tribune* in 1881. The assessment plan was, so said the Californian . . .

> 'the latest and most approved method. We have a big map of the mine hung up in the company's office, made by one of

the most competent artists on the coast. Now when we have a good map of the lower workings we don't need any workings to speak of. We photograph the Savage hoisting works from the top of Hale and Norcross trestle work – an entirely new view – and call it by our own name, the Bullion Block. I keep a man in Virginia at $60 a month to superintend the location and write weekly letters, and I stay in San Francisco in my office on Pine street, and levy the assessments every sixty days, that's as often as the law allows. I'm the president, board of trustees, secretary, treasurer, and everything. Of course, I draw a salary for all the offices, and when I get through drawing salaries, I turn the rest over to the agent in Virginia to pay off the hands. By not employing any hands he saves enough to pay himself. My regular income from that mine is $200,000 a year and never a pick stuck in the ground. This is what I consider scientific mining, sir. You get the silver out of the pockets of the stockholders and leave the vast argentiferous and auriferous deposits in your claim for your children, who can go right ahead and develop the mine just as soon as the public quit putting up.'

'But,' said the Utah man, 'my style of mining keeps a lot of men at work.'

'So does mine,' quoth the Golden Gate chap. 'Thousands of men are working night and day to pay assessments. It keeps the country as busy as a bee hive,' and the speaker sauntered to the telegraph office to order assessment number 36.

Australia's most successful miners were the scientific entrepreneurs, like the gentleman from San Francisco. Though production figures differ sharply between reliable reference works, one source gives Western Australia's gold output for 1894 as one million pounds, yet in that year nearly 350 new mining companies were registered on the London exchange, capitalized at £35,000,000. In the following year the number had exploded to 780. Evidently most of these were 'Bullion Blocks' so far as profit for the investors was reckoned, for within five years 640 of these companies had gone into bankruptcy.

How many men were made wealthy by this most scientific way of mining cannot be guessed. Whatever their number was, it would have been vastly increased had the enterprise required only the intent to work at the highest level of efficiency. Nevertheless, Australian gold mine employees working with their hands alone stole so much that the only estimate is too great to be repeated. The only one of these unincorporated miners who seems to have used his head was the Balaclava, Victoria, digger who had part of his skull shaved and a patch hairpiece made to cover the bare spot. Each day he would interlard a layer of gold between his head and the wiglet, and by this means he was able to acquire enough capital to buy a saloon which he appropriately named 'The Golden Patch'. Some of these manual workers would have done better to use their eyes. One prospector was murdered by his partner for his share of their gold and hastily thrust into an impromptu grave – too hastily for the murderer to notice what the police discovered when they dug up the body: that the sides of the grave were impregnated with gold. The killer was duly hanged and another man went on to make his pile with the claim, commemoratively named 'The Murdered Mate'.

The acquisitiveness of Australia's miners was characterized by the theft of specimens of each coin of the realm placed in the crypt of the first brick building erected in Coolgardie. Activity of this nature finally resulted in the establishment of a Criminal Investigation Bureau Gold Stealing Detective Unit, whose first staff members were inconvenienced in their searches by steel slivers and razors that seemed to have mysteriously found their way into miner's pockets.

When gold was unavailable for stealing some miners robbed dead companions, just to keep their hand in the game:

> Two diggers one day on Kangaroo Flat,
> Whilst driving an old hole came on a felt hat;
> And there they found, buried right under the dirt,
> Some old mouldy bones, and a rotten blue shirt:

Poor Sing-Hi'd gone there, but put up no prop,
And the top of the drive had come down on him whop;
And when his mates heard that he'd turned up his toes,
They said 'poor old chap', then divided his clothes.

Once again the repetition of themes across the Pacific occurs; a traditional American hobo song tells of the lamentable demise of a companion in the presence of his mourning comrade:

'Hark! I hear her whistling,
I must catch her on the fly;
I would like one scoop of beer
Once more before I die.'
The hobo stopped, his head fell back,
He'd sung his last refrain;
His old pal stole his coat and hat
And caught an East-bound train.

The Australians, to their credit, confined such ungentlemanly pilfering to the detested Chinamen. Americans traditionally observed no such niceties.

In the meliorating process of time criminal behavior softens into humor, but life on the two goldfields was not always amusing for victims of violent private enterprise. For the whole history of Australian mining the warning of Governor George Gipps of New South Wales to the Reverend Mr W. B. Clarke when that gentleman came to him with a nugget ten years before the official discovery of gold was prophetic: 'Put it away or we shall all have our throats cut'. Sutter in California and Suttor in Australia both had their properties destroyed by the gold rush, to begin with; in Australia the direct violence did not end in the diggings until 1966, when a policeman was finally appointed to the opal mining hell hole of Coober Pedy in South Australia's gibber desert. Until that time the miners were blowing one another out of their shafts with gelignite. Such Is Life.

SIX

Ways into the Wilderness

Stand at Menindie in October of 1844 on the dry side of the Darling River and watch the vanguard of civilization pass into the last frontier of Australia: Captain Charles Sturt (a veteran of the war against the Americans in 1812) and 15 men, 11 horses, 5 carts, 30 bullocks, 200 sheep, uncounted dogs, and that wonderful boat to sail the inland sea. Stand there again 14 months later and see them faltering back, 14 men now carrying their blind and nearly dead leader, full of wonderful adventures to tell one day – of the bone-dry Centre (no inland sea, alas!) beyond the Great Stony Desert; the waterhole they named Fort Grey where they were locked up by the sun for six months with all waters before them and behind scorched away in shade temperatures of 130°, of screws fallings out of boxes and nails out of boots; of dry flour losing 16 pounds a bag to evaporation; of live hair and nails and wool stopped growing; of a moon so bright as to be 'one of the most distressing things we had to endure'.

Stand at Menindie yet once more, in October of 1860. It is no longer a flat scrub in a ring of billabongs, but a community of shanties huddled around that essential nucleus of all outback settlements, the pub. Watch then the grandest expedition ever mounted in Australia lumber in to establish a base for the first penetration north through 'the ghastly blank' to the Gulf of Carpentaria. Two months earlier Castlemaine Superintendent of Police Robert O'Hara Burke led out of Melbourne a caravan of 17 motley men, 27 camels, 23 horses, and some 21 tons of food and equipment planned to last for 18 months, carried on a variety of wagons as motley as the personnel – including two great vehicles that could be converted into river boats. These now were strung out along the track behind them as Burke and his advance column came in to prepare their main camp.

No use to watch for Burke's return to Menindie a year later. Of the four men who made the desperate journey from the last depot on Cooper's Creek to the swamps on the Gulf more than 700 miles farther north, only one was to return; and at the beginning of October, 1861, even he was thought lost. The story of that tragic party is an example of the differences between truth and fiction, as Mark Twain distinguished them: fiction had to stick to possibilities. The Burke-Wills tragedy is an impossible truth.

Down from the north at the end of that October came Alfred W. Howitt, later an eminent anthropologist but then the rescuer of the one survivor of the lost party, the surveyor John King, found barely living through the hospitality of a tribe of wild aborigines.

The march of civilization meanwhile had accelerated to a wild sprint: Burke's expedition had been two months on the track from Melbourne to Menindie, but Howitt, leaving the city on the Fourth of July when rumor came south with an aborigine named Sambo that there was a party of white men at Cooper's Creek, made Menindie before the end of the month. And he went much of the way by public transportation – the American stagecoach line of Cobb and Co. More ironic still is the accomplishment of the famous pedestrian George 'Chinese' Morrison, who walked the whole 2,000 miles from the Gulf of Carpentaria down to Adelaide, alone, in less time than it took Burke and Wills to get to Cooper's Creek.

In a mountain in one of the crumbling ironstone ranges in Central Australia, far from the white man's roads, there is a cave on whose walls aborigines have painted something unique even for them: a positively Turnerian chronicle of the frontier's penetration. First appears a drawing of an aborigine moving barefoot through his nomadic range as his race had done for thousands of years; next, a white man on a horse followed by a man on a camel, a memory of an early expedition; then, astonishingly a white man on a bicycle. The fact that aborigines must have seen such a thing is corroborated by old bushmen who recall several eccentric cyclists. Finally, the paintings depict the most successful of the transport used by frontiersmen – the four-wheel-drive vehicle.

The difference between walking and riding – even a bicycle – is absolute. It is the difference between the Old Stone Age and the Technitronic Age, as it was a change of philosophy more than a change of tool technology that distinguished the Paleolithic from the Neolithic.

By choosing to walk, the aborigines made a commitment to be passive to the pressure of evolutionary laws. They allowed the environment to adapt them, while in other parts of the world other races of *homo sapiens*, imposing upon their intelligence, adapted their environment to themselves. Which was better is impossible to say, since we cannot give any certain definition for progress in human development. It used to be thought that population increase was the measure of biological success; now it is known that there is no more swift, no more certain way to extinction for any species than uncontrolled reproduction. That is the path of the wheel, the path of all civilization. It is comfortable all the way to the penultimate generation; payment is made by posterity, and what did posterity ever do for us, anyway? The aborigines' way is uncomfortable at best, desperate and hopeless at worst. It means not only cutting one's feet on the spinifex, but infanticide and abandonment of the aged, pain of diseases and injuries, a hard view of life and the instablity and insensitivity attending the alternative between finding water and death, and possessions limited by what you – or

143

more properly, your wife – can carry. But this way of life has delayed entropy for perhaps as long as two million years as man and several billion years in ancestral forms of man; all our ancestors were part of the environment and were molded by it. Even the dinosaurs, ridiculed by us for letting themselves become extinct, knocked around for 150 million years on this earth; man's chances of making one million from the time he decided to change nature by farming it are not such that he should make fun of other species. And it is all in the decision to use a horse instead of Shanks's mare. The bare foot needs no more than the brain to live in the wilderness, not for the length of an expedition, but for the whole of a lifetime. The horse leads to the truck and that requires a large capsule of advanced culture in its bed. Carnegie's 1896 expedition consisted of himself and two companions. If they had been aborigines, they would have taken several wooden spears (no stone points), a digging stick, and a winnowing dish, all of which could have been made along the way. But Carnegie had to have eight pack camels and one riding camel; various kinds of camel equipment (rope, twine, spare leather and canvas, and medicines – tar and oil, sulphur, kerosene); four galvanized iron water tanks; buckets, funnels, pipes, and waterbags; picks and shovels, tomahawks, a saw, an axe, a chisel, a brace, soldering irons, and other tools; one large tent, some smaller fly tents, four mosquito nets; cooking utensils; two 12-bore shotguns, four Colt revolvers, four Winchester rifles; medicines; a binocular camera; candles and soap; 28 dozen matches; blankets, boots, shirts, and other clothing; food to augment what they expected to forage: 200 pounds of rice, 70 pounds of oatmeal (Carnegie was a Scot), 140 pounds of sugar, 40 pounds of salt, 30 pounds of tea, 100 pounds of potatoes, 60 pounds of dried fruits, two dozen cans of fruit, two dozen cans of vegetables, four bottles of brandy and one bottle of rum – altogether, some two tons of equipment per man.

Nor was it easy to travel lighter. A. W. Canning, so tough

a bushman that he considered going without water for several days in shade temperatures of 120° no hardship, followed the same route as Carnegie in 1909 with a caravan of 70 camels, 500 goats to provide food for his expedition, and even more equipment than Carnegie. Over the years requirements have if anything increased. Today any sensible anthropologist would not venture into the bush without a four-wheel-drive truck equipped with augmented suspension; built-in extra tanks for fuel and water; food for at least twice the time he expects to be away; two spare tyres and wheels, a battery, a radio, tools, cooking utensils, medicines, fly and mosquito nets and blankets, to say nothing of his instruments and maps.

There are those, however who have chosen to enter the outback less well equipped. 'Chinese' Morrison, who walked not only from the top of the Australian continent to the bottom, but across China and India and Siberia as well, and had his hardest time surviving in the United States, does not appear quite so eccentric after all. At any rate he did better in imitating the aborigines than the aborigines are doing imitating the white man; the natives who are being exploited by used-car salesmen in Alice Springs pool the resources of much of their tribe to buy automobiles that manage to get various distances from that town into their tribal territory, thereafter to serve no purpose beyond marking the route along which they lie in eternal repose.

Some of the walkers over the wilderness pushed wheel-barrows and handcarts, like the American Mormons in their incredible treks over the plains in the winters following the pioneer movement of 1846.

There were more Australian outback cyclists than the man immortalized in the aboriginal cave painting. Before the various telegraph lines were erected to connect the gold towns of Western Australia, bicyclists were the Australian equivalent of the Pony Express, carrying messages and mail along tracks packed down by camels. Some of the cyclists achieved fame for exploits one cannot appreciate without experiencing the country through which they travelled. W. C. Snell, the first mayor of Leonora, pushed a bike 2,000 miles between Adelaide, South Australia, and Menzies, Western Australia, before any road had been made.

When one knows that bicyclists have traversed some of the worst frontier terrain, one begins to wonder whether some of the romanticized explorers did not make spinifex out of sagebrush, and mountains out of molehills. From the ashes of Frémont's campfires cities of the American West have sprung, so say the romantic historians, ignoring the fact that he followed trails laid down by unsung fur trappers. The nameless heroes of the Australian frontier were the overlanders and bullockies, plain workmen of the bush, as unpretentious as they were competent. And their opinion of the famous explorers was sometimes at odds with historical consensus. After the bodies of Burke and Wills were brought back to Melbourne the sorrowing residents buried them under a memorial block of granite weighing 36 tons, which sat as heavy on the city's conscience as it did on the explorers. Out in the bush there was little sympathy for men who had been guilty of the worst of sins – failure. Even Christ in bullocky folklore was made the subject of humor for getting lost for forty days in the desert – 'some bloody bushman he was!' Joseph Furphy, a bullock driver himself before he became 'Tom Collins', the author of Australia's frontier classic, *Such Is Life*, has Willoughby, an Englishman still unbrutalized after 15 years as a carrier, say a generous word for Burke and Wills. Mosey, closer to the earth earthy, will not have any of that muck:

'Hold on, hold on,' interrupted Mosey. 'Don't go no furder, for Gossake. Yer knockin' yerself bad, an' you don't know it. Wills was a pore harmless weed, so he kin pass; but look 'ere – there ain't a drover, nor yet a bullock driver, nor yet a stock-keeper, from 'ere to 'ell that could n't 'a' bossed that expegition straight through to the Gulf, an' back agen, an' never

146

turned a hair – with sich a season as Burke had. Don't sicken a man with yer Burke. He burked that expegition, right enough.' . . . 'They give him a lot o' credit for dyin' in the open . . . but I want to know what else a feller like him could do, when there was no git out? An' you'll see in Melb'n there, a statue of him made o' cast steel, or concrete, or somethin,' standin' as bold as brass in the middle o' the street. My word! An' all the thousands o' pore beggars that's died o' thirst an' hardship in the back country – all o' them a dash sight better men nor Burke knowed how to be – where's theyre statues? Don't talk rubbage to me. Why, there was no end to that feller's childishness.'

In view of Mosey's opinion, we should record that the American Ferguson, hired as foreman of the Burke and Wills expedition, quit before the excursion had reached Menindie.

Before the bullockies came the overlanders, cattle drovers who established cattle ranges immediately after and some-times before the explorers opened trails into the outback. They were tough men, not overly scrupulous in some cases, and so have in Australian folklore a commensurate reputation:

> Now there's a trade you all know well,
>   It's bringing cattle over;
> I'll tell you all about the time
>   When I became a drover.
> I made a line for Queensland,
>   To Kempsey I did wander;
> I picked up a mob of duffers there
>   And began as an overlander.

Chorus: So pass the bottle round, boys,
>   Don't let the pint pot stand there,
> For tonight we'll drink the health
>   Of every overlander.

When the cattle all were mustered
    And the outfit ready to start,
I saw the lads all mounted
    With their swags left in the cart.
I saw all kinds of men I had
    From Germany, France, and Flanders –
Doctors, lawyers, good and bad –
    In the mob of overlanders.

From the track I then fed out
    Where the grass was green and long,
When a squatter with a curse and shout
    Told me to move along.
I said, 'Me lad, you're very hard
    But don't you raise me dander,
For I'm a regular knowing card,
    I'm a Queensland overlander'.

He swore he'd impound my cattle
    But I bullied him that time;
They very seldom saw me out
    And never got the fine;
They think we live on store beef
    But no, I'm not a gander,
Whenever a straggler joins the mob,
    'He'll do,' says the overlander.

If ever our horses get done up
    Of course we set them free,
And you never expect a drover to walk
    If a pony he can see;
So now and then we pinch a prad
    And believe me, it's no slander
To say there's many a clever trick
    Done by the overlander.

Now I would scorn to prig a shirt,
  As all my mates will say;
But if we pass through a township
  Upon a washing day,
The dirty brats of kids will shout
  And quickly raise my dander,
Crying, 'Mother, quick, take in the clothes,
  Here comes an overlander!'

In town we drain the whisky glass
  And go to see the play;
We never think of being hard up
  Or how to spend the day;
We sheer up to the pretty girls
  Who rig themselves with grandeur,
And as long as we spend our check, my lads,
  They love the overlander.

A little girl in Sydneyside
  She said, 'Don't leave me lonely,'
I said, 'It's sad but my old prad
  Has room for one man only.'
So now, my lads, we're jogging back,
  This pony, she's a goer,
We'll pick up a job with a crawling mob
  Along the Maranowa.

Though the children of the outback settlements may well have warned their mothers that the clothes-pinchers were coming, many of these townships were founded by the bullockies. Unless there was some more compelling economic reason for making a town, such as a river junction, settlements sprang up at the twelve-mile stops, the distance that a bullock team averaged in a day's run, and naturally the first structure erected was the pub. The draft animals, the bullocks, were hybrids of domestic cattle and water buffalo brought in from the north; strong and steady, their only fault was a stubbornness comparable to that of the bullockies themselves.

Being somewhat more articulate than their oxen, the bullock-ies exhorted the animals to overcome their natural lethargy by driving them with 20-foot stockwhips and a notorious sharpness of tongue.

Aggravating the carriers' continuous annoyance was the impossible situation in which they worked. Few roads existed in much of the outback, and in any case the bullocks had to feed along the way; since the way was station property whose pasturage was minimal for its own stock, these teams of often more than two dozen oxen were on the one hand welcomed as indispensable transport of supplies and on the other as trespassers liable to confiscation. The bullockies' dilemma was moral as well as economic. Tom Collins has one of them complain, 'For my part, I'm sick and tired of study-ing why some people should be in a position where they have to go out of their way to do wrong, and other people are concerned to that extent that they can't live without doing wrong.' It was a situation that did not help to heal the division between owners and workers, for even when the owner was lenient towards the teamsters, it was only because he chose to be so. As Tom Collins explained,

> You must understand that these beasts had no legal right to be anywhere except traveling along the track, or floating down the river. If they scattered off the track – not being at-tended by some capable person – their owner would, there and then, and as often as this occurred, be liable for trespass; twenty times a day, if you like, and a shilling per head each time. If I wished to remove them across a five- or twenty-mile paddock, the only way I could legally do so would be by means of a balloon. The thousands of homeless bullocks and horses which carry on the land-transport trade had to live and work, or starve and work, on squatters' grass, year after year. So the right to live, being in the nature of a boon or bene-faction, went largely by favor. . . .

Yet to these men – the overlanders, drovers, and bullockies – Australia owes the location of its settlements, the direction of its roads, and the roads themselves. In the allotment of accolades to the many deserving candidates among Australian explorers, most should go to Edward John Eyre, the first white man to traverse the Nullarbor Plain, the first to see the great salt lake which was named after him, and the first to clarify by his own errors a route from Sydney to Melbourne. He became an explorer through apprenticeship as an overlander. His first overland journey was made with three bullock teams and 300 head of cattle just before Christmas, 1837, from Sydney to Adelaide. The purpose of his journey was not only the worthy one of bringing beef to the new South Australian colony, but the accomplishment of pioneering a stock route. He failed as a pioneer, but only just, and besides, his mistakes were made because he chose to rely upon the interpretations of another explorer, Sir Thomas Livingstone Mitchell, who had been aimlessly wandering around some of the deceptive stream beds in western New South Wales – so aimlessly, in fact, that the phrase 'to Major Mitchell' is still used in outback Australia to describe senseless meandering. Mitchell was knighted for his efforts (some of which were commendable enough) but Eyre might have perished for them, had he not picked up the tracks just laid by two other overlanders, Joseph Hawden and Charles Bonney, who paralleled his route into Adelaide with another 300 head of cattle. Eyre had the further humiliation of being passed by a mailman riding the first leg of a postal service set up by the enterprising Hawden. Eyre did become the first South Australian sheep overlander before going on to more memorable things – his epic Nullarbor exploration and the unhappy business in Jamaica, of which he became governor. History has still to make a decision on whether his suppression of Jamaicans occurred during a revolution or a civil disturbance, though either way it proved his ruin.

Eyre became an explorer and his name has not been forgotten. Other overlanders (of sheep as well as cattle) are not so well remembered – men like Nathaniel Buchanan, the

Duracks, John Gardiner, Ralph Milner, the Leslies – men who would follow rain clouds when there were no water holes, and who lost their stock when rain clouds failed. They have been excluded from romantic history made simple and appealing by restricting great adventure to the magnificent though often foolish efforts of notable explorers. It is the same in America; the image of quaintly garbed Pilgrims stepping from the *Mayflower* onto Plymouth Rock as if they were Armstrong and Aldrin putting tentative foot on the moon loses some of its lustre if it is known that before their landing some ten thousand Englishmen were annually fishing the Newfoundland banks. Often the distinction between the overlander and the explorer was just that the one had reason for plunging into new country and the other did not.

What small romance is allowed to the overlanders is merely incidental. The Faithfull Party is chronicled because ten of these sheep drovers were killed by aborigines. Sometimes the accomplishments of Harry Redford are recorded in print; his feat was the establishment of the Strzelecki Track while conducting the most audacious bit of cattle rustling in Australian annals of crime. Redford stole a thousand head of cattle from a station in central Queensland and drove them 1,500 miles down the Thomson, Barcoo, Cooper, and Strzelecki riverbeds. With every sympathy for his victims it seems a pity, perhaps, that after so remarkable an achievement Redford was caught. The jury at Roma, where he was tried, thought so too, for they acquitted him. The judge did not share their feeling; he severely censured them and suspended court sessions in the region for two years.

Besides the Strzelecki Track, Australia knows other famous stock routes: the Murranji Track, from the Victoria River in north-west Northern Territory to Newcastle Waters and Camooweal, Queensland; an amorphous route from north Queensland to the south – rather like the American Chisholm trail in its poor definition; the Birdsville Track, now the only road from the eastern edge of the Simpson to the east coast;

and the incredible Canning Stock Route, which has become a memory rather than a road since there are now other ways laid down for cattle.

The American cattle trails fared better in romantic history, legend, and folklore, not so much because of their economic importance, which was incalculable, but because cowboys, Indians, and gunfighters as well as cattle moved along them. The more orderly cattle routes of the East are remembered as poorly as the Australian trails – the Bay State Cow Path (the earliest to be made and the first to die: 1670-1770), the Three Mountain Trail, the Wilderness Road.

Everyone who has seen a Western on television or motion pictures knows of the American West's Chisholm Trail. But aside from inspiring the composition of one of the best bawdy American folksongs, the most that can be said for the Chisholm Trail is that it ran from somewhere in east central Texas by some now forgotten route to St Louis. In 1917, a committee was set up by the Old Time Trail Drivers' Association to map the correct route for history, but all that emerged from the conference was a mixture of error of fact and opinion. The committee could not even ascertain after which Chisholm the trail had been named; and the only certain thing about the route they accepted is that it was wrong. As for the trail's eponym, the only trail any known Chisholm made was the short wagon road from Wichita to Wichita Agency rutted out by the half-breed Jesse.

Osage Indian traders, carrying pelts, bear grease, snake oil, and other Indian commodities, blazed the Osage Trace from the Texas frontier to St Louis in 1810. By 1844 it had been incorporated into the most important cattle trail of all, the Texas Road, along which more than 200,000 longhorns were driven. Ironically, it was the Texas Road that put an end to the Indians as a social entity in this region; either by accident or design they got in the way of both sides fighting the Civil War in the West up and down the Texas Road.

At the end of the Civil War the Texas cattle industry had

burgeoned to 15 million head and had spilled over into the neighbouring states. To funnel all this meat to the ravenous eastern markets, other notable cattle roads were pounded out by longhorn hooves: the Western Trail (central Texas to Dodge City), the Goodnight-Loving Trail (central Texas through New Mexico to Colorado), the Cox Trail (central Kansas to Wichita), the California Trail (central Texas to San Francisco), the Northern Trail (Montana to Oregon), and the Oregon Cattle Trail (northern Missouri to Oregon).

The trails and their cowboys vanished about the same time as Turner's frontier, and for a variety of reasons too mundane to be part of the American Arthurian Legend: the incursion of sedentary land users around 1870, homesteaders who shot cattle straying on their land and juries that would not convict; the discovery that cattle could be raised almost everywhere, even in the cold northern states; the explosion of railroad building during the Great Barbecue; and the baby red-brown tick that caused 'Texas Fever', lethal to shorthorn cattle though tolerated by the carrier longhorns, which in turn were no longer tolerated by northern cattlemen.

In the United States, the American equivalent of the Australian bullock drivers were provided by cartage firms like Russell, Majors, and Waddell, which used 3,500 wagons pulled by 40,000 oxen. Swamped out of the American frontier legend by the railroads, the American bullockies are as little known to the layman as the fact that many of the Plains Indians had horse-drawn wagons – sometimes hundreds of them in a single movement. Somehow wagons do not seem proper in the American West unless they are in a circle surrounded by whooping Indians.

In the least accessible regions of Australia there are still cattle drovers and cattle drives, but in America the drovers have long since disappeared. In 1969 cattlemen and employees of the Great Western Land and Cattle Company recreated on old-time drive by running 600 head of cattle from New Mexico to summer range in Colorado, making 192 miles in

14 days. Some of the arduousness of the work was missing however; the drive's chuck wagon contained among other modern conveniences an electric deep freeze. But the adventure did include a genuine attack by Indians: in the tradition of Tom Collins's squatters in *Such Is Life*, for the Jicarilla Apache tried to impound the cattle for trespass and the Great Western company had to pay $50 a day to get the beef through.

While every hiving-off from a parent civilization is a chance for the young colony to begin again unhampered by the pressures, hardships, and debilities that prompted emigration, it is a chance no serious gambler would bet upon. Unless the motivating trauma for the colonists is so severe as to force rather than to permit casting off old traditions, material and immaterial, the useless baggage of the past is carried into the future. Americans are taught that the Puritans left England to make a new Jerusalem, cutting ties with their errant motherland, and so they did; those Puritans who stayed were ferocious enough as revolutionaries to cut the head off their king and to kill thousands who had no sin but patriotism. Americans are not so often told what the Puritan colonists said on their departure, best expressed by their pastor, Francis Higginson: 'We will not say, as the Separatists were wont to say at their leaving of England, Farewell Babylon, farewell Rome, but we will say, farewell dear England!' It took five purging wars, two of them against the mother country, for the United States to achieve what independence it has. Australia suffered not at all in its birth and weaning, and consequently it is closer still to Britain. Uniquely Australian contumely of the 'bloody Poms' is the first intimacy an American visitor attains Down Under, and he is able to reply with the same sentiment if not the same vigor, but no serious student of national character pays any more attention to the anglophobic expressions of the American and Australian than he would to the grumbling of a small boy sent to bed without his supper. In the Year of Our Lord 1969 Australians for the first time carried passports identifying them as Australian citizens and not British subjects.

Like every culture process, static or dynamic, the inertia of tradition can be detected in every part of the culture, even modes of transportation into the frontiers. Government agencies in Australia today buy British four-wheel-drive vehicles because they are British; their inferiority to American and American-distinguished-as-Japanese hard-country vehicles is as clear as the inferiority of the horse compared to the camel. There is as much probability of the Australian Commonwealth changing its practice here as there is of the British manufacturer taking off the eye-gouging window handles and knee-breaking dashboard that help to distinguish their product.

It was the same in the earliest phase of Australian frontier penetration. The British attachment to the horse as a beast of burden, friend, and drinking companion was carried to the new colony with the horse itself, and both the horse and its folklore persisted long after the horse was found to be useless any distance from a bridle path. In recalling the regular morning complaint of every explorer who packed his chances of survival along with the other gear on the back of his horses, one wonders how these men could justify their choice of a beast so nearly worthless in difficult country. Yet horses were the only proper means of exploratory transport during the first half century of Australian history. If the British had bestowed their affection upon hippopotami, Sturt's boat would have gone into the Great Stony Desert on a cart pulled by a hippopotamus.

It is the way of the world once again. Camels were brought to Egypt in 525 BC as the only practical beast of desert burden. Tradition in the western Dry World nevertheless opposed logic and evidence to preserve the horse and ox as draft animals for another half a millenium, and yielded only when the Romans forced the camel on the Berbers. It might be supposed that this precedent would have suggested an early trial of camels when the aridity of Australia's center was discovered. Not so; tradition kept the country free of camels until 1840.

One reason innovators are so often sacrificial pioneers is the unaccountable certainty that their introduction will fail absolutely and spectacularly, whether it be the steamboat, submarine, guillotine, electric chair, automobile, supermarket, or camel. The pioneer J. A. Horrocks broke away from the horse symbiosis in 1846 by becoming the first Australian explorer to use a camel. It killed him.

Camels also shared in the contrived bad fortune of the Burke and Wills expedition, and were in fact the first to suffer, for Victoria grew no suitable fodder for camels. A small thing for Burke, but a hard thing for the 24 camels he imported from Afghanistan and the half-dozen he bought, appropriately enough, from a local circus.

This poor beginning added to the burden of invidious folklore about the camel. Few other animals have been described so unfavorably by persons who have no knowledge of them whatever; they are so often held to be stupid, ill-tempered, stubborn and smelly. 'It must be admitted,' wrote the anthropologist Linton after enumerating the camel's faults, 'that the Arab does not agree with the European on this point. He regards the camel as a paragon of virtue and an epitome of loveliness. Pre-Islamic literature is full of poems extolling the beauties of the beast.' The Australians who tried both horses and camels in the hardest outback agree with the Arabs. Carnegie concluded after his harrowing trip through the western deserts,

I think there are few animals endowed with more good qualities than the much-abused camel – abused not only by the ignorant, which is excusable, but by travellers and writers who should know better. Patience, perseverance, intelligence, docility, and good temper under the most trying conditions, stand out pre-eminently amongst his virtues. Not that all camels are perfect – some are vicious and bad-tempered; so far as my experience goes these are the exceptions. Some few are vicious naturally, but the majority of bad-tempered camels are made so by ill-treatment. If a camel is constantly bullied, he will patiently wait his chance and take his revenge – and pick the right man too. 'Vice or bad temper,' says the indignant victim; 'Intelligence,' say I.

H. M. Barker, an old-time camel man who wrote a book about the camel as a contribution to human survival in case the hydrogen bomb went off and blew away his culture, was sufficiently annoyed by the *Encyclopaedia Britannica*'s summary of the camel as 'from first to last an undomesticated and savage animal, rendered serviceable by stupidity alone', to wax lyrical about 'my friend the camel' as well as any bushman could: 'A camel is one of the nicest animals there is' [sic]. He admits the camel will explode a half-gallon of vomit upon you once in a while, but only after extreme provocation – and what animal, including man, could help being sick during great torture such as was inflicted upon the camel by nose plugs. Giles in his *Australia Twice Traversed* recalls a stomach-turning scene of a camel driven nearly mad by flies after a nose plug was torn through its septum.

Barker makes the important point that alone among the introduced animals, the camel has fitted well and harmlessly into Australian desert ecology. It lives on forage that no other animal can tolerate, and its wide pads pack rather than break the desert pavement. The early South Australian pioneer Bull records that in the severe drought in the country above Port Augusta in 1882-1883 three quarters of the horses and bullocks died, 'yet the camels have worked through it all, in the most admirable way'.

Sir Thomas Elder imported 120 camels in 1862 and built a breeding station some 150 miles north of Port Augusta on the eastern edge of the dry Lake Torrens. Within a short time he evolved a breed far superior to its Asian ancestors. Having had experience with both kinds, Carnegie eagerly paid 18 times as much for Elder camels as he would have done for imported camels. Capable of carrying or pulling several times the limit of Asian camels, less susceptible to mange and other diseases, and with greater endurance, Elder's camels may have been the most striking development in camel breeding since the animal left Persia for Egypt two and a half thousand years ago. Ernest Giles, the explorer, got a week out of horses deprived of water; Tietkens, trained by Giles, marched his own camels 537 miles in 34 days without a drink. As for strength, Barker (who knew more about this than anyone else) notes that the heaviest load drawn by horses in Australia averaged two tons per animal, about one third of what the best camels could pull. The heaviest load lifted from a kneeling position by a camel, to Barker's knowledge, was 1,700 pounds – and that was in a betting situation (as one might guess for Australia) where the camel's owner wagered his camel could lift a full ton, but there were no takers. The only disadvantage in using camels in Australia was their inability to distinguish the deadly poisonous leaves of the ironwood tree and one or two other poisonous plants (there is a parallel in America: an Asian weed, halogeton, was introduced and is spreading against the native desert vegetation; it is poisonous to livestock).

All other criticisms of the camel in Australia were shifted from the animal to its keepers, the 'Afghans' (who in fact came from Karachi or Baluchistan), imported to take care of these strange beasts. The great explorers, all of whom had highly developed skills at humorous invective, poured vituperation on these sons of Allah. The only good that was ever spoken of them by men who knew them best was Barker's remark, 'Afghans were Mohammedans and drank neither beer nor spirits, so they were widely employed in carting the commodity they shunned'. Several of the camel explorers were particularly irritated by the notions these Muslims had about the capability of camels. Carnegie wrote,

There are one or two things that camels are quite unable to do, according to an Asiatic driver; one is to travel in wet weather. However, Europeans manage to work camels, wet or fine; the wily Afghan says 'Camel no do this,' 'Camel no do that,' because it doesn't suit his book that camel should do so – and a great many people think that he *must* know and is indispensable in the driving of camels; which seems to me to be no more sensible than to say that a chow-dog can only be managed by a Chinaman.

Ernest Giles, who made as great an improvement in camel equipment as Elder had done to the breed itself, encountered the same obstinacy. His camel driver argued that Giles's quickly removable camel pack was not fit to replace the old traditional method of fastening a load with ropes tied in a thousand knots. 'Camel he can't carry them that way,' said Saleh. Giles's reply was sharp. 'Camel he must and camel he shall,' and the consequence was that camel he did.

It seems possible that the camel era in Australia was ended by that Yankee mining engineer and President-to-be, Herbert Hoover. In 1903 he introduced a Panhard automobile from France and proved its superiority to other forms of transport by making 125 miles in one day. Hoover then brought in more automobiles and, as they became more reliable, they displaced the camel entirely. One can still see camels being used in the farthest outback by some natives, and the tracks of wild camels, descendants from those released when their usefulness came to an end, are everywhere in the deepest bush – though the camels themselves are better even than kangaroos in keeping out of sight. Their masters, the Afghans, also vanished with time. Unable to integrate into a culture inimically foreign, the Afghans either went back to India or lived out their lives in celibacy. Until very recently there was only one mosque in all Australia, built on what was once the city of Adelaide's camel paddock; the mosque is now buried away among workshops and warehouses in a poor section of town.

Environment's determination to establish camels on the American frontier aborted because of several largely historical circumstances not obtaining in Australia – the Civil War, the necessity of combating Indian cavalry with white cavalry, American disinterest in developing the poorest lands where camels are best, and the incomparable growth of railroads in the Reconstruction period.

Camels had been brought to Virginia in colonial times, as senseless an importation as the first camels to Tasmania in 1840, for both localities were impossibly rich for animals which evolution had adapted to poor country.

Camels do not seriously appear in American history until 1851, when Jefferson Davis, Chairman of the Senate Committee on Military Affairs, requested money to import 50 camels for military experimentation and breeding in the arid West. The federal government was then somewhat less generous in financing scientific and military projects than it is today, and Davis's application languished for four years. In this interim Davis became Secretary of War, encouraged the resignation of Captain Ulysses S. Grant for excessive drinking, and found support for his camel experiment in Lt Col. Robert E. Lee.

The agent Davis sent abroad to buy camels Major Mitchelled his way through much of the Near East (Salonica, Tunis, Constantinople, Balaclava, Alexandria, Smyrna), but finally bought his first consignment so cheaply that a second journey was authorized. This trip, concluded in 1857, brought the total importation to 75 camels, all debarked in Texas.

Before he could make any use of the camels, Davis was replaced as Secretary of War by John Buchanan Floyd. Floyd, however, shared Davis's interest in camels, and decided to try them on an expedition then being mounted to survey a wagon road from Fort Defiance, New Mexico, to the Colorado River. The leader of the expedition was Edward F. Beale, a long-time factotum for the government – as a messenger he had carried to the East in 1848 the first authenticated report of the California gold discovery – Superintendent of Indian Affairs for California and Nevada,

Surveyor-General of California, United States Minister to Austria. His expedition was both successful and uneventful; in a little less than four months he completed his survey, crossing the Colorado River fifteen miles north of Needles, California, on 19 October 1857, drowning in the process two mules, ten horses, and no camels. On emerging from the water on the California side he was welcomed by a Mohave Indian: 'God damn my soul eyes! How de do! How de do!'

Beale continued into Los Angeles and delighted the population, then a mere 1,500, with their first sight of a camel. Beale, always an inconsistent man, then left the camels in California and went off on another road survey, using as his scout the renowned Jesse Chisholm. This road, running from Fort Smith to the Colorado River, became the route for the Santa Fé Railroad.

Floyd, encouraged by the fine performance of the camels on Beale's 1857 survey, recommended purchase of a thousand more beasts. But the Civil War was imminent, and the camel's champions – Jefferson Davis, Robert E. Lee, and Floyd himself – were hardly the best advocates that might have been wished for. Floyd became a brigadier general for the Confederacy, surrendered too eagerly to General Grant, and was consequently relieved of his command by Confederate President Jefferson Davis. The camels drifted off like unwanted orphans; some ended the story as Australia's camels began – with the circus; some worked out their term as mine cart animals; most were used by the army. But the army and the camels did not fare well together; soldiers lost patience quickly with animals that refused to behave as stupidly as their horses, killed some and let others run away. Those that escaped into the California desert soon reverted to the wild, the cause of persistent stories of 'ghost camels' down almost to the present. The last of Beale's camels, 'Topsy', died in the Griffith Park Zoo in 1934. Recalling another Army servant who 'simply faded away,' General Douglas MacArthur remembered that his father, Arthur MacArthur, had used some camels for desultory transport when he was commander of the Thirteenth Infantry in New Mexico.

Jefferson Davis was not the only importer of camels to the United States, for American business enterprise has always followed the American military, even in its own territory. As early as 1854 an 'American Camel Company' was formed; another ambitiously named organization, the 'California and Utah Camel Association', went into incorporation a few years later with a capitalization of $12,000. A Mrs Watson, the English proprietor of a Texas ranch and a woman of mystery, imported forty camels in 1858 but refused to accept delivery, and the animals fell into the ownership of F. R. Lubbock, later governor of Texas. Most persistent of the camel importers and least successful was the San Francisco merchant Otto Esche, who in three shipments of camels from China in the early 1960s bought ninety Bactrians, half of which arrived dead. Some use was made of the live ones in mine cartage, but eventually all faded away like their army compatriots.

In America, too, Asian camel drivers were immigrated, and were found to be as unsatisfactory by American opinion as the Afghans were in Australia. Only one of them seems to have had any lasting good fortune – a Syrian who went to Mexico and established a family that apparently produced Plutarco Elias Calles, the revolutionary President of Mexico from 1924 to 1928.

At Menindie on the day Captain Robert O'Hara Burke led his magnificent expedition into the outpost, a steamboat belonging to river pioneer Francis Cadell paddled into the settlement with supplies. A fortuitous meeting this was – of the first of the important commercial entrepreneurs of the frontier and one of the last of the uncommercial probers of the habitable inland, both of them necessary but transitionary to more efficient methods of opening the wilderness.

River transportation in Australia beyond what in America

was called the 'fall line' – nonesuch in flat Australia – was limited to the Murray River. Every other stream of that degree of incursion had gone dry at one time or other. The Murray itself was hardly impressive; a Scottish engineer, one E. J. Brady, spoke for the consensus when he called it a 'dommed puddle hole'. Though it occupied geographically much the same comparative location as the Ohio River running into the Mississippi down to the Gulf, the Murray's resemblance to the great American waterway ceases at that point. No one would ever rhapsodize about the Murray as one American did about the Mississippi in 1844:

> The Mississippi! The great big rollin', tumblin', bilin', endless and almost shoreless Mississippi! There's a river for you! I don't care what John Bull may say, or any other ruffle-shirted fellow, about their old castles with their bloody murder legends. I tell you the United States is a great country! There ain't nobody else but Uncle Sam as could afford such a river as that!

In the same year that paean to the Mississippi was written the father of William Richard Randell took up a selection at Gumeracha, near Adelaide, South Australia, on the Torrens River. Even then young Randell had determined his life's purpose: to be the first to sail the first steamboat up the Murray River.

When the vague entity of South Australia was proclaimed in 1834, and Colonel William Light, the new Surveyor-General, was sent to locate a capital settlement, his orders directed him to find a site as close to the mouth of the Murray River as possible. This is a most confused area geographically, with shallows, indecisive lakes, lagoons, islands, and a unique ocean billabong called the Coorong, all where the Murray's outlet to the sea should be. Light was easily persuaded by the explorer Charles Sturt, an early visitor to this area, that the Murray mouth was not navigable, and so with some extenuation of his authority Light founded Adelaide on the

164

other side of the Mount Lofty Ranges at the first dry, solid ground supplied with reliable fresh water, the River Torrens.

It seemed neither possible nor right to some of the men who came with Light that the largest river on the continent could flow for more than 1,600 miles, gathering tributaries all the way, and still have too little strength to force its way clearly to the sea. Some of these influential pioneers sharply disagreed with Light's decision, but his judgment prevailed. One of Light's opponents on this question was the Governor, Sir John Hindmarsh, who attempted to prove that the Murray could be entered from the sea by sending a boat to enter it. Unhappily, he experienced the too-frequent bad luck of the camel pioneer J. A. Horrocks and others who risked their reputations on innovations: the boat overturned and a sailor was drowned. William J. S. Pullen, a former naval officer turned settler, also was a strenuous proponent of Murray navigability until he soured on the internecine fighting then tearing the nobly conceived colony apart – not only the relatively minor dispute about the Murray ingress, but far more bitter political controversy. Pullen returned to the navy and went off to the Arctic to lie icebound for two years while searching for the lost expedition of Sir John Franklin. One contemporary South Australian diarist remarked that he had 'gone to a more congenial clime'. The most unfortunate and unpleasant business of the recall of both Hindmarsh and his successor, George Gawler, and the Crown's indefensible repudiation of Gawler's public works bills, brought depression, panic, and near collapse of Adelaide in which the matter of Murray navigation fell out of official sight.

In 1852, 28-year-old, William Randell determined to fulfil his great ambition to be the first to sail a steamboat up the Murray River. He built a wooden steamboat on the station, the *Mary Ann*, inventing and fabricating parts himself in primitive conditions. Ingenious but makeshift, his boiler had to be strapped together in the absence of riveting equipment, and when it built up steam it caused some apprehension in onlookers by breathing like an accordion. For all its grotesquerie the *Mary Ann* worked, and early in 1853 Randell hauled it over the mountains and launched it on the Murray River. On this first trip Randell got about 150 miles up river just beyond the Murray's big bend, where shallow water forced him to turn back. In August he tried again, and ran into that inexorable law of cultural evolution that says when a thing is possible it is inevitable. An invention is made when the culture is ready for it, and the accredited inventor is only a person with the good luck of being at the right place at the right time. So it is that historians have arbitrarily chosen Fulton as the inventor of the steamboat though Fitch, Symington, Rumsey, Morey, Roosevelt, Jouffroy, Livingston, and God only knows how many Russians had equal claims in a situation of 'invention' where the only truth is that given the steam engine and given the boat, the steamboat is an inevitability. In short, when Randell passed the Murrumbidgee Junction in the *Mary Ann*, another steamboat passed him. This was the *Lady Augusta*, built in Sydney to the order of Francis Cadell, a Scot who had observed river navigation on the Mississippi. Of course the two boats immediately started a race, in Mississippi fashion; this one lasted for a month, each boat paying first attention to the profitable business of loading and unloading cargo.

Taking a quite inhumanistic view, one could say that the force that put steamboats on the Murray was neither Randell nor Cadell, who argued about the primacy for the rest of their lives, but economic opportunity, greed once again. Before the boats goods carriage between Sydney and Adelaide overland cost an unacceptable £12 a ton and took three months; after greed pulled the bullockies off the overland run and into the short and profitable goldfields business, something had to fill the economic niche. Cadell and Randell immediately became fierce competitors, as well they might have been, for property values rose a hundred per cent as soon as the boats went on the river. Another economic law went into operation right away – other competition soon glutted the river with steamboats. And finally, both Cadell and Randell were sacrificial pioneers: neither prospered at the end. Having cleared only a small profit, Randell left the river to manage his station when his father died in 1875. He received political reward by being elected to the South Australian parliament. Cadell's end was more adventurous. He over-extended his enterprise and went into bankruptcy in 1858. Continuing in a smaller line of business on the river, he was finally driven off entirely when the rivalry between New South Wales and Victoria, which shared the Murray as a boundary and resulted in customs regulations little short of piracy. Cadell sold his last small boat to New Zealand, did some trading with the Maori natives of that country, came back to Australia to explore Arnhem Land, went into whaling, pearling, and blackbirding (capture of Polynesians for slavery in Queensland). He came to a dramatic finish at the hands of Torres Strait islanders in 1879. Both the *Lady Augusta* and the *Mary Ann* were cannibalized for the construction of other boats, and their hulks still lie under silt on the river they were the first to conquer.

As with the Mississippi, the Murray riverboat era was rich in folklore. Both rivers had their share of delightful if senseless races: Randell once stoked his boilers with cargo bacon when his wood ran out; another captain was said to have fired up his boiler with coffins, one of which at least was occupied. Both rivers had their ferocious, all-in, all-out fighters; both made a romantic world for children that Mark Twain immortalized for his river; both changed their course in floods so that captains steamed their crafts far inland (in Australia the appropriately named *Wandering Jew* was said to have gone inland, never to be seen again); both amassed a treasury of songs and stories; and both were tied together by the inevitable Americans. The port of Wahgunyah, remembered for Captain Bill Jinks's mad but intrepid rush onto the sandbank, was a terminus for the American boat *Lady Daly*, and Gus Pierce, Peleg Jackson, and A. L. Blake, Yankees all, were among the most famous and colorful captains on the Murray. Both waterways declined as avenues of transport with the advent of the railroads. Australian railways were more vicious in their opposition to the boats: subsidies, under-cost rates, and dummy lines were used by railroads in both countries, but only in Australia were bridges built across the river so low that boats could not pass.

But before the railroads came the roads.

With all due and undue respect, with the greatest love and admiration for the country and its people, with understanding of the insuperable problems that both face in constructing ways for vehicular traffic, it must be said that Australian roads go some distance beyond the limits of belief. The South Australian pioneer, John Wrathall Bull, remembers that the track between Adelaide and the Kapunda copper mine was made by Captain Bagot dragging a stick behind him. Very little advance has been made since. Even the sealed highways, covered with bitumen (pronounced so as to cast doubt upon its ancestry), are like Hansel and Gretel's path through the forest – there are bits of asphalt here and there like their bits of bread, just enough for the sharp-eyed traveler to find his way. It may have had some alteration since, or it may have disappeared entirely, but in 1967 the section of the Eyre Highway running from Eucla to Madura along the Western Australia coast was surely the most harrowing track ever to be designated a public high-way. Its corrugations – which have been found to extend some twenty feet below the surface – will shake all but the toughest cars into their component parts; its cavernous ruts can drop a truck down to its door handles; its warning signals often are simply great boulders dropped in the middle of the road to provide the immovable object for the irresistible force of a vehicle racing along the top of the corrugations; its stretches of 'bulldust' absorb a whole car like so much flour and its deceptively navigable shoulders lure drivers into bogs that can bury their vehicles forevermore.

And that is the only highway connecting the settlements of Western Australia with the other states. The main highway between the two largest cities, Melbourne and Sydney, runs across a quicksand near Gundagai on which apparently the concrete was merely laid. In 1956 heavy trucks and the road itself sank into the swamp. This road had existed, after a fashion, in 1852, when one writer described it 'as consisting of gum-trees and public houses; the grass for your horse improving as the comfort for yourself becomes less.' In that year Earp's survey of the colony added to the Sydney-Melbourne track two other roads: from Sydney to the Hawkesbury and from Sydney to Parramatta; 'with the exception of these roads there are no means of internal transit whatever, though wool has to be brought down in bullock-drays from immense distances, in order to reach the port of shipment.' Even these roads in Earp's account were not 'roads in the English sense of the term, but a succession of openings through the forest, in which the chance of being lost is somewhat diminished.' That was the situation in 1852; in 1968 one reference source informs us that the Eyre Highway of Western Australia 'is now sealed to a point beyond Cocklebiddy on the Nullarbor Plain. Otherwise the highways are only partly stabilized though clearly defined.'

The first good roads made in Australia were tamped out by the flapjack feet of the camels, and so long as they were used by transit carriers that did not break the surface, they remained in reasonable condition. Rougher but more useful since they followed lines of genuine commerce instead of the mirage of the gold trail were the bullock-team tracks. In wet weather these roads would become bogs of remarkable depth and tenacity. The novelist Arthur Upfield recalled seeing efforts made to pull a bogged bullock cart out of its mire with an unprecedented number of camels, bullocks, and horses hitched to the line. The team moved but the cart did not – at least not in one piece; it was jerked to flinderjigs.

The condition of these roads was worsened, by the retention, wherever possible, of the good old British heavy coaches and clumsy two-wheeled wagons. To make the coach runs as British as possible among the gum trees, drivers warned the kangaroos of their approach with a bugle, and bush pubs were named after well known English taverns – pretensions that did not square with the Yass leg of the Melbourne-Sydney Royal Mail coach line, on which the transport was a two-wheeled cart.

So the Australians suffered until the gold rush brought in Freeman Cobb, James Swanton, John Lamber, and John Peck – all Americans who had had experience with the Wells Fargo line in the United States. With the financial and moral backing of the great entrepreneur George Train, these men formed in 1853 one of the legendary Australian institutions, 'Cobb and Co'. Though Cobb sold out to another American, James Rutherford, in 1859, the company continued under the famous name, running coaches until 1924. The coaches as well as the owners were American; the steel-springed English coaches which bashed their coach's occupants about so cruelly were replaced by leather-springed Concord coaches, which made passengers sea-sick. But no one really expected comfort; so far as the mail and goods coach lines were concerned, passengers were aboard to serve 'the useful purposes of dragging the carriage through the sand and dust when the horses collapsed, of hunting up the team in the mornings, and of lightening the load by walking. For this exceedingly comfortable journey they had the pleasure of paying at least £5.' It was the same on the American goldfields; the songs from the era are almost interchangeable:

> There's no respect for youth or age
> On board of a California stage;
> But pull and haul about for seats
> As bedbugs do among the sheets.

They started out in a thieving line
In eighteen hundred and forty-nine;
All opposition they defy,
So the people must 'root hog, or die'.

You're crowded in with Chinamen
As fattening hogs are in a pen;
And what will more a man provoke
Than musty plug tobacco smoke?

The ladies are compelled to sit
With dresses in tobacco spit;
The gentlemen don't seem to care
But talk on politics and swear.

The dust is deep in summer time,
The mountains very hard to climb;
And drivers often stop and yell
'Get out, all hands, and push up hill!'

The drivers, when they feel inclined
Will have you walking on behind,
And on your shoulder lug a pole
To help them through some muddy hole.

They promise when your fare you pay
'You'll have to walk but *half* the way';
Then add aside with cunning laugh,
'You'll push and pull the other half!'

Americans established a near-monopoly in Australian road
transport that has lasted, with few interruptions, down to the
present day. Cobb's line was predominant, but it had other
American rivals, like F. B. Clapp's Melbourne Tramways and
Omnibus Company, which held the city transport monopoly
until it was replaced by an American cable car in the 1880s.
During the Second World War a road from the east to Alice
Springs and then north to Darwin was an American project.
Most recently, American capital and management built the

encapsulated towns and the roads to them that distinguish the new mineral finds. And in 1969, Wells Fargo completed the circle by buying into Australia's Mercantile Bank.

The most improbable and astonishing road project ever undertaken in Australia is, however, the work of an Australian, Len Beadell, surveyor for a number of government agencies. With a party of five men, three trucks, a Land Rover, a bulldozer, and a grader, Beadell 'bushbashed' his 'Gunbarrel Highway' from the short road leading out of Alice Springs to the Carnegie homestead in Western Australia, from which an established road ran on to the coast.

Ostensibly made for scientific purposes (geodetic surveys and mineral exploration), Len Beadell's road has some possible military significance, but aside from that, it is a road to nowhere that few people can obtain permission to travel. The main east-west section was completed in 1963; since then Beadell has extended a northward leg through part of the Gibson and Great Sandy Deserts to North Nowhere. There is no possibility of its opening this vast area to settlement, and, in fact, the road is breaking up badly over nearly all its route. Since its bed is lower than the adjoining shoulders – having been simply pushed out by the bulldozer and scraper – it has become a watercourse for the infrequent but violent rains, so that it is fast reverting to the ultimate use claimed for it by Beadell: 'a means whereby a traveller could arrive at his destination without everlastingly consulting a compass for direction and observing the stars for position'. Fair enough, as the Aussies say; except that there are no destinations anywhere along the Gunbarrel Highway.

Comparisons between American and Australian roads are inescapably invidious, for nothing in the two countries differs so much in quantity and quality. There are only 80,000 miles of asphalt-concrete roads in all Australia while the United States has at least 3,000,000 miles and this figure is growing faster than one can calculate. On a population basis the difference may seem exaggerated, but this is an area of development not closely connected to population. Each nation has about 3,000,000 square miles, and whatever the population the various parts of the continent must be linked for national integrity if for no other reason. Some of the obstacles preventing road development in Australia are insurmountable; the inability of a small population to achieve standards easily attained by a large nation is in every case fundamental to technological inferiority in Australia. Japan can absorb a forty per cent import duty on its automobiles and still beat Australian competition – for the same reason Australia cannot spread a network of good roads around the country.

Another difficulty is the not-so-facetious observation that Australian roads have nowhere to go. Beadell's inland roads extend approximately 1,500 miles in one direction or other, yet there are no destinations along them, except Giles Meteorological Station (prohibited entry), Warburton Aboriginal Mission (prohibited entry), North West Reserve (prohibited entry), and one or two other places to which entry is forbidden; Alice Springs on one terminus and the Carnegie homestead on the other do not count, since access to these places is practicable only from the opposite direction to that of the road. In fact, Australia was not traversed from the point farthest west to the point farthest east until 1966 – and then only by an expedition distinguished by personnel as foolhardy as they were well supported by resource assistance. American roads, on the contrary, all lead somewhere. Typical is the Pennsylvania Turnpike, the first of the modern arterial high-speed highways; it followed for some of its route the Philadelphia-Lancaster Turnpike of 1794. The National Road ran through Turner's famous Cumberland Gap. These and all others – hundreds of them – fan out into a system of constantly dividing capillaries enmeshing every community of the United States. The places named in Australia's outback are in most cases stations – ranches – whose owners have less use for trespassers than they did in the days of Tom Collins's bullockies. Too many adventurous tourists are young Americans depending entirely on Australian hospitality and having no equipment except a Volkswagen and a touching ignorance. A few of these have an appeal to anyone's sense of the ridiculous, but a swarm of them is as noxious as a swarm of bushflies. The squatter's wished-for visitors fly in on their own planes.

It seems that one of the inherited instincts of the human species is a compulsion to learn mistakes by making them, not by absorbing the experience of others. Americans are as prone to this educational inefficiency as any other people. To an American observing Australian behavior, the Australians' obstinate refusal to learn by American errors is reprehensible. Sydneysiders are building their Opera House at a cost that will round off at perhaps a hundred million dollars yet its builders refuse even to consider providing parking facilities for more than five hundred automobiles. Impressive high-rise office buildings scrape the Sydney sky on lots that three or four years ago held milk bars, yet the same amount of parking space is considered adequate for old and new enterprise. A few superhighways have been built; these as often as not are constructed to sweep around in exciting great curves – a pattern corrected years ago in the United States when any deviation from a straight line was found to have a high incidence of fatal accidents.

These are simple, single errors; they are venial, tolerable. Double mistakes are sins against the Holy Ghost; there is no absolution for them in this world or the next. The Australian approach to the question of railroads is a quadruple-barreled error. The errors, two of which were committed by the United States, are these: first, preservation of a moribund system of transportation; second, supporting rail lines at the direct expense of roads; and thirdly (the British error), letting ownership reside in the hands of government.

There was a time when railroads were the means by which

the deserts could be made to bloom and great nations to arise. The American railroads a century ago were new, imaginative and magnificent, yet so corrupt that no one at the time understood that such excesses could open a country. Social and economic philosophers thought only of the corruption and the prodigality of the national wealth by a weak President and venal assistants, for who could have justified the bribery that gave railroad magnates one ninth of Louisiana; one eighth of California; one seventh of Nebraska; one fifth of Wisconsin, Iowa, Kansas, North Dakota, and Montana; and one fourth of Minnesota and Washington? There was without doubt an enormous amount of graft, bribery, and other forms of monetary corruption. The *Crédit Mobilier* by itself seduced into impeachable corruption members of Congress and the Senate, cabinet officers, the Vice President of the United States, and a future President. But the *Crédit Mobilier* built the Union Pacific Railroad. The moguls who projected the Northern Pacific Railroad were given land grants calculated to return the equivalent of a billion dollars in today's currency. But the Northern Pacific settled the northern plains states. In 1850 the federal government gave the promoters of the Illinois Central Railroad more than a million acres. But the Illinois Central populated the heart of America. The official government admission of 140,725,000 acres of public land given to railroads is shocking. But it was those grants and those railroads that brought ten million settlers into the wilderness. From a 16-mile locomotive line between the two Pennsylvania towns of Carbondale and Honesdale, American railroads grew within the century to a half million miles of track, about thirty per cent of the world total. And the nation's growth was parallel: from being a political entity rather like Sweden today – existing because it suited its powerful neighbors to permit it to exist – the United States became the most powerful country in the world.

But all that was a century ago. Japan watched the progress and, looking upon its own traditional stagnation, decided to follow the American lead. But time had already passed and the Japanese government questioned whether what had been best for the United States was so much as good for Japan. Herbert Spencer was brought in, that greatly underrated evolutionist before Darwin, philosopher, father of sociology, and railroad magnate, to suggest means of circumventing the inefficiencies and evils of economic natural selection. He did, and so Japan arbitrarily created its robber barons and industrial tycoons, thus saving years of needless contention among the rapacious.

That, too, was a long time ago. Today the railroads of the United States are collapsing. Several states have lost passenger service entirely. Only the very old and the very frightened will use trains for long distance travel. No locomotives exist outside switching yards anywhere in the nation. Trains that were revolutionary innovations a generation ago have been removed, unable to survive even as metatactic toys. There are people who would take these facts to be a sign of American economic decline, but they are like the Russian in the American story who boasted that his country had thousands of delousing stations while there was not one to be seen in the United States.

At this moment in economic history, as American railroad unions prepare to launch themselves into another national strike, another suicidal banzai charge against inevitability, sober men understand that railroads are as moribund as wool and mutton, as poor a carrier for a nation as the sheep's back. The government of the United States is quietly abandoning railroads in their terminal illness with only nominal assistance and no more grants of land. Federal money now goes into space transport and surface roads. By the transparent device of military necessity, the national government pays 90 per cent of main road building costs. The frontier is being buried under a sea of concrete.

What of Australia as the third millennium of the Christian era approaches?

– From a rail mileage of 243 in 1861 Australian railroads have in a century grown to a mileage of 25,000.

– Gauges vary from state to state, locality to locality: five feet three, four feet eight, three feet six, two feet six and two feet. In the Queensland sugar fields, gauge variance is hard to determine as workmen pick up sections of double track and move them about as needed.

– Half of the nation's locomotives are steam-driven.

– It is possible to walk (if one has the stamina and the supplies) for more than 2,000 miles in a straight line without crossing or paralleling a railroad in any direction.

– Some of Australia's locomotives were running when the Wright brothers were building their pioneer airplane.

– One of the nation's most famous railways, the 'Ghan' from Alice Springs to Adelaide, runs twice a week at an average speed of 17 miles per hour. If one considers its numerous breakdowns that may last for many days, the average drops to a walking speed or less.

These signs of underdevelopment and obsolescence would be fine in the United States, but they are not fine in Australia for the one reason that the Australian state and federal governments are dotingly paternalistic toward railroads, and not only put far too much of their transport development money into railroads, but actively obstruct and discourage road transport whenever it is remotely competitive with railroads. Road carriers, in accordance with the laws of culture change, have turned to technology to oppose the government in this matter: great engines have been developed to pull trains of heavy trailers – a half dozen or more in one hitch – right through the bush over the poorest tracks.

Meanwhile the state and commonwealth governments keep the railways cushioned safely in the past. Things have not changed much since Mark Twain noted three quarters of a century ago:

Along [the road] toiled occasional freight wagons, drawn by long double files of oxen. Those wagons were going on a journey of two hundred miles, I was told, and were running a successful opposition to the railway! The railways are owned and run by the government.

If Twain had ridden one of the secondary railroads, he would have been astonished – but probably pleased – to see that the man who gave the order for the train to resume after stopping at a small town was not the conductor but the local publican. This practice was observed almost to the present day. Outback railway towns do not consist of much more than the pub and the jail.

Australian railroads have done very little to open the frontier. The transcontinental railway runs in an absolutely straight line for 297 miles across the Nullarbor Plain. The map shows towns at intervals along the way, but these are as illusionary as that persistent 'town' of Eucla – less so, for Eucla's buildings (three old telegraph stations filled with drifting sand) are in their skeletons, archaeological ruins though they be, more ambitious structures than the corrugated-iron shanties that pass for settlements on the Trans-Australian Railway. From Kalgoorlie on the west to Port Pirie on the east, there is nothing at all for a full thousand miles – unless the train stops at Port Augusta, in which case there is nothing for 950 miles. Laid in such a barren region, the transcontinental railroad had an easy bed to run upon, but it could do no more to open the last frontier for possible settlement than the jet planes flying high across the continent.

The admirable Australian qualities of independence and tenacity prevent the nation's leaders from learning even from mistakes made in Britain. Government ownership of rail lines is nearly complete; only 650 miles of track lie in private hands, nearly all of it tied to special industries, and some of this quite hilarious, like the Kalgoorlie Firewood Company's line, which runs from Kalgoorlie into the bush – with the latter terminal being moved around as trees are cut down. No doubt the cozy socialism of publicly owned railways was attractive to the Labor Party and not wholly repugnant to conservatives, but its ramifications are worrying. Led by American example, the federal Australian government is pouring more money into vehicular roads now, bringing the total assistance to $280,000,000 a year. This sounds impressive until one listens harder to what it means. To make only one invidious comparison, the Victorian government is beginning the redevelopment of the Flinders Street Railway Station at a cost estimate (which means usually about two thirds of the actuality) of $112,000,000. Mark Twain noticed this gross inequity of expenditure on railway stations in 1896, despite the official adherence to the 'pioneer standard' of spending money on railways and not on buildings. Few Australians disagree with his view of Maryborough as a railway station with a town attached. Twain also remarked that there were 800 railway stations in Victoria 'and the business done at 80 of them doesn't foot up twenty shillings a week'. It is admirable theory for a country to own its own railroads and thus cut out the Hills, Harrimans, Cookes, Goulds, Drews, Fisks, Vanderbilts, and other predators of like mind, but practice and theory are different things. Cut out the robber barons and you bring in the pilferers. The man who steals the common off the goose is little punished for the reason that he contributes to the prosperity of the common; the man who steals the goose off the common does neither the common nor the goose any tangible good. The country that keeps its own railways does not get nation builders; it gets railway employees.

Stand at Menindie today on the dry side of the Darling River and see what the progress of a century has changed. The heat still addles men's brains, as it did when Burke passed through, and aridity still drops nails out of boots. The riverboats are gone. There is a pipeline running out to the wilderness paradise of Broken Hill, sending it sustenance like an umbilical cord. And the population has grown to 644 people. Such Is Life.

SEVEN

The Underground Frontier

In March 1969, the last working gold mine in the state of Victoria closed down. The death of the Wattle Gully mine was an absolute termination of the Victorian frontier, not an equivocal closure, like the riddling infiltration Turner accepted as signifying the end of the American West in 1890.

The 118 years between the first wild discoveries of dust and nuggets in 1851 and the economic strangulation of the Wattle Gully mine in 1969 were the Attack Phase of frontier conquest, that universal transitionary period when intruders come in only to take out. Final conquest means permanent occupation, a symbiotic relationship between settlers and the land wherein each gives the other something of value.

On most modern frontiers this attack phase is a mining operation in both the extractive and military sense. The attack is subsurficial, the frontier underground, with the land used only as a point of entry to the real or supposed riches underneath. Whether it is the gold diggings in Nubia's Wasi Alaki 3,200 years ago, of which the Pharaoh Rameses II said,

> if a few of the gold washers went thither, it was only the half of them that arrived, for they died of thirst on the road

or the American-Australian Pilbara iron operation in the far north-west of Australia, for which a capsule of civilization including a seaport, railroad, mining complex and a city is being imposed on the land without any integration with the land – a wilderness is not defeated so long as trespassers must flee from it or take refuge from it. Except for the atmosphere,

Pilbara might as well be on the moon as in the Hamersley Range.

A kind of madness is needed to put people in Pilbara, out at Wasi Alaki, or on the moon. Rational, normal human beings do not go to these hostile places because they have a fondness for the countryside. They must be pulled or driven to them by some very strong motive and, to say it once more, greed is only too adequate a stimulus. Very few other things over the whole history of mankind have been so often the object of greed as gold.

The value of gold is entirely in the mind, where madness lies. As a metallic substance, gold has a few unique or very unusual qualities that make it truly useful in modern space and electronic technology – its malleability, its inertness, its cryogenic superiority as a perfect conductor of electricity at absolute zero – but these characteristics cannot be cited as the reason for gold madness in earlier times. Malleability and gold's inability to compound directly with oxygen were known since gold was known, but the former was a defect in the metal so far as ancient use is considered. One cannot make a spear point out of boiled spaghetti. To be used even as a material symbol, gold must be combined with some sturdier metal. (It is of parenthetical interest to notice that the adjectival phrase '14-carat' common as a synonym for perfection augments the illusions surrounding gold – 14-carat gold is only 58.3 per cent pure.) Utility of gold – if we accept *use* as meaning a consumption of the product for purposes more directly affecting the organism, such as crude oil as the raw material for internal combustion engine power – did not exist in any significant degree until after the Second World War. To that time gold was only a symbol – one third of it employed in the somatic and other arts, two thirds put into coinage or in bars, the latter interestingly enough put back into underground vaults. With full allowance for the fact that beauty is in the eye of the beholder, pure gold is not an attractive substance; one walk through the gold room of the

University Museum in Philadelphia will convince almost anyone that 24-carat gold is a tawdry ornament. Electrum – an alloy of gold and silver – elicits many more cries of admiration than gold unalloyed.

Nevertheless, the delusion of gold is perhaps the most ancient form of civilized greed. Evidence of gold panning goes back at least 6,000 years, and signs of frenzy in the search for gold have also been plain throughout this time. The story of Jason and the Golden Fleece is a legendary sublimation of an expedition sent to rob working prospectors some three thousand years ago. This is the testimony of a cultural imperative: that technology depends for its stimulus upon urgent need. The practice of laying sheepskins in auriferous stream beds is an invention made independently in ancient Greece and in recent California, if in the latter case blankets are accepted in place of a fleece; at the present time in South Africa corduroy cotton fabric is used for the same purpose. Nearly all the technology of gold extraction and refining was known and used by the ancients: cupellation was used in the second century before Christ; amalgamation, in Roman times; and even the principle inherent in the extraction of gold by potassium cyanide – a process whose invention is accredited to MacArthur and the Forrests in 1887 and which made South Africa the world leader in gold production – has been known since time immemorial.

It is not scarcity alone that makes gold precious; on this criterion gold cannot be compared to tektites, particularly the Australian australites, believed to have been spun onto the earth when a tremendous meteor struck the moon and made the crater Tycho three quarters of a million years ago. Iron was a more valuable metal to Egyptians of the XIII Dynasty (a small block of meteoric iron placed under the head of the young pharaoh was the most precious object in the gold-glutted tomb of King Tutankhamen). A piece of canvas painted over by the hand of Leonardo da Vinci and called *Ginevra de' Benci* is worth fifteen thousand times its weight in gold. But one does not create nations with paintings and defective postage stamps. Gold is what made the world go round. It is unapproached in history as the most enduring form of currency. It kept medieval philosophers working for centuries at the persistent madness of alchemy. It sent men mad into the Australian and the American Wests. It made them attack the very earth in fury, a lunacy of destruction; if ever the anthropological 'Man from Mars' – that quintessentially objective observer – comes to look upon the gold fields of Western Australia, cratered for hundreds of miles like the surface of the moon, or the beds of Colorado streams, torn up and thrown out in massive heaps upon their banks, he will wonder how such things could have been done by so physically weak a creature. It would be hard for him to say how and impossible to say why, for it is all illusion. All the gold dug out of the Australian earth – ten per cent of the world total – is worth in today's American currency, only seven billion dollars: about as much as the United States spends every six weeks on social security and various welfare programs. Wattle Gully and all the hundreds of gold mines in Victoria were killed by the delusion that created them; for years they worked as all remaining gold mines must work, in a gamble against the future, supported in the meantime by government subsidies and the desperate hope that the International Monetary Fund will rescind its 1945 price freeze and allow people to renew their faith that gold is in fact worth all they are eager to pay for it. Neither purchasers nor sellers are in any way deterred by the Auriferal Paradox: gold up, money down. The best they can get out of a price release is a simple inflated equilibrium, with the Devil taking care of those living on fixed incomes.

The discovery of gold in America and Australia had to wait upon the usefulness of the illusion. Since its social function is to lure people into a presumably domesticable wilderness, gold had to lie officially unseen until the wilderness was in a historical position to be occupied. In America this meant until California was politically accessible to the manifest destiny of the United States; no sense in discovering western gold so long as Mexicans and Russians were in a better position to take both the gold and the land it lay in. It is no mere geological coincidence that gold was not discovered in California until 1848, the same year the Treaty of Guadalupe Hidalgo ceded the region to the United States.

The story of the discovery of gold in Australia is a classical example of how these geosocial accidents occur. It is the tale of how an Australian prospector in California named Edward Hargraves was struck by the resemblance of the Mother Lode country to land he knew back in Australia and just went back and picked up the first gold. Occurrences of this kind, of course, do not happen outside literature. And perhaps it is difficult to accept that huge amounts of gold, from dust to reefs to hundredweight nuggets, are found by thousands of people within a few months in an area that had been walked over for sixty years without anyone ever noticing the slightest sparkle of gold. Of course the least reference to history establishes the Hargraves tale as 24-carat romance.

Like most subjects of romance, Edward Hammond Hargraves had luck in extremes. Born in England, he went to sea in 1816 at the age of 14 as cabin boy to Captain John Lister. Two years later he debarked at Sydney and went into the bush to work on a cattle station. Leaving this employment quickly, he shipped aboard a French schooner to hunt tortoiseshell in Torres Strait. At Batavia typhus struck the crew; Hargraves was one of the few who survived. After a brief return to England Hargraves was back in Australia again and opting for a career on the land. He married, took up several pastoral holdings one after the other, failing at the production of everything except children. When news of the California rush reached him, he sold his few cattle for a pound a head, leaving his half-dozen children in the hands of his long-suffering wife, and bought passage to California in July of 1849. Hargraves wandered aimlessly around the California diggings for a year with six partners and a couple of aborigines.

The California adventure was unprofitable. The companions made little more than enough to keep alive, and in their poor circumstances and knowing Australians, it is easy to imagine them making the disparaging remark that there was more bloody gold in bloody Australia than in this bloody place. A clever remark bears much repeating over a glass of beer surrounded by Australians, and it may be suspected that Hargraves and his mates eventually came to believe it to be the bloody truth. In any event, three of them – Hargraves, Simpson Davison, and E. W. Rudder – claimed to have made this observation in letters to Australia and then suddenly decided to return home and follow it up. These letters figured later in the inevitable dispute about who had got the idea first. Unfortunately for Davison, his recipient lost or destroyed his letter; Rudder had his published in the *Sydney Morning Herald*; and Hargraves, one way or other, was able to produce his later.

Hargraves had his best luck as a prospector on board the ship back to Australia, for he arrived first in Australia to act upon their collective hunch. Davison lost time making a few last-minute sales in San Francisco (inefficient greed, this), and Rudder was shipwrecked on the Great Barrier Reef.

It is difficult to ascertain exactly what happened after Hargraves's arrival in Sydney from the confused reconstruction of the events made later, but somehow he got out to the area around Bathurst, where acquaintances of his – Mrs Lister and her son John, probably the relics of the Captain John Lister who had been his first master in the merchant marine, were living in some poverty. Young John Lister took Hargraves down to the creek and let him pan out a little gold – tuppence worth, according to one later account, all he was ever to find in Australia.

Although Hargraves on all the evidence seems to have been particularly ungifted at detecting gold in the ground (he was taken to Western Australia later to assess the possibility of goldfields there, and asserted there was none), he did have what all credible inventors and discoverers must have: the ability to talk others into belief and, if necessary, investment. Badgering Governor General Charles Fitzroy and Colonial Secretary Deas Thomson for a reward due the first discoverer of gold in Australia, Hargraves importuned rather than proved his claim. He had a little dust to support his argument, but Deas Thomson had been in America himself and was inclined to think that the gold had come from the $100,000 shipment brought to Australia on the same ship that returned Hargraves. By this time Hargraves had made so much noise that prospectors were streaming out to the Listers' homestead, which he had christened 'Ophir' in a burst of typical magniloquence and the memory of a similarly-named digging in California. He was given a reward of £500, two uniformed servants, and the title of 'Crown Commissioner for Exploration of the Gold-fields'. So passes Edward Hammond Hargraves into history.

The history of gold discovery in Australia is controversial to say the least. In 1823 a government surveyor named James McBrien had reported his discovery of gold in the Fish River Valley. As with all other documented and undocumented evidence of previous discoveries, Hargraves declared that he had no prior knowledge of this report. But let it not be doubted that there is a Providence above that sooner or later delivers the wicked into the hands of the righteous. In a manuscript collection in Sydney's Mitchell Library, un-catalogued and evidently unknown to the librarians, there is a note in Hargraves's own hand admitting his knowledge of McBrien's find prior to his Ophir discovery.

Both before and after McBrien's discovery, convicts who had gone into the bush came back with gold and were whipped for their labors, the authorities suspecting they had pounded nuggets out of stolen gold watches. The Reverend William Branwhite Clarke found gold in 1839. Count Edmund de Strzelecki discovered traces of gold in the same year. W. J. Smith came in from the bush with gold in 1846; several surveyors did the same in 1848. Louis Michel, William Campbell, T. Hiscock, James Esmonds, and Dr G. W. Bruhn were given rewards by the government in testimony of their primacy as gold discoverers. Esmonds was one of Hargraves's mates who also claimed to have found gold by equating the geology of Australia and America; Bruhn added a pretty American touch by finding his gold in the Jim Crow Range. And when Hargraves first went to see John Lister and his friend William Tom (another gold discoverer), there already were nuggets reposing upon the Listers' mantelpiece.

Gold was officially discovered in Australia in 1851 because that was the first year it was safe for the young colony to have the madness of gold in it. When Governor Gipps recoiled from the Reverend Mr Clarke's samples with the exclamation 'Put it away or we shall all have our throats cut,' he showed a wisdom beyond that of many more famous administrators. If California gold had to wait upon political union with the United States, Australian gold had to wait until there were enough settlers to give the colony stability. In fact, 1851 was a bit early; the discovery was permitted in that year because the authorities of Victoria and New South Wales were grievously apprehensive about the emigration to California of many of their people. Newspapers were employed to dissuade Australians from leaving their own country to follow the chimera, and succeeded fairly well until the first Sydney ship came in with 2,865 ounces of gold early in August of 1849. Nearly two thousand Sydneysiders left on the first ships to return to California. The Australian finds drew people away from more essential pursuits, but at least they stayed in the colony. After the Ballarat strikes, eighty per cent of Melbourne's police force resigned to join the rush; half the sailors in Melbourne's harbor quit, and those who stayed agreed to ship out for fifteen times the wages they had been paid for shipping in. The social upheaval is well illustrated by an anecdote told by a contemporary historian:

[A] gentleman, a large sheep-owner, and not a small man either in his own estimation, or in that of his own shepherds before the gold revolution, being in great trouble about shearing his flocks, went to a party of shearers at the gold diggings, to ask them to engage to shear his flock. He fancied in his innocence that by offering high wages they would come for a few days, and had fully made up his mind to give whatever they asked. He found the men lying indolently around their fire, and told his wishes. The men went inside and consulted with each other, and their speaker then advanced with gravity, and said they would do it. 'Well,' said our friend, 'let us have a written agreement,' and produced ink and paper. 'Now, what are the wages to put in?' 'All the wool!' and on no other terms would they come, so he was going away in disgust; but they called him back, and he, thinking the men had relented, returned eagerly. The men then said, 'Master, we want a cook, and if you will take the place we will give you 15s a day.'

Earp makes this sort of situation quite understandable by describing the fantastic encouragement ordinary workers were given to give up their regular toil – which anyway gave them little in the way of wages:

By the 10th of December, the yield had become astonishing, considering the small number of hands. The whole dividing range between New South Wales and Victoria, known as the Snowy Mountains, was one vast gold field. Neither labor nor carts could be readily got for the escort service. The *Melbourne Herald*, of the 10th of December, stated that a *ton and a half of gold* was waiting in Commissioner Powlett's tent for the escort. At Mount Alexander, a man obtained eighty pounds weight of gold in a single hour! And on the 20th of December, there had been collected, in Victoria alone, *ten tons, two hundred weights, eighty-two pounds, ten ounces, of gold!*

In Melbourne itself the people began to tear up the streets, which had been macadamized with quartz brought in from the gold region. Gold nuggets were thrown on the stage to popular actors and actresses as tokens of appreciation. As in San Francisco, gold dusted all they drank and ate.

Later, during the equally mad rush in Western Australia, gold became a similar obsession. The society column of one of Coolgardie's newspapers – which were as lively as the American goldfields journals – reported a wedding this way:

> The bride wore a rich cream quartz coloured silk with orange blossom outcrops. Miss Hickey was dressed in a reddish substance with sandstone leaders running through the main body. . . . Mrs Faahan wore a pale milk quartz combination with gold outcrops across the full breadth of the face. Mrs Burns appeared in a charming outfit, the main body being blue with trimmings all down the footwall side, with laminated leaders of dark slate.
>
> Miss Brennan set envious teeth on edge as she waltzed around in a slate-coloured robe, the principal outcrops being decorated with diorite coloured stringers . . . and many a digger wishes that for once he owned so good a claim. Miss Kennedy wore a kaolin coloured silk, while Miss Smith was arrayed from peg to peg in a slate coloured material relieved at the throat by a wide quartzite band. Miss Dwyer, in a rich limestone coloured creation, relieved at the datum points near neck and shoulders, looked as pretty as a picture.

The function of gold as a lure to settlement is nowhere shown so clearly as in Western Australia. This immense state, as large as the United States east of the Mississippi, was colonized first in 1827, on the comparatively rich south coast. In 1886, after nearly sixty years of settlement that saw desperately strenuous efforts on the part of the government to increase immigration – including the resumption of convict transportation – the population had risen to only 39,000. Then in the mid-1880s gold was discovered in several areas in the north and north-west of the state: Phil Saunders, Adam Johns, and E. T. Hardman re-enacted the Hargraves scenario in the Kimberleys; Jack Slattery and Charles Hall found gold at Hall's Creek, still the first outpost of civilization one meets after traversing a thousand miles of desert from the south; Gilles McPherson, an overlander, discovered the deep Murchison field and worked it quietly for a year rather than claim the finder's reward, which consequently went to two late comers. These are only a half dozen of the many prospectors whose names are in the archives of western gold discovery, too many to be manageable for legend, but each with his drama, comic and tragic. McPherson's life oscillated between extremes of luck. He found gold, nearly died of thirst, lost gold, found more, pointed out rich fields which others than himself profited from, penetrated the no-man's-land between the Gibson and Great Victoria deserts, and even wandered right across the western half of the continent to Alice Springs. The name of James Withnell also deserves mention: he picked up a stone to throw at a crow, saw he had a lump of gold in his hand, and naturally enough forgot the crow in the excitement of finding the shallow gold field of Pilbara – the same Pilbara that nearly a century later was to make billions of dollars for iron miners.

These northern discoveries brought hundreds of miners into a huge uninhabited region, but none of the diggings was rich enough to keep a rush going, and before long the area was again uninhabited except for those rogue males whose lives are wasted climbing the other side of barren mountains. The fields richest in gold and stories were those to the south, leading out of Perth, north-east to the western edge of the Great Victoria Desert. Once again there were ambiguous finds by early pioneers whose shuffling feet uncovered gold for more observant followers to find. The man whose claim began the roaring days of Western Australia was an experienced bushman named Arthur Bayley. He had worked his way down from the north, doing better on nearly all the goldfields than most (he was at one time associated with Gilles McPherson) before setting out with his partner William Ford to make the find he was certain existed. Sure enough he found

Fly Flat, soon to become the city of Coolgardie, the rich satellite of the Golden Mile a little distance to the east. Others had preceded Bayley and Ford in digging Fly Flat, but the only pair who staked a prior claim left their skeletons in a near-by gully. A few days after Bayley and his mate struck the field, other prospectors arrived; some they were able to mislead into continuing but some more clever had to be persuaded by pistols. It is not a pleasant story for anyone who believes in the nobility of man generally and Australians specifically. Had he been there, that mysterious author of the *Treasure of the Sierra Madre* could have told his Pardoner's Tale a generation earlier. The end of greed in the Bayley case did not settle upon the diggers, however, but upon the sedentary speculators whose money inflated the British Bubble. The Bubble burst in London in 1894 while 28,000 miners dug Fly Flat and drank beer produced in even greater quantities than gold from the community's three breweries.

In the center of Kalgoorlie today sits a remarkable statue of a gold prospector holding out an ever-flowing waterbag to thirsty pedestrians. The statue was erected in memory of Paddy Hannan, an Irish veteran who had prospected for gold in New Zealand, Queensland, New South Wales, Victoria, Tasmania, and South Australia, without any success whatsoever, until he stopped to shoe his horse 25 miles east of Coolgardie while searching for Mount Yule, a golden 'mountain the height and importance of which may be judged from the fact that no one was able to find it'. At his halt he saw enough color to make him tarry, and in a few days had six pounds of gold, which, in Carnegie's continuing account,

> transformed the silent bush into a populous town of 2,000 inhabitants, with its churches, clubs, hotels, and streets of offices and shops, surrounded by rich mines, and reminded of the cause of its existence by the ceaseless crashing of mills and stamps, grinding out gold at the rate of nearly 80,000 oz per month.

This was the Golden Mile of Boulder-Kalgoorlie, described

by its able historians Casey and Mayman as 'the richest few acres of gold-bearing country in the world.'

Hannan himself did not linger to share in the fortune that grew out of his chance discovery on 10 June 1893, but pursuing his bad luck as determinedly as before, went on to the short-lived boom at Menzies to the west.

The romance, irony, perversity of Fortune, comedy, tragedy, and inspiration indigenous to all gold rushes were as plentiful in Hannan's Find as anywhere in the legendry of gold. For the Irishman himself there were such little things as his gift of his first nugget to Clara Saunders, whose wedding (the first in Coolgardie) was described in those memorable terms of the mine; his mate Jack Carlson, discoverer of the Sons of Gwalia Mine, where Herbert Hoover worked; and on the other side of remarkability, the White Feather claim found near Hannan's own, by far the richest mine in the history of creation. What other hole just five feet long and four feet deep produced £760,000? Not all from the hole, obviously – only £60,000 there – but from those lambs leaping to slaughter who put £700,000 into the mine when it went on the London exchange as the 'Londonderry Gold Mining Company' – rechristened 'Plunderderry' when it collapsed.

After the romance, the ultimate awakening. If gold was discovered in California for the purpose of adding California to the United States and in eastern Australia for the purpose of dissuading its colonists from running off to California, gold was almost forcibly discovered in Western Australia to keep its few settlers from rushing to the mines of the eastern states. But in the end the effort largely failed. Except for some little resurgence prompted by discoveries of nickel in the area, Boulder today is a city 'dying in its sleep'. Most shops are shut down and real estate agents' windows are blocked out with advertisements offering houses for a fifth of their value elsewhere. Its twin city of Kalgoorlie is still the second city of Western Australia, but aborigines chase one another with spears through the center of town while Paddy Hannan and his waterbag look the other way. A few mines along the Golden Mile still churn out the slimes with enough profit from government subsidies to keep alive for the day when more valuable minerals than gold will bring back the days of '95 when its streets, like Melbourne's, were paved with gold. And Coolgardie, where Bayley made his strike, is a ghost town, its two pubs servicing perhaps 600 people in the large pastoral area surrounding it. There is a 'Denver City Hotel' to intrigue American visitors, but its proprietor knows nothing about its history or its name – 'I've only had this place 25 years, mate!'

Two hundred years before Bayley, Hannan, and the other modern claimants to first discovery of gold set foot in this country, Dutch mariners touched upon the Australian northwest, near Pilbara, noticed the golden promise of the earth, named the region *Terra Aurifera*, and went off to more practicable enterprises. Possibly they were very hard-headed Dutchmen who thought in the same direction as a *Punch* writer in the days of gold mania, who asked the rhetorical question,

> *What will be the ultimate effect of the discovery of the Diggins?* To raise prices, ruin fools, to demoralize a new country first, and settle it afterwards.

Prices are still high for commodities in Western Australia, its residents are wishful rather than foolish, and demoralization still precedes viable settlement. The failure of the West's gold lay not in its exhaustion but in gold itself. If this country is to succeed, it will be because of the worthier, baser metals, like iron, and the technology needed to produce them – technology that must bring in permanent settlers. In all its golden years the entire state of Western Australia yielded one billion dollars, less than half guaranteed in Pilbara's iron operations. Once more gold moidores yield to cheap tin trays and the waste of gold gives way to the wealth of iron.

Leaving gold and its specious worth, we can look upon coal and its supposed worthlessness to find a microcosm of the way culture works upon man to conquer his environment. Its hard anthracite truths are enfolded in illogical paradoxes whose very inevitability makes them harder for most people to accept. To see these inevitable truths and to extrapolate them into an understanding of how frontiers are overcome, we must begin at a time that many coal miners are assured by their Bibles never existed: the period when Europe was going through the greatest change in mankind's culture – the transition from the Palaeolithic to the Neolithic. Archaeologists digging up the remains of man's works in this distant time have uncovered in flint mines things discouragingly close to what is still happening in American and Australian mines. In Obourg, Belgium, they dug out a skeleton from the Old Stone Age, lying on its side, an antler pick near the bones of its hand. Elsewhere in northern Europe other human remains were found from that time, lying among their tools – picks of bone and antler, shovels of ox scapulae, crowbars of human femurs. Archaeologists of the far future may open the collapsed mines of America and find as many as a hundred thousand crushed men lying among their picks, shovels, and crowbars, and they will wonder how this could have happened in a time of advanced civilization and prosperity. They may fall back upon the mystical conclusion that Harry Caudill gives us in his sobering book *Night Comes to the Cumberlands*, that 'coal has always cursed the land in which it lies'. But this conclusion is too simple. For while it is true that coal mining has killed innumerable men and condemned a still greater number to inhuman squalor and suffering, yet more than any other substance it created the greatest, richest, and most humane civilization in the history of man.

The cultural stimulus of coal acted only upon modern western civilization. The earliest civilizations grew to incomplete maturity without coal, and they also disappeared, probably for the reason that workable coal deposits were absent. These cultures were built upon lesser metals like gold and silver and copper, yet what progress was made in those days came out of mining. The first anticipation of the alphabet was cut into an Egyptian copper mine by Jewish slaves nearly four thousand years ago. Much later Romans came to Britain for that island's mineral wealth – though not for coal, which was hardly known in Rome. Had they recognized the extent and value of the British coal deposits, they might have been masters of our own civilization – but that is the way of the world.

So far as extant documents testify, coal was unknown in Europe until the eleventh century AD (it was known and mined in ancient China, but like so many discoveries and inventions of that country, almost no practical use was made of it), but by the time of Elizabeth I the coal civilization was irresistibly on its way. Very few teachers of English literary history besmirch the romantic picture of Shakespeare's London by telling us there was coal dust on the fiddles in the Globe Theatre and often the spectators could not see the actors for the acrid smoke drifting down from the eternal clouds of smog hovering over its open roof. But it was this filthy substance, disgusting foreign visitors, that immediately raised England to its pride of place – not the defeat of the Armada or Elizabeth's cunning political machinations or even English sea power – and it was coal that directly or indirectly made the great advances in technology of the next three centuries that in turn caused the Industrial Revolution and today underlies the hope for our escape to cleaner, saner, and less despoiled planets.

In another of those ironic paradoxes that make the study of man and his works so frustrating for students seeking easy truths, it was the low intrinsic value of coal that whipped up invention. Since even marginal profit depended on enormous quantities of coal, mines went deeper and expenses went higher for the extractors. In the single problem (and there were many others) of pumping out sump water both human and equine energy quickly became intolerably expensive and inefficient, so 75 years before James Watt invented the steam engine, there were steam engines pumping water out of British mines. When Shakespeare was writing his first plays coal cars were already running on wooden rails from the British mines; by the eighteenth century the rails were metal; and early in the nineteenth century the cars were being pulled by locomotives (invented by mining engineers like Richard Trevithick and George Stephenson). The myriad inventions that fell out of the basic developments of mine technology cannot even be summarized here (though the automobile because of its incalculable effect on our modern civilization must be mentioned as one). Few of the artifacts made of iron and steel would have been possible without coal as the supplier of mill energy. And yet there are histories of inventions published today that do not even mention coal and its technology; many times more see the development of nations wholly in the interactions of politicians.

By the grace of coal the sun never set on the British Empire. The British sun shone on India, but it did not shine into the British mines. There, until Sir Humphrey Davy and others made the safety lamp, human beings were pecking coal from mine surfaces deep in the earth by the light glowing weakly from putrescent fish. There was no nonsense about human rights or the natural frailty of women in the mines. As man's first beast of burden, women until well into the nineteenth century brought coal out of the mines, crawling along narrow tunnels for hundreds of yards, naked in the hot, methanous, noisome atmosphere, with as much as 170 pounds of coal strapped to their backs; and on emerging from the tunnels, they sometimes had to climb up hundreds of feet of ladders to the surface.

It might be supposed that labor for such employment was hard to obtain, but with laws like the one enacted in the middle of the sixteenth century that empowered coal operators to seize, without further interference of law, any 'vagrants' and their children found in the vicinity and set them to permanent work in the mines, the collieries were able to get along. England had many conscientious foes of slavery, like Bishop 'Soapy Sam' Wilberforce, but they were opposed to slavery in Africa and America, not to the local variety.

Conditions for the unskilled workers at the bottom of the British industrial complex were brutalizing – which means it made brutes of them. From this class came the settlers of the second American frontier, Appalachia, the archetype of early underground-frontier enterprise in the United States. Most of them came over as indentured servants, which is quite the handsomest term ever coined for slaves. When they later spread out in penurious freedom through the mountain country, their savagery was honed to a fine edge. The Indians of the southern woodlands are generally regarded as the most savage aborigines ever met in historical times, but the frontiersmen tore them to pieces by day while their ferocious dogs tore them to pieces by night. They had no crafts except weapon making and no arts except singing, and they knew just enough about farming to keep themselves alive and to kill the land. Their entertainment was fighting, drinking, tobacco chewing, occasional religious orgies, and unrestrained copulation. They feared nothing except what their superstitious minds created. Considering the sanguine history of the mountain country from the extermination of the Indians, through the internecine fighting caused by the Civil War, the incredible clan feuds that ran on for nearly a century, and the continuous, indiscriminate killings over women, whisky, and elections, it is astonishing that the apparently effete coal entrepreneurs of the cities dared come in. But they did, and they defeated these mountain folk by a different kind of ferocity almost none of the natives understood. A farming mountaineer might 'slicker a furriner' by selling him mineral rights for fifty cents an acre, with the glee that we would have in selling outer space rights above our houses.

But the farmer's son would feel a 'mite juberous' about his Pap's cunning when he saw the operator extract as much as 20,000 tons of coal, plus oil, gas, and other minerals than coal, out of the fifty-cent investment. And his grandson's feelings can well be imagined when strip mining began around 1920 and his entire farm was scraped away.

There is an inevitability of cultural evolution in gold, iron, coal, and kangaroos – and inevitabilities are rarely pleasant. For coal, the hard fact of human inefficiency and the displacement of human beings by machines precipitated a nasty problem in the underground frontier. Human beings had to go, no question of that, in spite of all the John Stuart Mills of the realm of unrealistic theory. That fact was met in two ways by the miners in Appalachia – and elsewhere: most directly, by the way set down by such people as Kentucky's Aunt Molly Jackson. Aunt Molly saw only one solution: kill the operators and their lackeys. Her violence gained many supporters in the ignorant cities; she sang of the hardship of men forced to dig coal for 33 cents a ton – but what she did not mention was that coal operators then (in the early 1930s) were trying to sell coal at ten cents a ton. The cities' great sympathy for the miners forced the Department of the Interior to capitulate to John L. Lewis, the greatest statesman of American union history, and let him sketch out a plan for a miner's terrestrial heaven. This was the second approach to the hard inevitability, and few others than John L. Lewis understood what he was doing. Aunt Molly Jackson hated him because he did not encourage her violent philosophy, and she was out of the mines and driven out of the state by the time Secretary of the Interior J. A. Krug activated the heaven. In that paradise – which still exists – miners draw wages higher than in any other heavy industry ($160 a week base pay); hospitals are provided for them; universities are easily accessible for their children; they own their homes, automobiles, color television sets, and even yachts; and they all can look toward a large retirement pension. But it is a hard heaven to enter, as fantastic new machines displace human hands.

So now gigantic, grotesque, incredible machines roll on their own power over the coal fields: electric shovels 120 feet higher than the Statue of Liberty take out 300 tons of coal at a single bite and swing it a quarter of a mile away; 'coal moles' burrow tunnels into the earth, feeding coal with great steel claws into their voracious maws and excreting it behind at the rate of eight tons a minute onto conveyor belts; 'push-button miners' drive augers seven feet in diameter into coal seams traced by radar and load the extracted coal onto self-propelled conveyors that roll obediently into place from a three-storey spiral garage towed behind the auger, and 'Kolbe Wheels', which look like cantilever bridges set on tractors with a toothed Ferris Wheel at one end, buzz-saw coal out of mountains dropping it on conveyor belts that empty 450 feet behind. These machines need men to operate them – one each. And yet even these mechanized mines are doomed, as all products of the underground frontier are doomed, soon or late. The union and the operators publish prophecies of almost eternal prosperity – four trillion tons of coal to be converted into energy into the fortieth century. Similar technological miracles and similar prophecies come from the railroads, but these two moribund industries are like the two last survivors of a cannibal tribe, grinning at each other with sharpened teeth. Twenty-five years ago American locomotives burned 132 million tons of coal a year; today the locomotives are all gone, taking with them fifty per cent of coal's market. Now electric power producers are the largest remaining market for coal, but already the atom has impudently displaced coal in the center of Pennsylvania's great coal resources. Now the largest source of revenue for the railroads is coal hauling – but one of the cannibals has begun to eat the other: coal is being converted into electricity at the mine and shipped by wire.

The machines have not yet entirely replaced the human

miner. There are still about 143,000 miners remaining out of a peak force of more than 700,000. They are members of the union L. Lewis formed as their pathway to heaven – the United Mine Workers of America – but few as they are in the coal country, they are fewer still as the population grows, forming now an elite among folk thrown on the slag heap by the coal machines. And for those unemployed, the men whose ancestors were the toughest, most independent people in the Western World, life is now a shuffle down the rutted dirt streets to the local welfare agency to stand, hat in hand, whining plaints of disability where once their forefathers fought bears hand to claw.

Australia's coal history follows exactly the same path, but at different speeds, speeds that are not only accountable, but predictable. The first discovery of coal in Australia was made by those valiant escaped convicts, William and Mary Bryant, during their remarkable voyage from Sydney to Timor in 1796. Digging on the Hunter River field began in 1798, and exports (to India for rum) in 1799. By 1840 coal was an established industry, but development was almost negligible. Not until 1772 did production reach an annual total of a million long tons. One reason for the sluggishness was poor transportation. Aside from the delusion Australians cherish about living in a country too warm to warrant central heating, lack of economical transport to this day keeps coal out of houses less than a hundred miles from the Cessnock coal mines.

The interaction of coal and its miners in Australia was not significantly different from that in America. Newcastle, still a pleasant town by American coal field standards, settled into a Yankee pattern of violent solution to all its problems. Until about ten years ago, labor relations and technology in Australian coal mines were primitive to a degree. Horses were still being used to pull coal carts, mine tunnels were being shored up in a manner the fossilized flint miner of Obourg would have recognized, and mechanization was absolutely minimal.

There was one direct reason for this backwardness.

It is not a matter of opinion or even theory; it is a fact beyond influence or melioration by debate, national sensitivity, or propriety, that all the bitter troubles in Australian mines were deliberately created and aggravated by Communists. In one mine for which this book has direct, primary, and personally experienced documentation, there were forty-three strikes in one year, all of them for factitious reasons. No person without an ulterior reason for dissenting would object to this statement by an observer of Australian mining in the 1950s:

A boy's boots are hidden, a cap is missing, a path is muddy, a manager so far forgets himself as to help a man push a skip, a horse has a nasty smell, an SP bookmaker delays settlement, or the High Court declares invalid such 'progressive legislation' as the Bank Bill – these are some of the reasons for holding a pit top meeting that always results in the whole of the employees of that mine going home.

In 1953, 82 per cent of Australian strikes were called by just two unions – the Miners' Federation and the Waterside Workers. Other unions are controlled or heavily influenced by Communists. With the power to stop the production of energy and import-export, Communists could stop Australian economic life whenever they felt public opinion would not violently object – and with so long and deeply embedded a tradition of working-class sympathy, objection comes with much reluctance. For its part, the miners' union is hardly diffident about either its philosophy or intentions. The preamble to the constitution of the Miners' Federation says flatly in words taken verbatim from the manifesto of the Industrial Workers of the World when that organization was considerably to the left of the Communists:

We hold that there is a class struggle in society, and that the struggle is caused by the capitalist class owning the means of production, to which the working class must have access in

201

order to live. . . . Between these two classes the struggle must continue until capitalism is abolished. Capitalism can only be abolished by the workers uniting in one class-conscious organization to take and hold the means of production by revolutionary, political, and industrial action.

Conciliation on specious demands in Australian labor-relations has had the same result it always has everywhere, whether the issue is ceasing the bombing of North Vietnam or discrediting the ROTC on the campuses of American universities. Conciliation was tried at the Bellbird Mine in the mid-fifties; the workers were given more than they expected to get even after the Revolution. The result was that production dropped from 1,250 long tons a day to 800, with 51 strikes in 1955.

There can be only two alternatives in this situation: either the Revolution succeeds, or the men are driven out of the mines. The Communists are hopeful for the former alternative immediately, but they are not much discomforted by the probability of the latter, since all roads lead finally to Peking. Whether or not the displacement of man by the machine is best in the long run is not pertinent, since in the long run we will all be dead. On a short-term basis – which is as far ahead as reason can take us – the mine operators, public or private, must implement the cultural imperative and remove the inefficient human being from the mines and into something for which Nature has better fitted him. It is intolerable for an underdeveloped country like Australia to put up with a coal production of two long tons a day. In its isolated, insulated economy, Soviet Russia can continue with a production rate of 2.4 tons a day per man, while the United States production is 15.19. Even Russia must one day make an accommodation with reality. These figures are for 1964; the latest statistics (made available in October, 1969) give the 1967 United States coal production as 19.7 tons a day per man. Comparable figures for the Australian coal industry are not available, but without question they are second in the world, and rising swiftly. The intolerable situation continues: in June of 1972 the two unions – miners and longshoremen – achieved the demand of a 35-hour work week.

What happened to this stagnant industry was predictable a decade ago: mines completely in the control of the Miners' Federation were left to die while new mines, highly automated, were opened. And the other mines did die; employment in the Cessnock-Maitland area, traditionally the heart of Australian coalmining, has dropped nearly 80 per cent since 1954.

The Australian experience demonstrates another process of cultural evolution – the leap-frog progress of technology. All established societies accumulate barnacles of tradition, however advanced the societies may be. England was strangled by its reverence for things past. The United States should at least be concerned about an economic situation that prohibits the synthetic textile industry from producing 100 per cent Dacron fabrics and chooses instead to subsidize cotton and wool with 40 per cent of the clothing market that on functional considerations should be entirely synthetic. More and more the astute American businessman is putting his investment into areas where tradition has never existed or where it has been destroyed – Germany, Japan, and Australia. A few years ago the United States had electric coal shovels 270 feet tall moving under their own power against coal faces while Australian miners were limited to shovels they could hold in two hands. Now the largest electric shovel in the world is working Australian mines. On the same day the United States Bureau of the Census released its figures on American production of coal, the Australian government announced that an American mining firm presently operating eight collieries in New South Wales was beginning an enormous expansion to open new mines, build two ports, and construct railways. Earlier in 1969 it was revealed that a contract had been signed between Japan, as purchaser, and the Utah Construction and Mining Company of San Francisco, as seller, for one billion dollars worth of coking coal – from the Bowen Basin mines in central Queensland. The American company is building a new town and railway, together with a new seaport deep enough to handle 100,000-ton carriers, for the project. American firms have built up Australian black coal production from 19 million long tons in the mid-fifties to more than 40 million tons now, and lignite from 10 million tons to 20 million tons.

This is the pattern for all the other areas of Australia's underground frontier – and for the rest of Australian development as well. The government newsletter that made the announcement of the Bowen Basin coal sale to Japan (9 October 1969) revealed also negotiations for Japan's purchase of 1.344 billion dollars worth of Kimberley iron ore, and the important news of first production from Australia's largest oil field (1.3 billion barrels). A large share of the iron mines is owned by American companies, and the oil field is held by the ubiquitous Broken Hill Proprietary company and Esso-Standard of Australia. It is difficult to unravel the various companies by which American ownership of underground frontier operations is disguised; it is enough to say that without the American money these enterprises would not be in existence. In the more highly developed business of manufacturing, a survey made by the Australian Department of Trade and Industry in 1966 found 255 firms with equity share interest owned in the United States and 143 of these companies were wholly owned by American citizens. 'Australia's Own Car', the Holden, is made by General Motors-Holden, Pty. Ltd., one hundred per cent owned by American capital. Ford also has an appreciable share of the market in Australian-made automobiles; $A180,000,000 now and more than $A105,000,000 promised in new enterprise.

There are some Australians who do not like this much. The most prestigious critic of American capitalistic imperialism and neo-colonialism is the agrarian reformer Arthur Calwell, who led his Labor Party to ruination on the question of intervention in Vietnam. Mr Calwell has often put the point nicely; one of his frequent attacks on the American predators condemned countrymen's reliance on overseas capital as being not much different from 'mortgaging the house to pay the grocery bill'. He also reminds Australians from time to time that capitalism is just as much an enemy as communism, a judgment that led Australian historian Donald Horne to remark that statements of this kind would persuade younger people to regard Mr Calwell as insane. Horne, however, seems to favor an alternative explanation, that Mr Calwell is 'some relic of Early Man'. Younger critics on the Australian Left connect American capital intrusion with other disturbing things, like immigration; Neil McInnes, an intellectual of note, complained 'It is as though a part of Europe's population were being brought here so that US businessmen could supply them, more conveniently than in Europe, with cars, soap, and coco-pops.' It seems that Mr McInnes confused the last commodity with Coca Cola. The one serious and scholarly examination of the matter, Donald Brash's *American Investment in Australian Industry*, begins with an admission of what might be called guided objectivity:

> I have never held 'extremist' views on foreign investment, but it is fair to admit that, knowing something of the hostility generated by foreign capital both in this century and the last, I began this survey very conscious of the disadvantages of foreign investment. The survey was therefore framed substantially with Australian public sentiment.

Unless the ordinary Australian is more devious than Americans take him to be, Dr Brash's judgment on the public's attitude has been molded by his university's milieu, noticeably more inclined to the red side of the spectrum than that of the real world outside. What hostility exists against American capital investment has been generated by Mr Calwell and his supporters. Where money is going into the development of the underground frontier, the Australian public sentiment is one of amusement at American eagerness to buy anything.

One of the favorite stories around Alice Springs is the tale of the Aussie who threw a log chain around Ayers Rock, hitched it to a bullock team ten miles long, and dragged it off toward the Alice. 'Wotcher gonna do with that, mate?' asked a swagman. 'I reckon I'll flog it to the Yanks,' replied the bullocky. Flogging things to the Yanks is always good business; an opal found at Lightning Ridge by fossicker Jack Dunstan was sold in the field for $200; John D. Rockefeller bought it later for $1,500,000.

Still the criticism from Labor speakers is constant enough to annoy those who understand the necessities of underground frontier economics. Prime Minister Menzies' retort to a woman heckler when she interrupted one of his speeches containing references to overseas development of Australian resources, could hardly be deemed politic, but one can sympathize with his feeling. 'You're selling us out to the Yanks!' she shouted. Mr Menzies retorted, 'Well, if I may put it in pounds, Australian pounds, Madam, not in rubles. . . .'

There are many good people in Australia not conversant with economics but innocent of ulterior motives who fear leaving the back of the sheep to ride on the back of the tiger. No one can give absolute assurances of safety to those who seek help from America, but it is certain that the second law of thermodynamics applies in economics as well as in physics: heat does not flow from cold to heat, capital does not move from poor countries to rich ones. With the American acceleration of technology being matched by its acceleration in economic acumen – 60 per cent of major economic developments of the last generation were made by Americans – it is not likely that the Third World or the Second, for that matter, is ever going to catch up by itself. American overseas investment is incalculable, for more and more American enterprise abroad is being financed by foreign money, as the French economist Servan-Schreiber argued in his recent bestseller. Though scarcity of Australian capital for risk investment has brought about high interest rates, American firms are only too eager to borrow what is available. Persons interested in acquiring that monolith or other Australian real estate may now negotiate with the agents certified to make land sales: the Andoe-Whalen Investment Corporation, 111 Sutter Street, San Francisco.

H. G. Raggatt, for fourteen years the Secretary of the Australian Department of National Development, discussed the issue of overseas investment in Australia in a book published shortly before his death two years ago. As non-political as an official of the government can be, Raggatt defended American participation in Australian underground frontier development:

> Nobody appears to object to foreign companies spending millions of dollars on prospecting for oil, provided they are unsuccessful, but when they do find oil, their activities somehow are thought to be all wrong. It is churlish not to welcome a foreign company which is prepared to take risks we are not prepared to take ourselves.

On this point Raggatt certified that in his long tenure of office, of the many overseas firms that applied for licences to prospect the Australian outback, only two were at all reluctant to share the enterprise with Australian investors. Raggatt remembers his embarrassment when he had to answer 'none' when some of these companies asked what Australian investors were available. Most of the companies successful in their ventures offered stocks on the Australian exchange, but Australians have not shown any eagerness to share in the wealth. Francis Bacon was ignored when he advised against planting a colony with wicked condemned men, but Australians have tried to make up for it by obeying his stricture 'moil not too much underground; for the hope of mines is very uncertain'. This wariness is characteristic of Australian banks as well as of individuals; three banks in 1969 announced with obvious self-satisfaction that they lent Alcoa of Australia $A13,440,000 for improvements on its aluminum smelting plant at Port Henry. With Government backing assured, they felt the loan was a reasonably safe speculation in view of the $A180 million in overseas capital already tied into the project. The Australian automobile owner may be patriotic enough to volunteer gladly to fight for his country, but ask him to buy a brand of gasoline because it claims on billboards to be Australian is going a bit far; as more sophisticated advertisers understand, this appeal gets only the pity-sales. Those who buy on the basis of quality infer that any gasoline made in bloody Australia is not likely to be much bloody good. The ironic part of this is that in South Australia – and probably everywhere else – all brands of gasoline come from the same tanks at the same refinery.

Mr Calwell is not given to enumerating the many benefits to Australia of American investment: the development of the rich but economically inaccessible mineral and oil resources; the provision of technological and merchandising know-how; the stimulation to education; the construction of cities, railroads, roads, ports, and other public facilities; the organization of markets, which do not automatically appear when someone brings in an oil well; the almost emotional paternalism of American firms toward their Australian subsidiaries; the creation of tens of thousands of jobs; and of course the flood of money into the Australian economy. During the period 1966-1967, the infant oil industry disbursed more than one billion dollars; mineral production sold more than one billion dollars' worth of ore, 75 per cent of it to foreign buyers; and further investment, planned by the 164 firms comprising the Australian Mining Industry Council, exceeded two and a quarter billion dollars during 1969. With money pouring on this scale into the Australian economy, it is absurd to talk about capitalist oppression, except in so far as it makes the working class work: (the Australian unemployment rate is heading below one per cent).

Some of the Australian Labor Party's pity for the victims of capitalist affluence should be directed towards the poor capitalist himself. He too is caught in the grindstones of economic evolution. The Americans who have come to Australia loaded down with moneybags are a genial and harmless lot, once you get to know them. They do not mean to grind the faces of the poor or to forge chains for their legs. They cannot help themselves. As Justice Oliver Wendell Holmes wryly observed many years ago, the American system of free enterprise is a wickedly contradictory thing: it encourages industries to compete, but it does not let any of them win. It is a hell of a way to run a card game. From the first restrictive anti-trust laws to the current federal litigation against the 'conglomerates', the successful businessman is prevented from letting natural selection operate to its fullest, even though the end might be the practical communism of Edward Bellamy. Most of the American investors in Australia have opened the sluice gates of their capital to every possible working area of the world – including the Communist Bloc. The amount that gets into Australia is negligible; approximately 80 per cent of the Australian subsidiaries of American firms are less than three per cent of the parent company's size.

History, too, pleads for leniency toward American overseas investors. The United States was not born rich. Except for its stable government and early English investors, it would be as poor as Brazil, whose natural resources are great enough to make it another United States. We remember that the Pilgrim Fathers were themselves a business venture of a consortium of English investors. From their time until the tide of exchange began to run the other way, America depended on British capital. The astonishing success of the Erie Canal as a financial investment brought a flood of English money into similar projects, since that first waterway into the American West sold its bonds almost exclusively to British financiers. Much of the north-eastern United States today has forgotten canals, running to what once was the frontier. In Pennsylvania, Michigan, Indiana, Kentucky, Ohio, and Illinois canals were dug with British money. So long as the enterprise was in transportation, overseas investors put no reasonable limit on American credit. Even in the latter part of the nineteenth century, when foreign capital had to compete with domestic capital in American business, large sums of sterling flowed into the United States. One American economic historian estimates the European share of American railroad building in the 1880s as 40 per cent. Land banks, too, in the early frontier days relied upon English capital.

Not much English money went into American industries, however; England had no particular wish to encourage that kind of competition from its wayward offspring. England even went so far in selective assistance as to forbid the emigration of skilled mechanics. British investors were torn between fear and greed, and satisfied the latter by disguising the former; they did not invest directly in industrial enterprises that might make the young nation a shopkeeper instead of a shopper, but in transport enterprises which indirectly facilitated industrial enterprises. In a way, the choice was not as naïve as it was cunning; the circumlocution of finding was in effect a hedge against both loss and dishonor.

The adjective 'overseas' in Australian contexts of economic disapprobation means 'American'. One appreciates the euphemistic indirection, but the usage obscures the fact that only in the last year or so has American investment in Australia been greater than British. With its traditional instinct for the capillary, English finance became cagey when very large returns on risk capital appeared likely. Sir William Walkley, managing director of the 'Australian' gasoline company alluded to a half dozen paragraphs earlier, recalled his difficulties in obtaining a financial partner to explore an area of promise in north-western Australia in the late 1940s. Other Australian businessmen wanted no part of the speculation; that was expected. But London, too, showed no interest; as Walkley said, 'To British investors the project was about as promising as hunting for seals at Alice Springs.' Approaching the Americans, Walkley quickly found an interested man in Frank Morgan, vice president and director of exploration for Richfield, who lent Sir William geologists for further reconnaissance. Their report on the Exmouth area was favorable, and Richfield bought an operational base. After agonizing reappraisal the Richfield people withdrew. Here one must not be misled by superficial similarities between the American and British timidity; the Americans did not have much taste for the Labor government then in power. To appreciate their apprehension that the Labor Party would nationalize petroleum if any were found, one must know something about the Party's theoretician, Herbert Vere Evatt, foaled out of Maitland coal by Communism. Highly respected in his lifetime for brilliant mischief, Evatt has since been delivered into the hands of the righteous: he is remembered now chiefly for writing nice letters to Molotov. Richfield, to its credit, gave its operational base to Sir William's firm, and ultimately an American partner of some complexity in organization financed what became the first commercial oilfield discovered in Australia.

Investment in a rapidly developing economic frontier is like pouring water into a bucket: inevitably the bucket fills up. Frederick Jackson Turner would have made more sense if he had taken his eyes off that ghostly procession through the Cumberland Gap and looked instead on the flow of capital. The economic frontier closed about ten years after Turner's cartographic frontier, when the interest rate of domestic capital dropped below the point where foreign capital could compete with it. The process is universal and inevitable – and very long. Political statements to the contrary are to be placed somewhere between mischief and malice. Mr William McMahon, then Commonwealth treasurer, announced to the world (and Australian worriers and whingers) in 1969 that by 1973 Australia would not need any more 'overseas' investment capital. Scientifically conducted medical tests have established beyond any doubt that Mr McMahon is full of prunes.

Australia's capital reserves have expanded beyond the most optimistic forecasts made as recently as five years ago, but the country's underground frontier resources have grown so fast that all the available 'overseas' capital will find work and profit. The treasure of not gold but utility under Australia's surface makes even that abused term 'fabulous' inadequate to convey the wealth of it. Its extent and value are literally beyond belief. In 1802, when Napoleon was serving his most important guests on dinner plates of aluminum and lesser diners on gold, the mariner Matthew Flinders described in his journal mile after mile of 'reddish cliffs' on the west coast of Cape York peninsula. Later readers of his account would have identified this substance as bauxite, the ore of aluminum, but for their conviction that bauxite could not possibly exist in such quantity. In World War II the Gove air base was built on pure bauxite because no one believed it was bauxite. Eventually in 1955, Harry Evans, chief geologist of a BHP subsidiary, led a party of three geologists along the western Cape York coast inspecting possible oil country. He found the reddish cliffs and identified them as bauxite outcrops, but he still could not accept the fact:

As the journey down the coast revealed miles of bauxite cliffs, I kept thinking that, if all this is bauxite, then there must be something the matter with it; otherwise it would have been discovered and appreciated long ago.

It was indeed bauxite and there was nothing the matter with it. Matthew Flinders's maps were re-examined to locate deposits Evans had not seen. Now estimates set the probable amount of aluminum ore in this region at three billion tons, 30 per cent of the entire world's supply, and all of it easily accessible. The American firm of Kaiser owns 52 per cent of the development.

Directly across the continent to the west is the Hamersley Range and Pilbara, where the American vice-president of Kaiser, Tom Price, was brought to assess the iron ore deposits. He exulted,

There are untold millions of iron ore in the Pilbara deposits. I think this is one of the most massive ore-bodies in the world. There are mountains of iron ore there . . . it is just staggering. It is like trying to calculate how much air there is.

Later, after one of those mountains was named Tom Price (for the American official) an estimate was calculated: fifteen billion tons of 60 per cent iron ore – not including other large fields in the same region, such as the Ophthalmia Range, which had a different value for the explorer who named it after the eye disease he contracted there. At the Mount Newman complex in the Ophthalmia Range is presently being built, at an expenditure of $200,000,000, a town, a seaport, and a 260-mile railway to connect them. The enterprise is moving so fast that before the opening of the complex, two million tons of ore had been extracted and Japanese buyers had contracted for one and a half billion Australian dollars' worth of the ore. By the end of September, 1969, the iron mines of Western Australia had sold $A4,480,000,000 worth of iron. Kaiser Steel of Oakland holds 36 per cent of the Hamersley operations, the Australian public ten per cent. In this north-western treasure land lies Mount Whaleback, a single lump of seventy per cent pure iron ore of one billion tons. Nuzzled against it like a boatful of harpooners is a town of two thousand miners, all of whom came in after 1968.

Halfway between Cape York, where mariner-explorer Matthew Flinders saw the red cliffs, and the iron mountains of Western Australia, at whose seaport camels used to be debarked, is the Victoria River. Here the *Beagle*, carrying Charles Darwin on his epic voyage, stopped to caulk the ship's seams with oil in the form of asphalt – this in 1839, nearly 20 years before the great oil discovery at Titusville, Pennsylvania. In the last three or four years enough commercial oil fields have been found to justify the description of Australia as a mountain of iron floating in a sea of oil: for iron read also tin, uranium, copper, tungsten, lead, zinc, silver, nickel, phosphate, and, lest we forget, a little gold.

Natural gas and rarer substances: on the isolated tribal land of the still proud and fierce Wanindiljaugwa aborigines, Groote Eylandt, and on the western side of the Gulf of Carpentaria, there is manganese. Soviet enterprise produces a little of this newly important substance from this area, but the Russians have to drill through thousands of feet of rock to reach a seam about three feet thick. On Groote Eylandt they pushed 18 inches of topsoil away and revealed an island of manganese so pure the ore is loaded directly into ore ships.

A few hundred miles south-east of Groote Eylandt, in north central Queensland, is an oasis city – Mount Isa, where the American Smelting and Refining Company labored for many years without profit. Mount Isa is now the single largest producer of lead, silver, and zinc in the world, surrounded by more than one billion tons of phosphate.

Thus the underground frontier of Australia, the penultimate wilderness, rushes to a close; and exposes the last land frontier to assault. As Geoffrey Blainey understood, 'Possibly no other country in the world had been so quickly transformed by metals; the normal growth and achievement of several decades were crammed into one.'

EIGHT

Filling the Vacant Lands

High noon, the twenty-second day of April, 1889, on the poor side of the Cherokee Strip, three days beyond the last outpost of civilization. Ten thousand people, infant and aged, hale and infirm, along the border from dusty horizon to dusty horizon like all the sprinters in the world together for one great race, waiting for the bugler to sound the signal to explode them away from not much into nothing. In front, insinuative horses in a cavalry line, hooves chopping out their owners' tension upon the sparse vegetation; behind these, the vehicles of settlers with children and other impedimenta, buckboards, prairie schooners, democrat wagons, anything with wheels a horse could pull; the iron horses lined up on the steel arrow pointing into the wilderness, hissing and chuffing in hot impatience, waiting to pull the trains loaded above the roofs with more genteel homesteaders; and among all others, the men on foot, loads on their backs like astronauts (a *Harper's* reporter was to write of seeing a man running alongside the railroad track for six miles carrying a tent, blankets, digging tools, kitchen utensils, and a supply of food, until he literally fell on a land claim established by exhaustion). Captain Hays, the officer appointed to see that none of these competitors joined the Sooners already over the line, drops his arm, and the motley crowd bursts off in its mad dash into poverty.

Where did they think they were going when they rushed into country in which the Indians could not be persuaded to live? What did they think they would find? Contemporary photographs of the Oklahoma 'Unassigned Lands' show a flat plain empty as the moon, without a tree to mar the horizon or grass high enough to hide a man's ankle. They had failed already, many of them, in better country to the east; what did they hope to accomplish in a place whose principal natural product was buffalo dung?

Though they themselves would probably not have described it so, they were going to a poor man's picnic – the leftovers from that Great Barbecue the historian Vernon Parrington was to describe in the next century. The first guests a generation earlier had made fortunes not known since Midas, and if their leavings were not turkey breast, at least they were good giblets, 160 acres a claim, each man take his pick. Surely the time prophesied on the Mount twenty centuries before had at last arrived: the meek were possessing the earth. The land they could see from the starting line was hardly that of milk and honey, but perhaps this would come from the labor of the industrious. Had not some of the first frontier lands returned 10,000 per cent to investors? Were not four towns to be made on this first day – Norman, Kingfisher, Guthrie, and Oklahoma City?

They had been cruelly encouraged – from the Mount, from Washington, and by Horace Greeley, who advised from New York, 'Go west, young man, and grow up with the country.' Local poets caught the enthusiasm and gave them songs to sing:

> Come, all ye sons of labor
> Who wish to change your lot,
> Who've spunk enough to travel
> Beyond your native cot;
> Come, leave the crowded cities
> Where work is overdone
> And come with us to settle
> In western Kansas towns.

The soil is rich and loamy,
From three to ten feet deep;
The subsoil is cement and clay
That will the moisture keep
'Tis the bed of an inland sea
Drained off a long time ago,
And rich for grains and fruit and vines
Where ever you may go.

What more, ye sons of labor –
Than these can you desire :
Good health, good soil, good neighbors,
A climate all admire?
Two railroads now have we,
Free land is now all gone,
So come with us and settle
In peerless Lane County.

Some of the homesteaders on the Indian Territory starting line had fled from the proclaimed paradise of Lane County, Kansas, singing songs of their own making, not so poetic, but closer to reality :

No, don't get discouraged, you poor hungry men
For we are all here as free as a pig in a pen.
Just stick to your homestead and battle the fleas
And look to your Maker to send you a breeze.

Now, all you claim holders, I hope you will stay
And chew your hardtack till you are toothless and gray;
But as for myself I'll no longer remain
And starve like a dog on my Government claim.

So farewell to Lane County, the land of the free,
The land of the gopher, grasshopper, and flea;
I'll sing loud its praises and tell of its fame
While starving to death on my Government claim.

Before long the weaker of them were back, to hear the taunts of those who had remained impoverished on the Kansas claim, having chosen to bear those evils they had rather than fly to others they knew not of :

They are coming back to Kansas,
They are crossing on the bridge;
You can see their moving wagons
On the top of every ridge.

On the highways and the turnpikes
You can see their wagons come,
For they're coming back to Kansas
And they're coming on the run.

Who's a-coming back to Kansas?
Why, the migratory crowd
That left the state some months ago
With curses long and loud.

The boomers who stayed in Oklahoma to prove that life was possible where it was not comfortable, fought the land and won, literally by destroying it. Almost forty-one years to the day after the rush from the Cherokee Strip, the state of Oklahoma began to blow away in the first dust storm, and with it the other abused dry farming regions of Missouri, Texas, Arkansas, and eastern Colorado. As John Steinbeck described it in *The Grapes of Wrath*, dawn came, but no day; the corn abandoned its grasp on the loose earth and drifted away with windows and doors, but still the dust, too fine to be seen, sifted down like pollen on the chairs and the dishes just as it settled like snow outside on fence posts and roofs and wire and weeds.

A thousand miles to the east the people of more fortunate country saw unprecedented sunsets encarnadined by the western soil, as people in New Zealand were later to see their western sky reddened by wind-blown Australian earth. In Oklahoma the farms were abandoned as evolution reversed itself upon the people; hopeful farmers became hopeless nomads, pouring out of the ruined country to another, richer West, too late to find shares in it, except as menial hands to harvest for others:

California, Arizona, I make all your crops,
Then it's north up to Oregon to gather your hops;
Dig beets from your ground, cut the grapes from your vine
To set on your table your light sparkling wine.

I work in your orchards of peaches and prunes,
I sleep on the ground 'neath the light of your moon.
On the edge of your city you'll see us and then
We come with the dust and we go with the wind.

Australia has not yet had its John Steinbeck and Woody Guthrie to build memorials in story and song to the people who came too soon and too poorly equipped to fill the vacant lands, but every pioneer track in the Australian bush and desert has its skeletons of abandoned homesteads. Hundreds of miles of them run in lines, along the gold track in Western Australia and along the eastern shore of Lake Eyre. In wet but hospitable Arnhem Land, the same shacks can be seen dotted here and there on the huge pastoral stations which exist only because they cannibalized smaller land holdings as the 'cats' – Caterpillar tractors – ate the farms about whose American counterparts Steinbeck wrote and Guthrie sang.

Steinbeck, no less than others, saw the trouble that engulfed these last pioneers as only the evil machination of predatory exploiters – the bankers in America, the squatters in Australia. There were speculators, true enough, those who took up land for the purpose of selling it at a profit to the gullible. But this view is just another example of man's need to personalize situations inevitable in cultural evolution. Retributive anger, personal or vicarious, does not expend well against an invisible force; rage must have a villain.

After the rage, however, came the realization, as Huxley put it, that size is not grandeur, and territory does not make a nation. The last empty lands are vacant because there is nothing in them useful to man without a massive outlay in technology. These final frontiers can only be enriched by putting wealth in them, not by taking wealth out. And to put wealth in, one must have wealth to begin with. That cynical but perspicacious 'emigrant mechanic' Alexander Harris pointed out over a century ago that to become wealthy on Australian land one must first become rich. The ever-reliable Tom Collins, musing about the ironies of life while his bullocks illegally ate the squatters' grass, wrote for future America as for past Australia:

> The successful pioneer is the man who never spared others; the forgotten pioneer is the man who never spared himself, but, being a fool, built houses for wise men to live in, and omitted to gather moss. The former is the early bird; the latter is the early worm.

True enough, if hard. The worm is needed to make the soil, and the bird is needed to eat him, if evolution is to lead to superior creatures like man. The small pioneer is necessary to break the land as the land baron is necessary to take it away from him if evolution is to lead to nations. The speculator and beyond him the nation cannot live without the sacrificial pioneer. There can be no quicker way to put land into the hands of the large owner at a profit than by making good the promise that the meek shall inherit the earth. The little man's function in modern nations is to have a mouth to feed and to feed him at a price the land must first be cleared of the occupying hunting-gathering peoples; then the underground frontier must be worked to make capital and encourage the greedy. If this phase fails to draw in people, sheep or cattle farming will temporarily do the job until some other means fills the plains with customers. Robin Hood spent his life preying aimlessly on the odd friar because he thought it was profitable to rob the few rich instead of the many poor. In western New South Wales it takes 640 acres to keep one head of cattle alive; that same space in Woolloomooloo, crowded with poor, can make millionaires of many wise men. Knott's Berry Farm in California's Orange County opened that region with fruit trees to the horizon; now the trees are gone and houses of consumers fill the land. In a system of fluid profit, all movement makes profit for the wise man who is too efficient to depend on favorable outcomes only.

So it was with the various laws enacted by the United States government for the ostensible purpose of giving public lands to poor people: the Ordinance of 1785, the Land Law of 1796, the Land Law of 1800, the Land Law of 1804, the Land Law of 1820, the Preemption Act of 1842, the Graduation Act of 1854, the Homestead Act of 1862, the Timber Culture Act of 1873, the Desert Land Act of 1877, and the Timber and Stone Act of 1878. It is surely not necessary to pass so many acts merely to put small farmers on federal lands. It is useless to argue, as some historians have done, that each piece of land legislation was enacted to correct the abuses and loopholes of its predecessor, for as with every business activity, the intention behind every act was to exploit. Every advance made by small-time farmers in the long run meant advantage for the big landowners and businessmen who followed as every move of the amateur chess player opens boundless winning opportunities for his professional opponent. Settlers bursting into the manumitted public lands to buy farms at a dollar an acre did not calculate the incidental expenses – fencing at two to eight times the cost of the land; farm labor at the price demanded; lumber in a woodless plain for house and barn and outbuildings; professional plowmen, the only possessors of equipment capable of breaking the prairie soil, at two or three further dollars an acre; and legal fees – altogether, an average cost of a thousand dollars to start a farm too far from a railroad to make growing crops anything but a physical exercise. It was better to buy a farm near a railroad, but these were on those thirty-mile strips of land given railroads to run their tracks through, and they sold for somewhat more than a dollar an acre. Without the accessibility, the farmer was a bullocky with a team that had to eat its way across someone else's property. Railroad land, therefore, sold more farms at five dollars an acre than the government distributed under the Homestead Act. The best ground went much higher; land value along the Illinois Central Railroad rose 1,500 per cent when the trains began to roll. For their part, the railroads made no profit until they sold the land that gave right of way to the track. With the eastern states producing an insufficient stock of immediate customers, the railroad men went to Europe to gather up the Barefoot Men by distributing brochures, posters, and flyers all appealing to the peasants dreaming of becoming lords. The peasants responded in even larger numbers than the Dust Bowl refugees were to respond to similar advertisements for fruit pickers in California in the 1930s. Eventually all classes were to do well by the transactions; the railroads prospered immediately, making money even when they were losing money (the Northern Pacific went bankrupt in the 1873 panic, but its officials sold their holdings for a hundred per cent profit). The small farmer's success did not become apparent until the time of his grandchildren, while the large farmers by combining their holdings made a profit for the time being. In the Upper Mississippi Valley, 32,646 farms were owned by 3,800 men; one of these landlords owned 322 farms in Illinois and 845 in Missouri, Kansas, and Nebraska. Only 10 per cent of the land opened by the Homestead Act went to small settlers, leaving the other ninety per cent for the wise men who held mortgages or who had rented their land to tenant farmers. In a typical Nebraska township twenty years after its first settlement, half of the original farm owners had left, and 77 per cent of the remainder were under mortgage. One of the protest folksongs summed it up, 'Worm or beetle, drouth or tempest on a farmer's land may fall; but for first-class ruination, trust a mortgage 'gainst them all.'

The failure of idealism and the triumph of harsh reality had much the same effect in Australia. Lord Sydney's notion that the new colony was a jail better than any of His Majesty's prisons because it could support itself was quickly proved to be the foolishness of an armchair colonist. Within two years of the first landing at Port Jackson, Governor Phillip was forced into experimenting with an idea, inconceivable in 1788. He gave a convict named James Ruse 30 acres of land to farm. Ruse was a good worker and his farm succeeded; those who followed him did not have his estimation of the value of hard work, so he was in fact a poor guide to what occurred elsewhere. In any event, his 'Experiment Farm' in the near-by arable fields of Parramatta did so well that a land policy was established, first for the military and later for other settlers: a hundred acres to non-commissioned officers, fifty to privates (who presumably did not need so much to eat). A thousand acres were cleared and planted in 1791 and what farming could be done in the region of Port Jackson was undertaken. Ruse himself gets as much attention in Australian history as could be expected for a convict in a country whose history has been written by owners of convicts and their descendants. But his accomplishment is there, on his tombstone, for all who pass by to see.

> My Mother Reread Me Tenderley
> With Me She Took Much Paines
> And When I Arrived in This Coelney
> I Sowd the Forst Grain

Until 1831 free land grants were the usual method of land acquisition in the eastern Australian colonies; thereafter private and public sales displaced the gratuities. As in the United States after the West was opened by gold and other lures, the Australian government, for all its traditional disregard for the will of the proletariat, had to capitulate to established fact. The explosion of population into the eastern interior after good soil was found on the other side of the Blue Mountains put settlers on land from which they could not be removed by anything short of starvation. Starvation for the majority, however, was not long in coming, since the Riverina Basin was fertile only in comparison to the useless land bordering it. The notion of a farm's size, imported along with other perishable ideas from England, had to be abandoned.

The 'squatters' – the big landowners who acquired their estates by taking them – knew no more about economic theory than Merino sheep breeders knew about the Mendelian laws, but they knew what would work in the settlement of hard country, the spirit of the law and sometimes its letter notwithstanding. The small selector, the Australian counterpart of the American homesteaders, came to terms with reality when he tried to cash his promissory note. He found at once that the good land had been taken – by the simple device of selection of certain lands by the hired dummies of forehanded squatters, who used devices like 'peacocking' (selecting watered places, making adjoining property worthless to other buyers) to achieve their ends. If the acreage for which a selector applied was worth anything, he invariably found himself with a neighbor who did not want neighbors and who had a swagful of tricks to discourage anyone who came too close. The selector found too that his claim was often a 'clearing lease' which gave him a tenure just long enough to cut back the mallee and clear off the brush. 'This', said Earp in 1852, 'is so risky and unpromising that the person making such an undertaking should immediately chalk off all his expenses to experience.' The selector also found himself bogged down in a morass of legal requirements, expensive in time and money. In short, the land he took up so cheaply at a pound an acre worked out to a thousand pounds or more before he could begin to set his farming experience and business acumen – usually both entirely lacking – against an inimical Nature and hostile competitors.

The archetypical description of life on a small selection is Steele Rudd's series of anecdotes later burlesqued as 'Dad and Dave'. Originally they had more tragedy than comedy, for they were thinly fictionalized vignettes of Rudd's own boyhood on a hardscrabble farm in outback New South Wales, where the only humor was Nature's own – cruel irony, the fun of misfortune, wherein even good luck can be bad. One of the few concessions life makes to the human condition is to let the past seem better than it was; so in Rudd's tales there is a wry grin in Dad's scraping a piece of burnt toast to produce 'tea leaves' or in Mother's shaking out an empty bag for enough flour to make biscuits. Less funny, however, is the paradox of 'A Splendid Year for Corn'. After a series of bad years, Dad's field prospers, and he goes off to sell his crop, pay his debts, and give his family a small measure of what comforts an old bark hut could allow. But he finds the buyers few and reluctant; it seems that others have had splendid harvests as well:

At last he was offered ninepence halfpenny per bushel, delivered at the railway station. Ninepence halfpenny per bushel, delivered at the railway station! Oh, my country! And fivepence per bushel out of that to a carrier to take it there! Australia, my mother!

Whenever prosperity means disaster, the small man is revealed as an abomination to himself and to the country he occupies so inefficiently. It goes against human nature to favor a squatter in the struggle for Australian land, but the development of a new country cannot be left to poor people. The squatters contended against national sympathy for the underdog – an attitude with which Australia has always been blighted – and discrimination against them in law. With the advantage of hindsight, we must agree that

What the squatters defeated was really an attempt to break up their great pastoral estates for the sake of planting a few small farmers on the occasional pieces that could grow crops, which would have been more wasteful than the extravagant slaughter of the buffalo on our plains for the sake of their tongues.

Compassion has finally to give way to reality and the lovable Dad Rudds are inevitably defeated by predators like the multimillionaire 'Hungry' Tyson, who left his money to no one and his name to everyone as a synonym for greed. In the wheatlands of New South Wales in the time of Tyson and the Rudds, Dad was an anachronism; he was a small farmer in a great region of hundreds of thousands of acres of cultivated land, half of which was held by 677 people. Farther inland, owners grew less and holdings grew larger. The Duracks, a South Australian family eminent now in art and literature as well as in land acquisition, owned in Western Australia a station the size and shape of Belgium. Alexandria Station spread over 11,262 square miles. The largest station of all was Victoria River Downs, a private cattle property; at 35,000 square miles it was about the size of Austria. The immense runs of Tyson's time are being reduced now so that land can be used more efficiently, but stations are still reckoned in square miles instead of acres.

Although there was no place for small farmers in this kind of economy, here and there remain refuge areas inhabited by the 'cockies' – 'cockatoo farmers' – so named because they could be depended on to raise cockatoos and nothing more. Since cockatoos in these places were so numerous that when they sat on fence wires they pushed the posts down to ground level, they compared well with the po' white trash farmers of America's southland:

> Pa didn't raise no corn this year,
> Pa didn't raise no t'maters;
> Had bad luck with the cabbage crop –
> But oh, my God! them 'taters!

> Sixty cent p'taters!
> Nigh six-bit p'taters!
> Had bad luck with the cabbage crop,
> But oh, my God! them 'taters!

And below the cockies and 'tater farmers on the social scale were those nameless nomads, the hired hands like Dad Rudd's 'Cranky Jack', who worked like horses and spent like hardened employers. The Victorian outback still remembers the 'Cockies of Bungaree':

> Come all you weary travelers, that's out of work, just mind:
> You take a trip to Bungaree and plenty there you'll find;
> Have a trial with the cockies, you can take it straight from me –
> I'm very sure you'll rue the day you first saw Bungaree.
>
> Well, how I come this weary way I mean to let you know:
> Being out of employment, I didn't know where to go.
> So I went to the register office, and there I did agree
> To take a job of clearing for a cocky in Bungaree.
>
> Well, it's early the very next morning it was the usual go:
> He rattled a plate for breakfast before the cock did crow;
> The stars were shining glorious and the moon was high, you see;
> I thought before the sun would rise I'd die in Bungaree.
>
> By the time I came in to supper it was just on half-past nine,
> And when I had it ate, well, I reckoned it was my bed time;
> But the cocky, he came over to me and he said with a merry laugh,
> 'I want yez now for an hour or two to cut a bit of chaff.'
>
> When the work was over I'd to nurse the youngest child;
> Whenever I cracked a bit of a joke, the missus she would smile;
> The old fellow got jealous, looked like he'd murder me,
> And there he sat and whipped the cat, that cocky in Bungaree.

Well, when I'd done my first week's work I reckoned
 I'd had enough.
I went up to that cocky and I asked him for my stuff;
I came down into Ballarat and it didn't take me long –
I went straight in to Sayers' Hotel and blued my one
 pound one.

Ten thousand miles away on a frontier as hard as the
hinterland of Victoria there was an American swagman who
sang, unsuspecting of the similar identity of the two Wests:

My name is Charlie Brannan, from Charleston I come.
I've travelled this wide world over, some ups and downs
 I've had;
I've travelled this wide world over, some ups and downs
 I've saw –
But I never knew what misery was till I hit old Arkansaw.

I stepped behind the depot to dodge that blizzard wind,
I met a walking skeleton whose name was Thomas
 Quinn;
His hair hung down like rat-tails on his long and lantern
 jaw –
He invited me to his hotel, the best in Arkansaw.

I followed my conductor to his respected place
Where pity and starvation was seen on every face;
His bread it was corn-dodger, his meat I could not
 chaw –
But he charged me a half a dollar in the state of Arkansaw.

[*Spoken*] But I didn't like the work, ner the farm, ner the
farmer, ner his wife, ner *none* of his children, so I went up to
him one day and I told him, I said, 'Mister, I'm quittin' this
job and you can pay me off *right now*.' He says, 'Okay, son, if
that's the way you feel about it,' and he handed me a mink
skin. I told him, I said, 'Hell, brother, I don't want this thing,
I want my money.' He said, 'Son, that's what we use for
currency down here in Arkansaw.' So I took it and I went on

into town to see if I could find me some drinkin' whisky. I went on into a saloon and I th'owed the mink skin down on the bar, and derned if the bartender didn't give me a pint! Then he picked up my mink skin and blowed the hair back on it, and handed me three possum hides and fourteen rabbit skins for change.

Well, I'm goin' to the Indian Territory and marry me
   a squaw
And bid farewell to the canebrakes of the state of
   Arkansaw;
If ever you see me comin' again, I'll extend to you my
   paw –
But it'll be through a telescope from me to Arkansaw.

When H. S. Trotman came up the Canning Stock Route in 1906 on the well-digging expedition he bought a few supplies from Jock Ingles at Flora Valley and got a can of sardines for change. He was as dismayed as Charlie Brannan until Jock assured him that the Hall Creek storekeeper would give him a drink for it.

The only great difference in the pastoral economy of the Australian and American Wests is the status of sheep and sheepmen. In the United States both are regarded with scorn; in Australia they are much valued and deferred to. Folklore again is a good measure of attitudes, however unreliable it may be as a record of historical events. Most of Australia's folksongs deal with sheep and shearing but in America there is not one English-language song about sheep or the shearing of them. This has been a great puzzle to American folklorists, though the answer is simple enough. There are two reasons for the degradation of American sheep and shepherds, one ecological, the other social. American fleece was considered golden only in the early part of the last century when shepherds had the South-west to themselves. Raised first by Spanish missionaries, sheep were ready by the hundreds of thousands when gold was discovered to feed and clothe the prospectors. This first, short-lived prosperity encouraged sheepmen to intrude into the eastern cattle country, where they were tolerated until cattle overstocking made cattlemen look around for a better reason to account for declining profits than their own greed, and a whole body of censorious folk-lore about sheep was invented to justify declaring war against the sheepmen. In Australia shepherds were murdered by the natives; in the United States, by cattlemen. And the sheep were killed as well. Since cattlemen were the early possessors of the inland West and therefore the makers of the law, the sheepmen were outlaws in an almost literal sense. In folk courts like those of Judge Roy Bean and R. C. Barry, crimes committed by cattlemen were expiated by Chinamen or sheepmen. During the ruinous winter of 1887, some 'busted' cattlemen sank into sheep raising; their defection was held by cowboys to be a good thing in general, for it raised the level of intelligence in both industries. Open war between the two kinds of pastoralists broke out in 1890 and it is during this time that most of the killing in the romantic West occurred. The cattlemen outnumbered sheepmen, for cattle tending required more hands than sheep raising, and the war consisted of more massacres than battles. Sheep were killed, herders were murdered, homes and huts were burned. The usual recourse of a defeated force – to retreat into poorer country – was not a possible alternative for sheepmen, since sheep need better pasturage than cattle. Ultimately intimidation, violence, and abuse discouraged most native-born sheepmen, and foreign immigrants – principally the Basques – took over the sheep industry. The few English-speaking American shepherds remaining were both afraid and ashamed to call attention to themselves publicly and they never formed cohesive in-groups like cowboys, and so they never sang about their trials, troubles, or pleasures. They worked clandestinely, the garbage collectors of the West.

In Australia the situation was quite different. As in every

situation of tolerance, there was little or no competition. Sheep and cattle filled different econiches – the sheep to good country, the cattle to poor. Apple trees do not contend with codfish, so both live in amity. Sheep country in Australia is land with twenty to thirty inches of rainfall; too little rainfall makes insufficient pasturage, too much causes fleece rot and internal parasites. On the other hand, cattle thrive in semi-desert country. On this point it should be noted – especially in view of the unresolved contradictions in Australian explorers' reports concerning how long cattle and horses can go without water – that even human beings can live without imbibed water if their food has enough water in it; so also cattle. Wombats and koalas are almost habitual in obtaining water from their solid food.

Socially, Australian sheepmen had the advantages of a rare historical phenomenon, one of the few instances in cultural evolution where a significant event can be attributed to one man. In this case, the pioneer was John Macarthur, thought by sheepmen to be the Father of His Country.

Macarthur was born to contention and perfected his dubious gift in a life of gratuitous controversy. A lieutenant in the notorious New South Wales Corps at its commissioning in 1789, Macarthur spent his enforced leisure in cultivating the first fifty-acre farm in the colony, securing a reward for his work. Although he was encouraged in sheep raising by the polymathic and ubiquitous Sir Joseph Banks, whose intention was to free England from its dependency on Spanish wool, Macarthur's motivation lay not in his stars but in himself. The establishment of sheep in Australia gave him a chance to fight both Nature and man. The first sheep imported had not reproduced themselves; that was Nature's challenge; the human obstacle was the prestigious Governor Philip Gidley King. Macarthur, presuming upon his assigned importance in the colony, fought with King and his supporters about the direction of subsistence development; he had bred up a small flock of Merino sheep brought to Australia in 1796, via South

Africa. Since the Spanish Merinos and the few that had been taken to England were forbidden exportation, Macarthur's exploit in getting them in two directions reminds Americans of Thomas Jefferson's smuggling of silkworms into the United States. The contention reached an intolerable climax when Macarthur shot his superior officer, Lt Col. William Peterson, in a duel at Parramatta. King sent Macarthur back to London under arrest, accompanied by a letter saying that if Macarthur should be vindicated and returned in any official capacity, he might as well be sent back as Governor, since he already had half the colony.

While this unpleasant business was festering in Australia, another matter of great importance to Macarthur was developing in England, deriving from something that happened on the ninth of July, 1801, just about the time Macarthur was shooting Colonel Peterson:

> It is perhaps not unreasonable to mark this date as one of the significant moments in the commercial annals of the world. Seldom can we identify a particular day as that on which historical conception occurred but this summer morning in Soho Square has just that element of mild romance, briefly noted as a journal entry of most unromantic tinge:
> 'July 9 Mr Lacock call'd upon me & paid me the balance of his account £36.1.6. I delivered to him 8 fleeces from N. S. Wales to be examind and Reportd upon.

The fleeces, pronounced as good as any in His Majesty's Flock despite their coming from a deprived colony, were Macarthur's, sent off to London a year before his own expulsion.

When Macarthur arrived in London a perfunctory court martial was held, since it could not be avoided. He was dismissed from the army as much to free him for his pastoral occupation as for punishment. His success with the South African Merinos caused great excitement among officials to whom the development of British sheep was as important as the more publicized historical events of that turbulent period. During his sojourn in England Macarthur worked to destroy all obstacles to his Australian sheep enterprise, including the circumvention of the royal embargo on sheep. He stimulated the industry in England as well by making unprecedentedly high bids for breeding stock. In 1805 Macarthur returned to Australia with not only a virtual absolution of the charges King made against him, but with a 5000-acre grant and provisions for another 5,000, convict labor, and further sheep from His Majesty's Flock. Governor King was having more than enough troubles at that time with other malcontents, and he received Macarthur with an amity that Macarthur returned in a manner quite in contradiction to his character. However, when King was replaced by Captain Bligh, Macarthur's hostility broke out again – one could not imagine any other situation when two men like Macarthur and Bligh came together – and ended in open rebellion. Macarthur's man in the army, Lt Col. Johnston, deposed Bligh and Macarthur assumed the office of 'Colonial Secretary', and under that usurped title governed the colony. The irregularity was too great to be condoned by any orderly system of colonial administration, and Macarthur returned to England to have his position certified, which of course it could not be. He was gently prevented thereafter from returning to Australia, and his prospering sheep flock was managed by his wife and nephew until 1817, when he was at last permitted to return on condition he stay out of public affairs. He did not confine his energies to private enterprise, but by that time in his life his misanthropy had grown to such a level that it was dissipated over the whole of the population. He was certified as a lunatic and died in that condition two years after his commitment, in 1832.

There are few places in the world of nations where lunacy in high places is a disqualification from fame and respect, and one of them is not Australia. Macarthur's position, assumed and assigned, and his solid work in making sheep pastoralism the main economy of the new nation, created a status that has grown rather than diminished. Today the highest prestige one can inherit is an ancestry of woolly aristocracy; nothing else in trade or the professions approaches it. It is the equivalent of New York's four hundred families or Philadelphia's Main Liners, except that it cannot be bought into; and it is a prestige that is precipitated on the sheep and the laborers who work with them. To be a 'dinkum Aussie', a working man must have spent some time in a shearing shed. Shearing is the only manual trade respected by its practitioners to the extent of producing competition on the job and national heroes in its history. Australia's Jack Dempsey is Jackie Howe, who shore 321 sheep with hand shears in 8 hours and 40 minutes. The inevitable Americans and their technology have begun to erode this noble trade at last; their earlier contribution of breeding wrinkled-skin mutations with twice as much skin (and therefore twice as much fleece) aborted through diseases caused by Australian blowflies, but now shearing itself is threatened not only by synthetic fabrics and completely mechanized shearing, but by an invented substance that when injected into a sheep allows the fleece to be peeled off like an orange rind. Such Is Life.

A poor land, a hard frontier, must be prepared for human habitation. The recommendation tendered earlier, to keep poor people off poor land, does not derive from either social or economic discrimination; it is an evolutionary necessity. Where the water of human life must be drained out of mallee roots, a man does not grow watermelons, however good his will and strong his determination. When an expanding civilization is confronted by an arid frontier, its developers can only settle permanently with the aid of technology to overcome nature. Americans have accomplished miracles in settling and cultivating certain areas – the San Joaquin Valley and the Imperial Valley which are now rich agricultural land, and Las Vegas and Palm Springs which yield a more direct extraction of profit. The bulk of the underdeveloped American West is, however, still undisturbed desert.

The Australian West suffers from a major difficulty, presently insoluble: namely the absence of permanent water over regions larger than some European nations and the unreliability of rain over the whole continent. A graph of droughts in Australian history communicates the frightening regularity of this occurrence: a catastrophic drought every twelve years or so, with minor fluctuations between – and permuted with these continental periods, local irregularities of rainfall. Summarizing only the droughts in this century, in 1902, the entire continent dried up and half the sheep in Australia died. 1904 was nearly as bad; in South Australia the wheat crop was reduced to 1.41 bushels an acre. Drought struck again in 1927, and this, followed shortly by the world-wide economic depression, almost ruined the country. In 1940 a nation-wide drought began a three-year rainless period culminating in the disastrous year of 1944, when ten million sheep died and the total loss of the wheat crop in New South Wales kept Australia from emerging from the war into prosperity, as did the United States. A half million cattle died of thirst and lack of forage in 1951, another million died the following year. The pioneer advisor Earp warned in 1852 against too much optimism and too little rain; he noted that sheep were selling in Sydney for a shilling a head and sixpence on the stations if one could find the bankrupt settler to buy them from. In 1852, a shilling was worth a great deal more than in 1967, when sheep again were selling in the irrigated fruitlands of the Loxton area of South Australia for a shilling – and even at that price useless except as fertilizer. One Loxton horticulturalist who bought several hundred sheep at this price to kill and bury in his orchard, made so little from his ten thousand fruit trees that he had to take other employment to keep himself alive. The hundreds of war veterans whom the government had settled on special grant lands in this region also felt the pressures of Nature and economics, and many simply walked off their farms. And as recently as 1967, under the new decimal currency, live sheep were offered at five cents a head. Remembering that sheep are raised in comparatively good country, one can imagine what a severe drought means in regions of perpetual aridity.

The government responded to the intolerable condition of prospectors rushing after gold on the Western Australian goldfields only when death was promised for such foolishness, by closing Coolgardie to incoming miners in 1894. This was a totally useless measure, however. An attempt to supply water by digging out rockholes between Southern Cross and Coolgardie cost the government almost as much money as the goldfields were producing, but the meagre supply so provided had to be replaced early in the new century by a scheme of such ambition that its inventor, C. Y. O'Connor, shot himself in frustration before it was completed. But completed it had to be, and completed it was, in 1904 – a giant pipeline carrying water 346 miles from the Perth area to Coolgardie. The importance of the achievement was recognized immediately and O'Connor could well have emulated the famous Irish corpse at Finnegan's Wake and leapt up to share in the celebration as the conduits opened, for, as one participant remembered, 'Never have I heard so much talk about water and seen so little drunk'. The system has been enlarged and expanded since, but basically this same pipeline is still the only source of water for the inhabited parts of inland Western Australia.

Inadequate water supply was a problem also in the California goldfields, but not so difficult that it could not be solved by private enterprise. The first agriculturalist of note in California was John A. Sutter, famous now for the discovery of gold which he deplored. Sutter constructed a fort and a colony with irrigated fields. The pioneer of large-scale irrigation was the camel innovator, Edward Fitzgerald Beale, who made the San Joaquin Valley 'one of the greatest centers of irrigated agriculture in the world during the 1850s'.

For some reason beyond the fact that their water resources are greater, Americans have been far more energetic in irrigation pioneering than Australians, who need it more. All the important irrigation schemes in Australia have either been proposed or built by Americans. The first notable achievement was that of the Chaffey brothers, Canadian born but early immigrants to the United States. Having settled in California, George and William Chaffey built the first settlement irrigated with a concrete pipeline. George was the more enterprising of the two – so much so, in fact, that he invites comparison with his bustling contemporary, George Francis Train. George Chaffey became president of the Los Angeles Electric Company, and made Los Angeles the first American city to be lighted solely by electricity – an accomplishment worth mention in view of the persistence of gas street lighting in Philadelphia more than a half century later. He was also the founder of the city of Ontario, California, which has a population now of more than 50,000.

Alfred Deakin, later to become Prime Minister of Australia, visited California in 1885 to study American methods of irrigation, and consulted with the Chaffeys. He persuaded them to come to Australia, and after some consideration and a little deception by Deakin's careless agent on the matter of their compensation, they settled on the Mildura region in north-western Victoria, then unanimously regarded as hopeless. In exchange for a twenty-year license to work a quarter of a million acres, the Chaffeys agreed to put £300,000 into a permanent irrigation system. Their early achievements brought about such fear of success in those who had sworn themselves to the project's failure that the detractors really had to work at proving the hopelessness they predicted. Newspapers argued that the water line from the Murray River would break, settlers refused to pay water rates, banks refused to continue financing the project, and so the Chaffeys went bankrupt. When Deakin became Prime Minister, he apologized for the shabby treatment and poor faith that met the Chaffeys' efforts. George returned to California, where he founded the city of East Whittier, established the La Habra citrus industry with irrigation, and in his greatest accomplishment, created one of the most remarkable results of artificially directed water seen anywhere – the Imperial Valley. At the time of his coming this was an uninhabited million-acre desert; he left it an oasis of tropical lushness with a population of 70,000.

William Benjamin Chaffey remained in Australia, working to pay off the bankruptcy debts. With his genius and persistence, he founded the cities of Mildura and Renmark making them the center of a region so rich in agriculture and horticulture that its residents are today agitating for separation as an independent State. William Chaffey died in 1926, a much revered old man.

The leap-frog nature of technological evolution accounts in part for the magnitude and sophistication of the Snowy Mountains Irrigation and Hydro-Electric Project, one of the largest and most complex public works of its kind in the world. Its builders, the Six Companies, which constructed the Hoover Dam on the border of Nevada and California, served their apprenticeship on many schemes in America and exercised their mastery in Australia on a project that had been talked about for nearly a hundred years. The Snowy Mountains, despite their insignificance by international standards, are known as the Australian Alps and provide the best water catchment on the Australian continent. Before the irrigation project their runoff flowed into an area already adequately supplied with rain, so the scheme of getting the excess water to deprived regions did not require much imagination to conceive. But the fruition of schemes in a country poorly supplied with financial resources and population takes time, and it was not until 1949 that the federal government constituted the Snowy Mountains Hydro-Electric Authority. Nearing completion now, the Snowy Mountains project has expended about one billion dollars in the construction of nine large dams and many more smaller catchments, ten power stations, 80 miles of aqueducts, and a hundred miles of tunnels. When finished it will supply four million kilowatts of power and two million acre feet of irrigation water – an Australian TVA.

Around much of the perimeter of Australia, private American investment is developing agricultural regions that need only a minimum amount of work to irrigate them with existing coastal river resources. A few of these projects have failed, largely because enthusiasm was not matched by technical skill; the large rice plantation of Humpty Doo on the Adelaide River forty miles south-east of Darwin collapsed because land was not properly levelled and rats and wild buffalo damaged the crop. Another ambitious American project is located at a place with an equally strange name, Wee Waa, in north-eastern New South Wales, where irrigation from the Keepit Dam is fostering a cotton industry. If Art Linkletter, the television personality, owns half the land attributed to him by local inhabitants around the whole south-western quarter of the Australian coast, Art Linkletter will be the richest man on earth. Rejected as a foundling, this unassuming television personality seems to be avenging himself on the country of his birth by buying it up. The Esperance area alone which Linkletter has bought along with other Hollywood entertainment people (Anne Baxter, who tried valiantly to live the life of Mabel Rudd with her pastoralist husband not far from where Dad selected 'Shingle Hut'; Robert Cummings; Rhonda Fleming) will someday be another San Diego. This beautiful seacoast town was surrounded by three million useless acres of scrub until the discovery by Australian scientists of the importance of trace elements – miniscule quantities of rare minerals – in land fertility. Probably only motion picture stars could have been persuaded to invest in a project that called for putting cobalt grindstones into a sheep's stomach so that the animal could be a lifetime depositor of cobalt dust. The method is no more revolutionary than the concept, which is simply the recognition of land as a plane dimension on which science can combine nutriments to grow obligate cultigens: to put it another way, to create an ecological situation as artificial and as beautiful as a bluegrass lawn. Quite apart from its potentiality as an agricultural region, Esperance has much more to recommend it than Miami, Las Vegas, or Palm Springs when they began to make themselves by cosmetic surgery into tourist retreats. No need to drive alligators out or water in; all that is necessary is to persuade the affluent leisure class that this is the place to go.

Like almost every other fortune-making idea, it is a contradiction of logic that the most profitable crop that can be put on vacant land is people. There is scarcely any limit to the number of them that can be piled up in high-rise apartments or to the amount of money they can be made to return – so long as there is somewhere an agricultural base to feed them. The difficulty is in finding means to bring people into an area of exploitation, now that gold is no longer a viable lure.

Man only mimics Nature when he uses deception to satisfy greed. No real estate agent who ever sold desert homesites in California or swamp lots in Florida could conceive a swindle as outrageous as the flower of the *Orphys* orchid, which by an evolutionary process only Lamarck could explain, has come to resemble so closely a female wasp in appearance, size, smell, and the winsome embellishment of titillating tactile hairs, that a pollenating male wasp is lured into copulating with it. No harm is done in using an unworthy means to a worthy end in this case: the flower is pollenated, the wasp is happy – and if he isn't, serves him right for being such a filthy beast. Let her who has never put rouge on her lips or powder on her cheeks cast the first aspersion. A swamp can become Miami and Peter Pan can fly if people wish hard enough for fancy to be fact.

However dearly Americans would like it to be true, they did not invent the real estate swindle. The colonies of New

South Wales, Tasmania, Western Australia, and Queensland got their settlers by force; South Australia had to dissemble. Shortly after its establishment, the new city of Adelaide encouraged immigrants by means reprehensible enough for an American to have perpetrated them. As a contemporary writer complained,

> An influential agent in the South Australian interest not only produced a magnificently-coloured plan of the new city, divided into streets and squares, but, by a further stroke of imagination, anchored a 400 ton ship in the Torrens, opposite Government House—the River Torrens being a chain of pools in which the most desperate suicide would ordinarily have difficulty in drowning himself, and across which a child may generally step dryshod!

This was at a time when the State Treasury was a borrowed safe sheltered in a tent, containing one shilling and sixpence; when the Governor and his wife lived in a hut and when a formal ball at the Government House meant travelling over country tracks carrying one's own chairs to sit upon. This is not to say that South Australia was not at that time a land of opportunity;

> Young men of spirit were not satisfied to retire into the bush and look after a flock of silly sheep while it was possible to buy a section of land at a pound an acre, give it a fine name as a village site, sell the same land at £10 an acre, for a bill the bank would discount, and live in style at the Southern Cross Hotel. . . .

Pessimists like Charles Sturt, who, on the basis of his exploration before the first settlement, warned that the country was subject to severe and unpredictable droughts, were ignored. The settlers could not know without years of recorded observation that the land sloping down to the Murray lost rainfall at the rate of an inch a mile, but the Surveyor General, G. W. Goyder, proclaimed in 1865 that the southern limit of saltbush was the Rubicon of settlement that colonists passed at their own risk. Today, over a century later, Goyder's Line is still as effective as an electrified fence in keeping people to the south. Though South Australia is the grain field of the continent, the northern half of the state is uninhabited.

Thus Australia faces at a most critical time in its history the problem that took the United States a century to solve: the filling of vacant lands with people who could integrate with the established culture and be molded by it into a homogeneity of population. The possibility of failure is like the certainty of personal death – no one dares think about it. Certainly the desert lands will one day be occupied, as our own homes will be occupied, but by whom?

When time allows a choice, English-speaking colonies take English immigrants, even the complaining kind, and failing that, are happy enough to receive Scots bearing no thistles. Britons make up the majority of Australian immigrants still – two thirds of 1967's migrants – but there are too few of them to fill a hundredth of Australia's needs. Most of England now is shoddy, shabby, desperate, and despairing, even if London swings; but leaving England for Australia makes as much sense to an English slum-dweller as leaving a burning barn makes to a horse.

Irish are said to be welcome, though they present special problems of discipline by stubbornly refusing to follow the straight direction of George Moore: 'It is the plain duty of every Irishman to dissociate himself from all memories of Ireland – Ireland being a fatal disease, fatal to Englishmen and doubly fatal to Irishmen.' But the Land of Broken Heads was exhausted by the call of America a century earlier, when the Irish were the most persistent and numerous of the beggars at America's feast.

Even before the Great Barbecue was spread, there was more than enough for all who wished to dine. The metaphor is not overdrawn; a million and a half Irish starved to death after the total failure of the potato crop in 1845. Almost as many more emigrated to America. England would have provided the most accessible port of debarkation had not England been for seven hundred years the land of Ireland's oppression. Few Irishmen went there out of choice. More than a hundred thousand fled to Canada as a way to the free country to the south. As Thomas Colley Grattan put it in his Irish way, 'The shores of England are farther off in his heart's geography than those of Massachusetts or New York.' Partly for that reason Irish were reluctant to go to Australia, which in any case was where the British had sent them as a punishment. Another reason was more material in the Irish mind: relief food had come in large quantities from America, and always the Irishman has followed the potato.

Inhumanity to man occurs as often as a factor of numbers as of race. America's negroes to this fifth generation and more demand reparation for having been brought from a bad master to a better, yet the negro slave in mid-nineteenth century America was valued far above the Irishman. Slave ships were horrors except when compared to the 'coffin ships' that carried Irish migrants. The slaves could be sold on arrival but the Irish could not. There are records of transport vessels carrying half of the water required to maintain the lives of their Irish passengers and no food at all. Despite the fearful hardships of those days, the Irish fought as hard to get to America as they fought upon arriving, almost as if they knew that in five generations they would own the Presidency of the United States. One and a quarter million of them came in the two decades between 1840 and 1860, and continued to arrive later in numbers lessened only by the exhaustion of the home population. Today Ireland is a diminished country with no significant contribution of settlers to make towards Australia's need.

Thousands of southern European migrants – Greeks and Italians especially – have been and still are coming to Australia. These people have been and are being accepted in spite of their outlandish ways. Their presence is perhaps made more evident because they tend to take up trade and employment in areas of commerce which the old-time Australian meets every day (the neighborhood food store or 'deli' is almost always owned by Greeks and Italians), so that it might appear to the casual observer that the migrant scheme is bringing in many more people than is actually the case. On the whole the non-English-speaking peoples are integrating well, though there are definite signs, vociferously denied, that the Mafia is established already, and it does remain true that some Australians would prefer to be free of any person who learned another language than English at his mother's breast. Ironically, there is at least one case of an aborigine who made the transition from desert savagery to white civilization, reacting unfavorably to Italian immigration. Having made himself a solid part of Adelaide's white, though grimy, lower-class community, he moved out of his neighborhood with the angry complaint that there were 'too bloody many Italians coming in'.

Looking at the effect of immigration in other parts of the world (Fiji, as one example among many, where peoples of India poured in and drove the native Fijians into the central badlands without having any effect whatever on India's overpopulation), Australians hold as tenaciously as possible to the one human right supported by any kind of evidence other than verbal repetition – for a group to choose its own members. Until 1965, when the Labor Party and the Communists within it found it expedient to be less frank about their attitude, all groups in Australia openly subscribed to the policy stated on the masthead of that most Australian of all periodicals, the Sydney *Bulletin:* 'Australia for the White Man'. When world opinion – surely the least useful source of advice to which any nation can be subjected, since it only represents out-group feeling – made this explicitness inexpedient, the Australians went on restricting the kind and quality of its immigrants by such cunning devices as literacy tests – which immigrants had to complete successfully in any language the immigration officer chose. Nor is this sort of thing confined only to Australia, for the United States' most heartless department, the Immigration and Naturalization Service, continues in practice the quota system which has been formally abolished. By the device of pleading that there are insufficient means to process Australian immigrants to the United States, America has been able to keep the number of Australian white migrants down to the old figure of seventy a year. There are many cases, not publicized, of families being split up because exceptions are rarely made to this policy. The United States would no doubt find itself in a most embarrassing position, were someone to expose this inhumane and hypocritical behavior. The daughter of a Soviet dictator is welcomed into the United States, while that of an American citizen born in Australia is excluded. Unhappily this is another parallel between Australia and America.

In most cases of exclusion by general policy there is on the side of the excluders an overwhelming body of evidence. If the immigrant belongs to a nation whose nationalism is not worn away by his choosing to live in a new country, admitting him is dangerous business. America admits Moslems and pays for its liberality by having one of them assassinate a Presidential candidate. Australia admitted Moslems to drive its camels and paid for its liberality by one of the nastiest cases of racial violence in its history – again an incident little publicized. In that tightly integrated town of Broken Hill there were two Islamic Turks peddling ice cream from their cart. When World War I exploded from the pistol of that Serbian assassin, these two ice cream hawkers rolled their cart to the railroad track, turned it on its side, and began firing rifle bullets into a passing train, thus becoming the first enemies to fire the first shots of the war on Australian soil. That in itself would have been bad enough, but the reaction was worse: gangs of Australians attacked their neighbors of foreign origin in reprisal, proving once more, where no further proof is needed, that prejudice against the identifiable foreigner is strongly latent in all of us.

The largest and most troublesome nationality of immigrants to both Australia and America was the Chinese. The fact that they had little to do with the causes of the trouble is irrelevant; their very presence, their very appearance, their very character were sufficient to account for severe and, in America at least, inhuman repression.

Chinese were first brought to Australia after the convict system and its fountainhead of cheap labor were stopped in 1840 and employers in whom wisdom was entirely whelmed by expedience looked outside their culture for cheap and dumb workers. The plan might in practice have become a system uncomfortably close to American slavery if the gold strikes had not caused the Chinese to down their garden hoes and take up picks. In spite of the white man's haste to satisfy greed with gold in the early 1850s the Chinese swarmed over the goldfields so quickly and in such numbers that the wonder of it is why trouble did not erupt sooner. The almost certain failure in its finding that makes gold valuable in the first place should have driven disappointed white prospectors to blame their bad luck on the Chinese. Interestingly and ominously enough for American critics of Australian intolerance, the first serious uprising against Chinese on the goldfields occurred on the Fourth of July, 1854, in Bendigo. There is no question about American instigation, but their lead was followed enthusiastically enough by the Australians, and the general opinion thus manifested on the Victorian diggings resulted in a Chinese exclusion law in the state the following year. The Chinese – or, to be more accurate, those Australians and Americans who were making money transporting them to the diggings – responded by making landings on the coast of South Australia, a long and arduous walk into Victoria, but ingress for all that. The lonely Coorong is empty now of obvious archaeological evidence of the migration, but a century ago it held a line of shanties and sly-grog shops to guide the coolie prospector on his way to gold. Another anti-Chinese riot erupted in Victoria in 1857, again on the Fourth of July; and while this one pricked the conscience of the uninvolved Australians, the state of South Australia acknowledged the protest by excluding Chinese. New South Wales allowed the Chinese a port of entry until gold was discovered there; the Chinese began to swarm in and very soon American prospectors again sparked off a riot so that an exclusion act was passed in that state as well.

It must not be thought that Australians had stood by innocently while Americans attacked the Chinese. There is evidence enough that Australians joined in heartily whenever the Chinese were knocked about. One song from the Victorian goldfields tells how a bored prospector found amusement for his idle hands:

> And when of reading we were tired, and of cards had
> had enough,
> We'd set to and pelt the Chinese who were washing out
> their stuff.

A song from the 'Kelly country' records how the outlaw hero established non-verbal communication with a Chinese cook during the holdup at Jerilderie:

> They mustered up the servants and locked them in a
> room,
> Saying 'Do as we command you, or death will be your
> doom'.
> The Chinaman cook 'no savvied', his face was full of
> fear,
> But Ned soon made him savvy with a straight left to the
> ear.

Queensland was the next state to experience Chinese immigration to its goldfields; there the white miners were actually driven out by hordes of Chinese in the 1870s. In the Northern Territory by 1894, it is documented that 2,055 of the 2,120 gold miners on those sparse fields were Chinese, and that they removed 34,093 ounces of gold from the Territory (and from the country, to give Australians a further cause for complaint) while Australians gleaned a mere 450 ounces. Finally in 1901, defying Colonial Office opposition, an immigration act was passed excluding all Chinese. Since the Chinese miners brought almost no women with them, their population rapidly declined. Those who stayed during the amortization went into the less rewarding trades of market gardening and cabinet making.

Chinese laundrymen in the United States had their trade forced on them as market gardening was forced on the Chinese in Australia. The first Chinese immigrants, one couple only, came to the American goldfields in 1848 – a small start to a mass migration which swamped the California diggings in the 1860s. The American miners needed no aid from foreigners in their violent reaction to Chinese competition; vigilante groups were assembled almost everywhere the Chinese appeared, one with the expressive name of 'The Pick-Handle Brigade'. Though their numbers ran close to a hundred thousand in 1870, the Chinese had to assume a docile demeanor, accept low pay for employment that no white man would accept, and the usual calumny:

> Washee, washee, morn till night,
> No get drunk, no go fight;
> No give sasee Melican man,
> Workee hardee all he can.

> Melican loafee all day long,
> Spit on Chinee, say no wrong;
> Stealee muchee, when he couldee,
> Lie 'bout Chinee, say no goodee.

Chinamen redundant in laundries carried earth in shoulder baskets to raise the beds of the western and transcontinental railroads; others went into their ghetto in San Francisco and lived on opium and tong wars.

The few Australian demonstrations against Chinese miners

are in no way to be compared with American violent repression of Chinese whenever they appeared in any numbers. At one intended lynching of a Chinese during the almost continuous harassment of the 'Celestials' on the Denver Cherry Creek diggings in the 1880s, it is remembered that only one white man was brave enough to defend the victim – a gunman-gambler who confronted the mob with two irrefutable arguments: his pistol and the question 'If you kill Wong, who in hell will do my laundry? Get out, you sons of bitches'.

In evaluating the various immigrants to the United States while that nation was being born in 1782, St Jean de Crevecoeur drew from his opinion data of success what we may take as sincere if not scientific demography:

> out of twelve families of emigrants of each country, generally seven Scotch will succeed, nine Germans, and four Irish. The Scotch are frugal and laborious, but their wives cannot work so hard as German women. . . . The Irish do not prosper so well; they love to drink and quarrel; they are litigious, and soon take to the gun, which is the ruin of everything. . . .

Whenever they are quite safe from Irish eavesdroppers, both Australian and American natives will admit the validity of de Crevecoeur's estimation. The second most numerous nationality to contribute toward the five million immigrants who flooded into the United States during the middle decades of the nineteenth century was German, and judging by what records exist for making nebulous inferences, no other group integrated so well or made so great a contribution to the national culture.

Though their settlements in Australia were very much smaller, the Germans have a similar record in Australia, substantiating Horne's judgment,

> If entry in the Australian *Who's Who* is any kind of a test, the proportion of migrants who achieve success is more than double the proportion of native Australians who achieve success.

The pattern of German settlement in Australia is best seen in South Australia, where the Germans established their first and their strongest communities. With the assistance of one of the important but comparatively unknown early settlers, G. F. Angas, Germans came over in congregations, following their Lutheran pastors. They accepted the exploitation of land speculators philosophically where the Irish would have demanded the cracking of skulls. The colonial historian John Wrathall Bull records that owing to their vulnerability as foreigners with no English landing in a colony suffering from repudiation of colonial credit, the first Germans had to pay seven pounds an acre for land officially evaluated at one, plus heavy interest to bankers and the usual cost of provisions and stock. Yet their industriousness never flagged; at their first harvest they were hauling vegetables in carts over the Mount Lofty Ranges into Adelaide along a route that to this present time requires the use of winching devices by those who choose to use it.

Except for Hahndorf, Klemzig, and Lobethal, the seventy towns founded by the South Australian Germans are now disguised by English names imposed by rather silly nationalistic feelings during the First World War. The 'German towns' are distinguishable, however, because they still look the most 'Australian' of all colonial settlements. The annual wine festival at Hahndorf, whose first wine seller had been a sergeant at the Battle of Waterloo, follows straight after the John Martin Christmas Parade and the Anzac celebrations as the state's most traditional replication of the spirit of the old colony. German success as pioneers in grain growing and exportation is lost in their unapproached reputation as Australia's first great vignerons. Almost all the names of Australia's wines recall the German pioneers: C. A. Soberls of Tanunda; Benno Seppelt of Greenock; T. G. Hermann, maker of Quelltaler; J. Gramp, vintner to the proletariat; Gottlieb and Chris Hoffmann – these are only a few of the eminent names among the fifty thousand Germans who made the fifty towns in the Barossa valley world-famous vineyards despite the almost unsurmountable prejudice against 'domestic' wines that California wine makers know only too well. It may surprise those who think that knowledge of French wines is the only mark of a gentleman, to learn that California and Australia provide as near perfect climatic conditions for the production of wine as can be hoped for anywhere in the world. Indeed, when blight destroyed vineyards in Europe, regrowth was started with cuttings from Californian and Australian vineyards, and today it is not unusual for the sons of French winemakers to go to California and Australia to study how wines are best made. These minds are impregnable to either fact or logic; no wine to them is fit to drink unless it has had bare French feet in it.

Germans, by and large, are not much discriminated against in Australia; they even have the assurance that the names of their towns will not be changed in the next war. But relatively few Germans have chosen to migrate to Australia since settlers do not ordinarily move from rich countries to poor, and so regardless of the close proximity of the communist threat, Germans prefer to remain at home, Volkswagen-makers to the world.

Recognizing that life itself is a denial of entropy and a violation of the Second Law, and in no case much deterred from profitable action by any law of man, God, or Nature, Americans emigrated to Australia in effective if not appreciable numbers from the moment there was enough money in the antipodes to make enterprise and exploitation worth the voyage. Some of the first merchants were Americans, bringing not only business acumen but colorful behavior to Australia. Timothy Goodwin Pitman carried the Revolutionary trade of tea-mongery to Sydney and accumulated so much capital and respect that W. C. Wentworth (the first native Australian statesman, and founder of a dynasty of public service represented today by his grandson, also W. C. Wentworth, the eminent Minister for Aboriginal Affairs) overrode the law to make him a citizen. Prosper de Mestre, who left France for America before he was born, came to Australia in 1818 at the age of 25, became a congenial competitor of Pitman as a George Street tea merchant and an uncongenial competitor to a dinkum Aussie, which in those days meant a convict, manacled or manumitted. This fellow prosecuted de Mestre under an old statute prohibiting foreigners from engaging in trade on colonial soil; de Mestre countered successfully with an equally unusual law depriving emancipated convicts from suing in a court of justice. To stop further trouble of this sort, the Government enacted special legislation to give de Mestre British subject status, as had been done for Pitman. Later in life, however, the validity of de Mestre's citizenship was contested, but Chief Justice Forbes ruled that since he had been born at sea in a British ship, he had been an Englishman all the time.

American emigrants of this kidney gradually exerted upon the growing nation an influence beyond their numerical share. The inimitable George Francis Train, who could have molded the country into an American image all by himself had he stayed long enough, confided in a letter home in 1853, 'You will be surprised to see how fast this place is becoming Americanized!' Some Australians agreed, without finding anything about the situation to approve of. In 1855 an irritated Melbournian complained,

> There are barely 3,000 Americans in Victoria, compared with more than 35,000 other foreigners, and yet, from the very design of the town, to the presence of those hideous telegraph posts, everything speaks of the land of the Stars and Stripes.

In this matter of community design, America's heaviest imprint upon Australia is the national capital of Canberra (unless one accepts the Hell Gate Bridge in New York as the model on which the Sydney Harbour Bridge was copied).

Following another American lead in locating the national capital in a compromise site between a contending north and south, Canberra was built on the truly magnificent designs of a Chicago architect, Walter Burley Griffin. Feeble efforts at criticism are made from time to time by persons compelled by architectural faddism, but Osmar White's recent estimation of Canberra as 'the most calculated, the most self-conscious, and the most handsome' of Australian cities is likely to persist until urban sprawl engulfs its origins. The creation of Lake Burley Griffin in 1964 and the fastest growth rate of imposing public and private building in Australia have put Canberra quite out of reach of its contenders for White's superlatives. Its critics are forced to abandon logic completely when their objections are faced down even by names suggested by Australians for the capital city – 'Venus', 'Paxedwardus', 'Sydmeladpernrisho', 'Wheatwoolgold', and, inevitably, 'Labourall' and 'Labour City'. They can do no better than repeat what that ferocious Premier of New South Wales, George Dibbs, replied when asked his opinion of Griffin's native city: 'Damn Chicago'.

The United States insinuated its natives into Dibbs's own profession as well. John Greeley Jenkins came from Pennsylvania to Australia as an itinerant salesman for a publishing company and stayed to become a book salesman and importer. His career went from strength to strength and he eventually attained the premiership of South Australia and later, eminent positions in the national government. It all proved rather too much for him, however, and he quitted politics to hit the road as an international drummer.

At least as colorful and ferocious as Dibbs was King O'Malley, born on the Fourth of July in 1858 as a reincarnation of Davy Crockett. Working shrewdly under the guise of a professional backwoods American thumper, O'Malley made a fortune in various private enterprises while ascending the Australian political ladder to federal cabinet status. As Minister for Home Affairs in 1913 O'Malley drove the first construction peg in Canberra. He left politics shortly afterwards, having broken with the then Prime Minister, Billy Hughes. The dispute was unfortunate, for the two men were much of a sameness. Hughes's frank dismissal of Woodrow Wilson's ethereal international notions as 'bloody nonsense' when most of the world thought the President's utterances had drifted down from the Mount itself, were typical of the man and his American style. And finally there is the wife of former Prime Minister Gorton, still an American citizen when her husband was elected to the highest office in Australia.

One source of emigration to Australia has been visits from the American armed services. Curiously, the 1908 visit to Sydney Harbour of the American Great White Fleet, which encouraged only a few crewmen to return later as immigrants, had a surprisingly favorable impact on Australia, though there were those who resented the American presence, like the poet Bernard O'Dowd who damned the fleet as a 'wan array of hell-ships vomiting their Will-to-Slay'.

Since World War II, from whose lethal dangers the United States protected Australia (Australians generally believed the American presence was for Australia's protection, a notion that few Americans have chosen to dispel), American servicemen have been greeted in Australia with more good will than anywhere in the world, including America. Some American soldiers and sailors have few opportunities to see civilized Australia – like those stationed at that invisible but nevertheless enormous American installation on the North West Cape, said to be a communications base, but most servicemen get down to Sydney's King's Cross quickly enough. Those magnificent battles over Australian women fought by Americans and Australians in the Second World War still continue as fifteen hundred soldiers a week prowl the Cross searching for Rest and Recreation. More of these men return as permanent settlers than entirely pleases the United States government.

As the already great influence of the United States upon

Australian culture accelerates the two peoples and the two cultures become ever more compatible. Prime Minister Menzies' great reputation as a statesman almost vanished at one word when he suggested that the unit of currency in the new decimal system be called a 'royal'. 'Dollar' it had to be, and 'dollar' it was. With eighty per cent of film footage on Australian television coming from the United States and much of the rest imitative of American programs, Australian culture is being Yankified so fast that the youngest Australians would understand Tom Collins's *Such Is Life* no better than Americans. If such an area of culture can be put into figures, at least 25 per cent of the indigenously developed Australian language has disappeared in the last ten years; no 'dinkum Aussie' would now refer to himself as such. Even the Great Australian Adjective 'bloody' is being displaced by the American vulgar copulatory adjective – in situations of male fraternity, the new word is used to a greater extent than it was in the American army during World War II, if such a thing can be imagined, and almost as frequently as American conversationalists use the expression 'you know' and American social scientists write the neologism 'and/or'. On the most distant frontier the old Strine is spoken, but with the Postmaster-General's plan to use the NASA satellite ATSi as a reflector to replace the cumbersome relay telegraph communications system with a simple transceiver to ordinary private telephone lines, the great outback family now cohered by listening in to one another's conversations will fragmentate and fall even more rapidly under American influence. It has even been suggested – by an Australian – that within the visible future

the Army-Navy gridiron game will eventually supplant the Geelong-St Kilda League final even in Melbourne livingrooms . . . for all spectator sport is only as successful as the number of spectators it draws, and a game [televised by satellite] with a billion spectators will eventually swamp out even the attractions to Melbournians of Australian Rules.

The only antagonism toward Americans of any significance

is to be found in Australian Intellectual cells, and since their attitudes are shared by their American counterparts, one can foresee a situation where the intellectuals of one nation speak only to the intellectuals of the other and cease thereafter to trouble honest citizens of either country. While Monash University philosophers agonize over the selfishly exclusive American possession of Herbert Marcuse, the Australian man in the street is worried about the distressing fact that 95 per cent of his automobile industry, 97 per cent of his pharmaceutical, and 95 per cent of his petroleum refining and distribution are owned by overseas capital.

It is proper that the ordinary citizen of Australia should concern himself with the ectoplasmic spectre of American possession of his economy, for this is a worry possible only in conventional thinking. By the time the unconventional truths of Keynesian economics filter down to the common man, they will be as obsolete as Marxian economics. The real danger to the Average Australian, his culture, and his country is not one fully apprehended by him, partly because it is contradictory to the received truths of conventional economics and partly because it will not bear thinking about. The last Western frontier is demonstrating that very rare phenomenon, that riches may ultimately lead to ruin, for the more Australia prospers, the more critical becomes its problem of insufficient population. It is a mansion of great wealth, occupied by a small, defenceless family, with beggars at its feast and wolves at its door.

In August 1969, unemployment in affluent America was five per cent; in Australia it had dropped to below one per cent, with fewer than fifty thousand unemployed in the entire nation. At the same time there were 38,000 unfilled jobs listed. Distilling the facts out of the figures, one could say there was no unemployment at all in Australia. The gross national product increased nearly twelve per cent in 1969 – double the 1964 rate; yet there remain a wealth of areas still to be developed. The cotton industry grew 78 per cent in

1969, but is nevertheless far below its potential. There is a fat profit awaiting the man who puts buffalo meat on the American hamburger market. At the moment Australian cattlemen suppose Americans to have the same poor opinion of buffalo as they do, but Americans think 'buffalo' means 'bison' (while Australians think 'bison' is somefin a bloke warshes his fyce in), and if the price put on the meat is commensurate with its presumed rarity, there is no reason why someone cannot make his fortune. Prejudice alone keeps kangaroos off the meat market; Australians think 'roo meat is fit only for dogs, that it rots faster than the flesh of other animals, and that a person's stomach is turned by its peculiar blue color (dyeing of 'roo meat is required by law for the same sort of reasons that led Wisconsin a decade ago to permit dairymen to color butter yellow but forbade the margarine manufacturers to use a similar cosmetic on their product). In fact, kangaroo meat is certainly not an acquired taste for anyone who likes eating beef. It has a higher protein count than the flesh of any other edible animal, and once again, to the American imagination it is an exotic delicacy. Even if 'roo flesh were less acceptable than horse meat to human carnivores in Australia, it should be forced on them to spare the frontier's delicate surface the damage caused by ungulate hooves. Unfortunately, Australian beef, lamb, and wool sales are embarrassingly high already to American competitors. Economic diplomats had frequent meetings during 1969 to reach an agreeable balance between Australian exports and American imports. As Americans scale their tastes and budgets down from steak to hamburger, they eat more Australian beef. American cattlemen had already begun to complain in 1963, when Australian exports to hamburger chains in the United States rose three thousand per cent over the 1959 figure. In fact, the noisy clamor raised by Australian politicians about American exploitation of Australian industry and resources is, some American observers suspect, merely a ploy to disguise the real situation of imbalance against the United States. The average

Australian or American knows little of this; however, he does not even suspect the importance of the Cuban crisis in forcing the United States to ease restrictions on Australian sugar that were causing some bloody oaths to be uttered in the state of Queensland. American wool growers have been demanding high tariffs for years; they will not be pleased to know that Australian wool production in 1969 went some 60,000,000 pounds weight over the previous record established in 1968. Australians are, perhaps, most concerned about the production of wheat on their frontiers. Yet with only 4 per cent of the world's acreage Australia is producing fourteen per cent of the world's export wheat. Meanwhile American unsold wheat stockpiles grow, even with enormous quantities being 'sold' to India.

Though the English-speaking man in the street does not know very much about Australia's present and future wealth, men in other streets speaking very unfamiliar languages know about it, and their hungry eyes have been directed to the south for a long time. It is true – true beyond one's power to describe to anyone who has not been there – that Australia on the other side of the fringing frontier line is uninhabited because it is uninhabitable; that it is a 'ghastly blank' with Antarctica's power to kill an inadequately equipped intruder; that its hundreds of thousands of square miles of red desert sand ridges can never support permanent human settlement – but these are unacceptable truths to the beggars who stand watching Australia's feast from the other side of the water frontier. If Australia is an empty wilderness, too dry to support more than twenty million people at a Western standard of living, how can it produce so much wheat that it can sell 73 per cent of the harvest to starving Asian countries? The thought must sometimes enter even the friendly Japanese mind that what at the time seemed only a delaying setback at the Battle of the Coral Sea might with a more strenuous effort have given the overpopulated Japanese islands the whole of a continent it is now buying by the millions of tons for

258

billions of dollars. A nation whose trains are drawn by steam locomotives may appear backward to one in which trains are obsolescent, but how must it look to a country whose principal transport is a pair of yoked baskets over a coolie's shoulder? Australia's space alone, the sand and aridity notwithstanding, is an irresistible temptation to a population nearing a billion individuals. And now the great wealth evoked by American capital investment is being directed towards a friendly cousin after being turned out by hostile foreigners among whom they planted oil installations and other good things susceptible to nationalization.

And so the probings begin: savage tribesmen of 'East Irian' raid across the line into Australian New Guinea to kill and eat people under Australian protection while their putative spokesmen demand political independence; Communist anthropologists make maps of northern Australian shores while ostensibly making ethnographic studies; Asian nations claim earlier discoveries of Australia than those made by the Dutch and English; American Kremlin songbirds sing protest songs to sympathetic Australian audiences, asking that racist barriers be let down to admit Melanesians and Chinese and Indians and Indonesians and Malaysians and other gentle folk so that the world will respect Australia; aborigines with a nominal education are thrust through Australian universities and out into the world by fifth-column Communists intent on condemning their white countrymen.

Any nation subjected to unremitted accusation sooner or later begins to suspect the possibility that it might actually be guilty; Prime Minister Billy Hughes told President Wilson bluntly that Australia would preserve its national integrity in any way it bloody well wished, regardless of what the rest of the world thought. That time of plain talk is gone forever. The signs of guilt accepted for an uncommitted sin are clearly visible on the Australian national countenance, though the Australian soul is clean by any standard of morality. Americans who know no more about Australia than its location

259

somewhere off the coast of southern California – or Mexico? – know all about the abominable 'White Australia' policy, and people being what they are, God help us all, such Americans are not so considerate of Australian sensitivity on this saddle-gall of an issue that they refrain from asking about it. Carrying more guilt now than they can easily bear on the question of white oppression of black, Americans assume that a white Australia is oppressing a black somebody-or-other-they-are-not-sure-whom. Australians patiently try to make their critics understand that what Americans see as the Far East is Australia's Near North, that there is an enormous yellow cloud right above Australia's head, so heavy that it must pour out its contents soon. They can argue further that the opposite of white for them is yellow, and that the accusation of *tu quoque* can hit the American much harder than the Australian. What about the White American policy, for that matter? Is it not a fact that Australia admits more Chinese immigrants than the United States – a great differential when the population of twelve million is set against a population of two hundred million? And the bruited foreign aid of the United States – is it not a fact that Australia gives more help per capita to poor nations than the United States?

Logic and reason cannot survive when the data on which they work are incorrect; the humanity of man itself loses its tenuous hold on existence when the incorrectness of what purport to be factual data is a deliberate creation – no matter how virtuous the purpose of contrived dishonesty may be. Australia is often said to be any vague number of years behind the United States in any vague area of culture. This imputed lag may be real enough in some things – Australia is as far behind in hot dogs as America is in meat pies – but in most of the diffusing culture traits there is no greater backwardness for either country than either country believes necessary. In one item Australia is entirely too close to the United States: distortion of factual reference works. In this one area of belief the free West held inviolable, the force of new sociopolitical expediency has begun to corrupt reference books in both countries. For most of its long history a pioneer in scholarship, the *Encyclopaedia Britannica*, yielded truth to moral force a generation ago, as its first substantial critic, Joseph McCabe, argued fruitlessly the last years of his life. The year of 1969 saw the prestigious quick-fact American reference annual *The World Almanac* succumb to the need to repair past injustice with present falsity. In the same year the new *Australian Encyclopaedia* followed this pernicious American lead. In its article on Afghans in Australia, it said

> By and large, the Afghans were esteemed by all who came in contact with them. In their time they made an important and welcome contribution to life in the interior of Australia.

The remark is not only entirely gratuitous, but internally false and quite inconsistent with historical fact. It would be much closer to absolute truth to say that the Afghans were thoroughly disliked by all who came in contact with them. Whether the dislike of the Afghans was morally justifiable or substantiated by any qualities acceptable to either the Afghan or Australian culture is a question that can and perhaps should be discussed, but the dislike is a fact and must be maintained by any persons to whom truth is a virtue. This is only a small thing, but so, we were told two thousand years ago, is a mustard seed.

The fact of Australia's peril is not to be obscured by any kindness toward the underprivileged or over-pigmented peoples of the world. It is a fact that no other contiguous areas on earth have greater disparity in population than Australia and the south-east of Asia. The island of Java, immediately to Australia's north, has a population density of 1,234 persons per square mile. The North Point district of Hong Kong has a density of 1,200,000 persons per square mile. China has a total population of 740,000,000 – 21 per cent of the earth's population. India has another 500,000,000. The several new nations once comprising French Indo-China and the archipelagic nations between the mainland and Australia, teem with humanity crowded for room. All of these overpopulated and underfed nations look to the last vacant land in the south, and most claim it by right of prior discovery. Most could take it by force. The Indonesian army and navy could crush Australia in a matter of hours, if unhindered by the United States. Of course neither Indonesia nor India would do such a thing. Yet although they have given assurances that they will not attack Australia, the thought has nevertheless crosssed their minds. What, for instance, is suggested by the following remark, made 25 years ago, when the pressures were far below the present critical point?

> India's population today exceeds 400 millions and at the lowest minimum of 1,400 calories she can only feed less than 300 million people! That is, more than a hundred million people or roughly as many as there are in this country [the United States] are either starving or are on the brink of starvation. In nearby Australia for example, people average 3,000 calories a day. The basic reason for this difference is that some 8 million people have twice the area of land that 400 million people in India have today.

Since Dr Chandrasekhar made his ominous comparison, the population of Australia has risen by 4.8 million; India's, in spite of the suggested impossibility, by 200 million. Are the covetous glances fewer and less urgent now than in 1946? The people of Australia once took heart in the belief that India's religion did not permit the taking of life and her politics did not permit the taking of territory. Both prohibitions were shattered at once when the sanctimonious Indian Prime Minister Nehru expropriated without any pretence to moral rectitude the Portuguese colony of Goa. China, of course, does not pretend to any Western notions of the sacredness of life, except when talking to the bourgeoisie. 'Peace' means 'War' in China, as it did long before Orwell. The *T'ai-p'ing*, which is translated 'Peace', in which the Southern Ming

262

peasants fought the Manchu government troops, killed between 20,000,000 and 30,000,000 people. The Communists consolidated their position as the popular rulers of China by the *Hsiao Mieh* ('deprivation of existence') pogrom, which according to some estimates killed 20,000,000 Chinese. Even Peking admitted 2,910,000 executions. These were Chinese killing Chinese. Is it to be believed that if Australia's frontier is finally settled by China, the 12.7 million Australian Foreign Devils will be accommodated to *Realpolitik* more humanely?

Yes, it is so to be believed. Australians, like Americans, are Englishmen at bottom, and by that heritage they fall into the weakness noted exactly five hundred years ago by Sir Thomas Malory, when he grieved for the abandonment of their country and their greatest leader by the fictional but typical English in the time of Arthur:

> Alas, this is a great default of all Englishmen, for there may no thing please us no term. And so fared the people at that time; they were better pleased with Sir Mordred than they were with King Arthur, and much people drew unto Sir Mordred, and said they would abide with him for better and for worse. . . . And the most party of all England held with Sir Mordred, the people were so new fangle.

America's ability to nominate for its President a man who had just returned from leading the World Council of Churches in the condemnation of his country is matched by Australia's will to have no thing please them no term. The Labor Party from its foundation to 1965 publicly and vociferously upheld the policy of excluding undesirable immigrants, particularly Asian immigrants. *The Worker* of Brisbane warned in 1901 against

> the sinuous movements of the deadly coloured alien biped lurking in the scrub with a cane knife in his mudhook waiting to butcher the first casual white victim that comes along. . . .

The Worker continued with a call to arms against anyone who by voting against the Labor Party would 'be bequeathing a terrible birthright to his children in the shape of the coloured alien curse'. This manifesto against Asianization of the nation was one of the foundation stones of the Labor Party until out of fear or perfidy its Peking-oriented minority declared that their country after all was an Asian nation.

Of course, Australian folksongs have not failed to make a typical contribution to this subject:

> I asked a fellow for shearing once along the Marthaguy.
> He said, 'We shear non-union here.' 'I call it "scab",'
>   says I;
> I took a look along the board before I turned to go –
> There was twenty flaming Chinamen shearing in a row.
> So shift, boys, shift, for there isn't any doubt,
> It's time to make a move with the leprosy about.
> Was I to raise my hat to him? Was I his blasted dog?
> So I left his scabby station at the old jig-jog.

But alas, the great default. Removed from his Australian tap roots by some fifty overseas visits to paradises on the left of reality, Albert Monk, the twenty-year president of the Labor Party's strongest organized supporting group, the Australian Council of Trade Unions, said on returning from one of his visits to Communist China, 'China's government is not communist at all . . . there is no sign of a food shortage . . . no evidence of oppression . . . economic policy is sound'.

Lo ye, all Englishmen, see ye not what a mischief here was? For the hope of a place in the rice paddy, a basket to carry on their shoulders, these men have made a covenant with death, and with hell are at agreement.

Few today will stand boldly forward and say, as Donald Horne said unequivocally in 1959 and less certainly in 1964,

> we do not want our living standards swamped; we do not want to import race disturbances; and (rightly or wrongly) we wish to preserve in Australia a predominantly European kind of culture. Above all we simply assert our right as a nation to control immigration in whatever way we choose.

The Australian Bureau of Census and Statistics says Australia will have a population of 23 million by the year 2000. At the present rate of increase, Asia will have added a billion to its population in that time. So, despite a massive effort to encourage immigration, Australia can look forward at best to being outnumbered in the race for population by 500 to one.

All the vacant lands of the Western world are being examined by the security of covetousness. An Indian economist given access to America's ear by an American publisher 25 years ago wrote:

> Where there are vast open spaces, as in Amazonia and Australia, an exclusive policy of restricting immigration militates against the demands of world economy and productivity . . . vast arid areas in North America which are now settled only by cattlemen can be brought under the plough and harrow if Chinese and Indian immigration is encouraged on a reasonable scale. . . . In the world of the future, a balance of economic resources and populations has to be reckoned with. Standards of living and economic opportunities for all peoples should gradually approximate, if the world is to be saved from recurrent demographic crises and aggressions.

That is straighter talk than Mr Mukerjee would get from us; in terms of Asian politeness he says 'Open your frontiers or they will be opened'. Battened on Pakistan, India looks to Australia as another Bangla Desh.

Desperate necessity makes odd bedfellows. The only conceivable way Australia can survive as Australia – as the nation that has been built up during the last two centuries – is to seek protection from the one country that can provide it, the United States. Treaties exist to this end, of course; but America's surrender in Vietnam has destroyed the credibility of its assurances. Its treaties are no longer negotiable currency in free Asia and Oceania. Its failure to meet the seizure of the *Pueblo* with instant and massive retaliatory force and its consequent acceptance of more than a year of aggravated humiliation reduce its reliability as a protector of its own people abroad. The only situation one can believe the United States would respond to with effective military action – that is, action on the homeland of the invader instead of the homeland of the invaded – would be invasion of the United States itself.

Although one is speaking to an inevitability not subject to the will of any man or group of men, if Australians could do what clearly is best for their country, they would conjoin with the other United States. There is no question that for America it would be better to have a free and friendly neighbor – as Australia has always been – than another blood relative with all the disabilities that relationship assures; but Australia's dilemma is not soluble by an empty continent in a swarming world.

When England explicitly abandoned Australia to its apparently certain death as a nation during the Second World War, Prime Minister Curtin in his New Year message to the Australian people on the 29th of December 1941 declared,

> Without any inhibitions of any kind, I make it quite clear that Australia looks to America, free of any pangs as to our traditional links or kinship with the United Kingdom. . . . We know . . . that Australia can go and Britain can still hold on. We are, therefore, determined that Australia shall not go, and we shall exert all our energies towards the shaping of a plan, with the United States as its key-stone, which will give our country some confidence of being able to hold out. . . .

Like the utterances of all prophets, Prime Minister Curtin's declaration of shifting dependency had more substance than its time understood. It has been often proposed, by persons without influence or responsibility that Australia be incorporated into America as another Pacific state. Australia is more than that, though California seceded would be the fifth nation in the world. Australia is five states and a territory. It could be five States still in a new Western nation, the United

States of Austramerica, joining the two last Wests in what all the many parallels of their history and mutual influence adumbrate as a Manifest Destiny. The union is the only hope – for America.

NINE

Retreat from the Frontier:
Australian Immigration Today

England in August of 1971 called strongly to her wandering boy James Johnson. In the sceptered isle the thin sun of British summer warmed the coal dust sifting down upon its industrial cities, Nature's first green was black, the pubs were filled with nine hundred thousand jolly unemployed men swilling tepid beer, the surly employed work force were either on strike or about to down tools, and the telly offered the proletariat vicarious sharing of the lives of rag pickers and dustmen – *the real meaning of Life, Fred.* For James Johnson, suffering through the half-hearted winter in the emerald city of Adelaide, the magnetism of nostalgia was irresistible; *oh, to be in England, now that Welfare's there.* He gathered up his wife and ten of their thirteen children (three having escaped) and fled the land of lazy sunshine. But not without giving the Australian newsmongers the traditional press conference of prestigious returning migrants.

'The Australians are grabbers,' James declared. 'They want money for everything.' The hellish climate of South Australia had eroded the health of his children and the hellish fees of South Australian physicians had eroded the health of his pocketbook. He had found no gold at all in the streets and the jobs offered him did not square with the dignity of a member of the British working class. He had even been sent into the bush to labor for weeks on end, deprived of the comforting embrace of Mum – with the sad result that his marital duties could not be fulfilled. The evidence was irrefutable: not one new child in nearly three years. He admitted he had no skilled trade, having been too busy with other things during his marriage, but he had expected better treatment from the Australians as a celebrity of the first magnitude. When the Tea Tree Gully Jaycees had brought him and his clan to Australia in 1968 as part of its Operation Opportunity, he was the most prolific father among the year's immigrants. Feeding his family's fifteen mouths out of his own pocket was an inhuman oppression, he had been compelled to pay rent for the two-storey house they occupied, and the 130° heat was enervating, he maintained, citing again the failure of his family to grow.

Poor James – a victim of an historical process. He expected the usual inundation of sympathy Australians pour weekly on the returning migrant family chosen to fill the four-column sob space once reserved for unwed mothers, lost dogs, wolf children, and other unfortunates, but he was the inevitable last straw. Even the *London Evening News* disowned him, calling him and his kind 'a pain in the neck'. Australian newspapers reversed for a few days their editorial policy to publish letters from satisfied migrants, most of whom expressed their complete satisfaction with Johnson's departure to join the 'spineless young men and scruffy women making the most of Britain's dirty, slovenly, and lazy Welfare State'. Johnson's neighbours in the Adelaide suburb of Elizabeth went to press also, annotating his comments; 'each visit to the doctor cost him eighty cents'; 'first quality steak was seventy cents a pound'; 'a whole side of lamb cost two dollars'; with government assistance he could have bought an adequate brick house with garage and all mod. cons. for $10,000. The father-in-law of one of Johnson's escaped children who had married an Australian had a reminiscence or two to set the record straight. Once, he said, he visited Johnson's home and found the Johnson's had not even unpacked – in the $30,000, six-bedroom house that had been given him rent free. After three months the landlord decided to ask $15 weekly rent, to which oppression Johnson responded by moving out. The father-in-law conceded that Johnson did indeed show some signs of suffering from the heat, which in Adelaide's history once got up to 117°; he had come home unexpectedly to find Johnson there, lying in the swimming pool amid thousands of ice cubes.

Johnson was no unique sinner among the latter-day pioneers; he was just another 'moaning Pom'. The new frontiersmen are less sturdy, less steady than those who followed Cook and Flinders to the land Down Under. They go back to the misty isles in such numbers that an unexpected industry has grown up to accommodate them. The Clayton Travel Pty. Ltd. is typical; its continuing box in the *Adelaide Advertiser* reads,

MIGRANTS

RETURNING TO UK, LACK THE FULL FARE

TRAVEL NOW ★ PAY LATER

FROM $50 DEPOSIT

THE CLAYTON PROVEN PLAN IS UNBEATABLE
DEAL DIRECT WITH US IN ADELAIDE
BOOK YOUR CHOICE OF SHIP AND ROUTE
WE ARRANGE FINANCE IN UK OVER 1 TO 2 YEARS
PLEASE POST COUPON TO REPRESENTATIVE

The lemming-drive to go back 'ome has produced one familial enterprise worthy of being American: the father of the family runs an agency which advertises in England for migrants, painting luvly pictures in damp gray tones of Australia, and arranging passage to the Antipodes; his son runs another agency which ships them all back again as soon as disillusion sets in. So wonderful a thing it is to be a reasonable creature, said Benjamin Franklin, for it enables us to find or make a reason for anything we have a mind to do. With the ingenuity and resourcefulness that sent the vanguard of Western imperialism over the watery edge of the Third World, the disaffected immigrants of the 1970s return at last like plucked chickens to roost, but with fresh reasons. One British migrant complained of being put under bond for good behaviour simply because he set fire to the home of a contractor who refused to give him a proper job. A whole mass movement began, drawing centripetally to it other migrants of less happy climes, of an epizootic of alcoholism in laboring gentlemen who back home bent only the least elbow; the high alcoholic content of Australian beer had made unwitting boozers of abstemious men. It was all enough to drive them off their chumps – literally; one third of first-time admissions to the Claremont Hospital Psychiatric Division were migrants among whom schizophrenia was rampant.

So successful have the English been in educating the rest of the world to high quality standards of complaint that Australia now has multitudes of migrants of other colors, creeds, and chromosomes whingeing at a respectably elevated standard. Some Turks are protesting because the Australian government will not allow them the *laisser faire* to grow their traditional crop of opium poppies. Meno Ellas, of uncertain provenance, got himself into so much newsprint that the authorities eventually deported him, and all he did was complain that his art as an acid-rock hippie musician could not flourish in the Philistinic Australian air.

Ellas was replaced in the papers by a Malayan gentleman hungering for education, one Long Fong Ying, expressing bitterness of Oriental intensity over the government's demand that he hurry up and finish a non-degree accounting course he had been noodling over for ten years. Humberto Urriola, late of Brazil (where the Australians observe a gentleman's agreement not to recruit) stormed out of the country because the Australians used his inability to speak English as the reason for giving him employment that stultified his irrepressible need to create. But the prize for imaginative innovation must surely go to the eight British night-shift miners who downed tools because, they said, a ghost waved and groaned at them. 'The British make great strikers', commented the Australian Labor Party.

Urriola's grizzle about language difficulties is most often echoed by returning migrants. A gaggle of Hungarian immigrants threw stones at Australian tanks because the Aussies refuse to give them the courtesy of learning Hungarian, instead of the other way around. They have been encouraged by such idle-handed churchmen as Mr Alan Mathieson of the Dandenong Church of Christ, who thinks it would be only right and proper for Australians to put down that beer and learn to speak Sicilian. 'Why shouldn't we learn their language?' he asked. The ordinary Australian man-in-the-pub, if specifically asked the question, would throw an un-Christian glass of beer in his sallow face with the admonition to 'get stuffed, y' baastid'.

Gentler Australians who form do-gooding organizations like the Good Neighbour Council and the Friendship Groups set up evening classes in English to help the H*Y*M*A*N-K*A*P*L*A*N*S from southern Europe. These volunteers are for the most part very sweet ladies, who mean no more harm than the Doughnut Dugout dear souls of Knutsford who nearly destroyed General George S. Patton, Jr. Their essential failing is their inability to appreciate that Australian English 'Strine' has some marked differences from the tongue that Shakespeare spoke. One of their pupils went with great confidence from class to a tobacconist's shop to buy a pack of Turf (a brand name, not a componential description) cigarettes and came out with bewilderment and a copy of the Melbourne scandal sheet *Truth*. And what, in a practical sense, is the use to a man who has acquired the phrase 'Who has stolen my umbrella?' in a dry country where the artifact in question is known only as a 'brolly'?

There are more non-English speakers among the new

pioneers than one can conveniently poke a stick at. In Melbourne, according to one survey, sixty-five per cent; 25,000 in Wollongong, a tenth of that old city's population; in New South Wales, a hundred primary schools reported at least forty per cent non-English speakers. Altogether, since the migrant program began, a million new Australian *families* have arrived without the wherewithal to speak to the old Australians. Some of these unfortunate people did make an effort to learn some English before their departure from Old Europe; not that it did them much good when confronted by the Strine-speakers. The government, whose politicians are bilingual in the English of their peers and the English of their unwashed constituents, are recognizing the need. The government of New South Wales has issued *A Migrant's Guide to N.S.W., Australia,* with translations of common terms in English and Strine, so that the new innocents abroad can nut out what an Aussie means when he says *'Well, I was going crook at this galah because I took a sickie to shout a good sort a couple of middies and he threatened to dob me in, I told him not to come the raw prawn or I would do my block and so he shot through'.**

It is doubtless hard on the newcomer to overcome the physiological linguistic difficulties when they are aggravated by psychological sets. I personally have gone without butter in several small Australian settlements because I absolutely would not let my tongue utter a pronunciational abomination like 'but-teh'. I should rather have a copy of the Melbourne *Truth*. Nevertheless, more co-operation might be expected from the southern European migrants. It is to be doubted that language ever before stopped the true pioneer in a new country. Where is the spirit of that Mohave Indian who

---

* 'Well, I was venting my anger on a fool because I took a day off because of pretended illness to buy a good-looking girl two ten-ounce beers and he threatened to inform on me. I told him not to attempt it or I would lose control of my temper and so he left unexpectedly.'

greeted Edward Beale with that delightful if untraditional salutation, 'God damn my soul eyes! How de do! How de do!' or the Pitjandjara who threatened the explorer Ernest Giles in his minstrel vocabulary when that worthy man tried to cross the Centre in 1874? What has become of men like Columbus, who made the word *cannibal* to describe the first Americans his countrymen met?

Though the government and the little old ladies are doing all one might reasonably require of a congenitally indolent people, English is not spreading among the migrants at a rate sufficient to satisfy anyone. Without the common language the contracting force known to anthropologists as *campanilismo* works strenuously to petrify the natural separation of the new comers from the old. Italians live with Italians in Little Italys like Leichhardt, New Park, Spring Hill, and Teneriffe in Sydney, and similar urban divisions in other cities. Yugoslavs confine their knifings to other Yugoslavs, contributing in this endeavor almost nothing to the native Australians. One might as well be in inner-core Chicago, where recently a documentary television special was made with the utterances of militant negro youths translated in subtitles at the bottom of the screen.

Much of what is easily put down to discrimination is a self-imposed retreat. Instead of integrating, migrants – especially those from eastern and southern Europe, form their own shopping areas, social clubs, schools, churches, restaurants, kangaroo courts, and techniques of knife-fighting.

At bottom what the trouble is for the new arrivals is culture shock – that shift in behaviour, often small, that warns the intruder he is among strange people from whom he must retreat. The kind of thing Americans find in Paris, where, until recently, one could see behind the Arc de Triomphe a gentlemen's *pissoir* where the occupants' legs were visible and their discharge equally so. On this one subject, newly arrived American men turn and run up the stairs when they enter a men's room and find a little old lady there to hand them a sheet of toilet paper. Or, having got past that psychological hurdle, finding the toilet consisting of a block of concrete (marble, in the better places) with a central hole flanked by two slightly depressed intaglio footprints – nomad toilets, they are called. In Australia these places are closer to what Americans are familiar with – but then there is Australian toilet paper, an unpleasant experience. If he goes from that situation to a restaurant where they put passion fruit seeds on the spaghetti and make hamburgers out of pork, his next move may well be back home.

Newcomers of all nationalities starve to death if they enter an Australian weekend unprovided with provender, since everything closes down in some cities Friday afternoon. One can hit Perth at the beginning of a weekend and not see anyone about except policemen enforcing the commercial curfew. Bloody shocking, as the Australians say. Some improvement is presently noticeable; the state of Victoria introduced a small while back the American practice of keeping shops open on Friday nights – but they are balancing that concession by closing them on Saturday morning. An American in Brisbane will lose weight quickly while he looks about for restaurants serving recognizable food. He may, if he is very fortunate, find Mama Luigi's, where Italian food of a sort is available. The trouble there is that Mama Luigi's does not advertise and has no sign over its door. It's like a whorehouse – one has to know where it is to find it, and then one has to sneak up on it furtively.

The 'ghettoes' produced by culture shock and the need to stay among people one accepts as sane are more a creation of their residents than of their outside oppressors, but since ghetto dwelling is not in best fashion nowadays, the residents of these culture pockets turn the opprobrium against the people outside. That attitude of mind is subsumed now under the neologism *racism*. Never mind that race has almost nothing to do with it in Australia, where 99 out of a hundred urban Australians have never seen a part-blood aborigine and

999 out of a thousand have never seen a full-blood; if there is a need, it will be filled. Thus the Australian Council of Churches, as a relief from condemning America, caught an Australian school teacher instructing his migrant pupils with a blackboard drawing of a long-haired, soiled, peace-loving youth whom he identified with a chorus of students repeating, 'This is a hippie. We don't like him. He is dirty'.

The Australian hippie, a weedy pathetic thing compared to the genuine American variety, is discriminated against. He cannot yet be hated for himself alone. He must fall therefore into the overcrowded category of an underprivileged race to qualify for his rightful share of contempt. Racism and its loathsome offspring, antiracism, dying in America, are all the rage now Down Under, a wonderful, finger-burning social toy everybody is fighting to play with, and people who would be insufferable bores in England and the United States still take headlines in Australia. Consider the case of Mrs Sophie van Rood and her undescribed husband, who have been living on militant sanctimony in a succession of countries and who have found their econiche at last in Australia. She got a big spread in the *Adelaide Advertiser* in August of 1971 under the headline RACIALISM HERE HORRIFYING. 'What drives a woman', asked the lead paragraph, 'with three children, a loving husband, four cats and a gem of a house to stand out in the rain and campaign against [sic] such a controversial issue as racialism?' Mrs van Rood, who hides behind darkened granny glasses as big as saucers, answers from her tender heart, 'I'm neither a crank nor a fanatic – I'm doing this because I care deeply about people and I believe with all my heart that all men are equal, whatever the color of their skin'. Pretty obviously she has never met any fullblood members of the aboriginal race; if she had, the first thing they would have done would have been to eat her four cats. Aborigines are very fond of *putjikata* (pussycats).

Racism is so popular now that we have the amusing phenomenon of minority migrants fighting among themselves. In

July, 1971, the Japanese ambassador Shizuo Saito published a book titled *Australian Despatches* containing a small complaint about the reluctance of the Australian government to admit Japanese immigrants. The Japanese wish to populate Australia is sincere – no question of that. It took the American Pacific fleet to keep them out when they came in through the Coral Sea, and several of them tried to immigrate via submarines in Sydney Harbor. In any event, said Mr Saito-san, it was not fair to exclude Japanese when such folk as Turks were assisted. Turks are not white men, he pointed out. Turks are touchy people, though quite lovable in the dormant state. Somehow Mr Saito's remarks crossed the language barrier. What the bloody hell does he mean, asked the Turks, saying we are not white? We are not only white, they affirmed, but bloody upper-class whites. A racist-religious war threatened, with Turks screaming for the vengeance of Allah from their minarets in Adelaide's factitious slum mosque. An influential peacemaker managed to quiet them down. It was all a mistake, he said. 'Japanese may be yellow, but they're great.' There was some further agitation about the term 'Jap', whether it applied to fat ones or some less nourished. The Japanese did not like to be spoken to this way. An Occidental spokesman threw the *tu quoque* at them, reminding them they used the opprobrious term *gaijin* for white persons. The Japanese answered that their 'discrimination is against all foreigners, not just one nation . . . this is the nut of the problem'. Happily this crisis fizzled out on the fuse – perhaps because the majority of dervishing Turks were insulated behind the culture barrier. Twenty-six of them were found living in one south Melbourne house, and knew little of what was going on outside. One smaller Turkish family was discovered at the time of the Saito *contretemps* to have been living for three months in Australia thinking they were in Germany.

Those Turks who knew they were in Australia had more to annoy them than being deprived of a poppy-growing livelihood and horrid remarks from Japanese. Mrs G. N. Frost, executive officer of the Playgrounds and Recreation Association of Victoria, revealed that Greek children will not play with Italian children and Italian and Greek children will not play with Turkish children. Bussing is on the horizon.

It was all too confusing. The Americans did not have this chaos with their minorities. Perhaps what the Australians, new and old, needed was an amalgamation and simplification of out-groups. Pete Seeger suggested again the mass importation of Melanesians – Oceanic negroes. Walter Lippmann allowed that variety was great, and so in the long run was civil turmoil; he advised less integration. Craig McGregor, author of the popular novel *Don't Talk to Me of Love*, argued that American negroes should be imported. He declared that the black race is going to take over the world presently anyhow and the Australians should assist the inevitable millennium. He did his part by moving to Harlem. He has not been heard from since. Some unkind racists offered the observation that Mr McGregor was a descendant of the Scot who introduced the thistle to Australia.

Not yet fully Americanized, the Australians are at the moment content to let South Africa enjoy the guilt of racism. The Australian Council of Trades Unions announced forthwith that any airline flying the South African rugby team in Australia will be declared 'black'. In the long and glorious history of Australian labor militancy, the term 'black' meant 'worthy to be boycotted and struck by non-scab union workingmen'. But in this surge of new semantics, some Laborites must be puzzled over the curious situation of a group being declared black because they are white.

Perhaps Labor for its myriad sins is suffering most grievously from the contention between the Good People and the Bad. In simple truth they do not know where in hell they are – though they surely are in Hell, or are headed that way. Only a handful of years ago the Labor leader Arthur Calwell summed up the Labor Party's position on the heathen Chinee as immigrant by saying 'Two Wongs don't make a white'. But the numerous visits to China by Mr Monk and other influential Labor gentlemen proved to their satisfaction that the Chinese they met with were pretty damned dumb and therefore might make excellent constituents of Labor districts. Acting on this political discovery and knowing nothing of the Vito Marcantonio story in New York, the Labor Party sent a delegation to China and spread the word that the lid was off, that massive immigration from Asia would be permitted as soon as the Laborites captured national office. Labor Party officials lack, among other things, the subtle touch in political deviousness, and immediately the Labor policy on immigration was a disaster. M. J. Young, Federal ALP secretary, straightened out the misunderstanding. 'The fact is,' he said, 'the Labor Party, as a government, may not bring in one migrant from anywhere. This is something that has to be determined when you are in government. To concerned Australians, who do not expend much profundity of thought in the interpretation of political utterances, that was *orright*. *She'll be right, mate.*

As for the conservatives in the Liberal and Country party, there was Hubert Opperman, new at riding political coattails, who picked up Labor's ball and took it to Sir Peter Heydon, the permanent head of the Department of Immigration, persuading him that domestic worker loss would be offset internationally by letting in non-whites. Heydon changed immigration policy to read 'well qualified people wishing to settle in Australia will be considered on the basis of their suitability as settlers, their ability to integrate readily and their possession of qualifications which are in fact positively useful to Australia'. A bit transparent this; what he was saying was that the racist policy would be continued. No Japs and no Chinks either. Caught in the subterfuge, the only thing Sir Peter could do to escape the dilemma's horns was to die, which he did with grace and promptitude. The official obituary said of him, 'He was closely and personally associated with many of the changes in emphases and attitudes in relation to the immigration programme during the past decade.' Well – one should hope so for the permanent head of the Department of Immigration.

If Australian Immigration is caught now and then in equivocation, one must appreciate its difficulty. They must all follow the directions of the loud majority of Australians as expressed earthily in the pubs, but speak with the fine inscrutability that Australians will not master until the Chinese come in and take over the reins of government. But a survey reported in Arthur Huck's book *The Chinese in Australia* disclosed that only three per cent of Australians wanted negroes to be recruited as immigrants – and the Chinese three per cent likewise. Pretty much the same went for the bloody Irish; only 32 per cent in that survey wanted recruitment of Irish, a people often considered members of the white race. In assessing Australian attitudes, we must remember the Great Australian Joke, which has to do with two Irishmen standing outside the kangaroo enclosure at the Dublin zoo. 'Ehhh, whut are them things leppin' about, Martin?' asks Pat. 'Ah, Patrick, I'm ashamed o' yer ignorance. Sure and they're kangaroos – *natives of Australia.*' 'Ah, Jaysus, Mary, and Joseph,' wailed Pat, 'me sister married one o' thim things.'

Whatever the ultimate source of their xenophobia, the Aussies have become as disillusioned with massive immigration as Americans have with bussing. Pete Seeger's appeal for a prefabricated black problem has had a disappointing response; up to September of 1970 only five Melanesians had been permitted entry, and from the rest of the Pacific, only two others. Seven in all. Considering the circumstance that the overwhelming bulk of immigrants into Australia are British, the vote of opposition to further immigration is startling: sixty per cent of Australians want it stopped, and only ten per cent think there are too few migrants. That ten per cent is significant in a country which, like the United States, can be relied upon for a solid thirty per cent nut vote that will favor anything. There are exceptions of course in that depthless spring of lunatics with which all nations are afflicted; there exists even a band of philanthropists who are putting up money and effort to accomplish the immigration of Chinese forgers of American currency. But the migrant population now – eighteen per cent – is certainly near its acceptable limit.

The United States, a stentorian declaimer of democracy, has told its people bussing is like spinach; it is good for them whether they like it or not, and they'd bloody well better learn to swallow it. Australia, on the other hand, which makes no pretence at all of respecting the opinions of the Great Unwashed, is responding to the will of the people. The rate of new immigration for 1972 has been announced: 100,000, down 30,000. The cut is unavoidable, we are informed; inflationary pressures alone demand a cutback. And then there is the burden of supporting integration services once the immigrants are in.

Economists show that only a quarter of the $A1.5 billion spent for immigration recruiting would be enough to buy out all overseas investment in the new mining enterprises. The anti-pollutionists have got into the argument as well; they say the side effects of population growth, the spoilage of the environment by people, require a cessation of immigration. Working out of this reasoning, demographers argue that the birthrate for Britons and native-born Australians is less than three per 10,000 population, while that of eastern Europeans is more than ten. Therefore, the more prolific nationalities must be restrained by a neo-Malthusian device of keeping the baastids out. If these reasons do not satisfy, the government is prepared to issue its best reasons – no reason at all. It simply does not approve certain applicants. In 1970 only five out of three hundred applicants for passage assistance from persons of non-European descent living in Great Britain were approved; none were approved for non-European applicants outside Britain.

The Australian immigration authorities are managing the selective system with all its contradictions with deadly efficiency, but one wishes for the winsome hypocrisy of old, before the Natal Act of 1901 was replaced years ago. Under that law, the language test was an insurmountable obstacle against undesirable aliens. It was simple. Before being permitted to enter Australia for the purpose of residence, an applicant had to pass a literacy test – in whatever language the immigration authorities nominated. A fairly typical case was that of Mrs Mary Freer, an Englishwoman of ambiguous character, who was required to translate a passage read to her in Italian. With that desperate but futile resourcefulness that motivated her illiterate forebears who tried to read passages from the Bible on the scaffold so as to escape hanging by benefit of clergy, Mrs Freer clapped her hands over her ears and pleaded she could not pass the test because she could not hear it. Only one person came close to beating the literacy test, a Czech political activist named Egon Kisch, who was given his test in Gaelic. He took the matter to court and proved that Gaelic was not a language. The Irish were driven mad, but the immigration people simply gave Mr Kisch another test – in Portuguese. He failed.

Probably the new restrictiveness would be more vociferously opposed from the glassy Tower of Babel on the East River if the tide of demography were not running against the conquest of the last frontier. Australia is not the only rich nation conducting a feast at whose doors the beggars beat. West Germany calls louder to the poor; it has brought in nearly two million 'guest workers' since its postwar prosperity began by such inducements as old age pensions to be paid in the country of the temporary immigrant's origin. The Italian dreams now of working for a time in Germany and retiring on German pensions to the fountain under his own olive trees. Does he not fear the Russian bear, breathing fire over the Wall? Does he fear living on the slopes of Vesuvius?

These immutable movements to and fro are bewildering

the Australians. As they cut, so they bind up. Queensland is spending $185,000 this year to send didjeridu players abroad to attract migrants. Would anyone come to Australia because there are didjeridus there? As that sensible Frenchman said years ago on another matter, this is nonsense, and one does not give reasons for nonsense.

Meanwhile, standing almost alone in these swirls of movement and counter-movement on the last frontier are the Americans. Many mature Americans feel that somehow the America they knew is gurgling down a cosmic drain along with vaudeville, steam locomotives, buggy whips, and the Catholic Church. There must be some place to hide. But can it be beyond the borders of America? Such things cannot be. Perhaps no other people on earth of any consequence are constitutionally less inclined to abandon their homeland than Americans; outside its spiritual boundaries they are as lost as a Pitjandjara native straying into Aranda territory. Something of their souls is gone. Only the oddest of them can put real roots down anywhere but in American soil. But now in America the old spirit, the holding spirit, is vanishing. Perhaps there is no longer any *tjukurpa*, any *alchera*, no spirit of the land part of their spirit.

When their souls were strong, the Americans had no business knowing anything of the outside world with which they did business. They do not learn foreign languages, they do not learn geography. Few veterans of the Viet Nam war can place the country on a map. The average American who escaped going to the Pacific wars knows little about Australia beyond the suspicion that it is somewhat sizeable, offshore from Los Angeles, vaguely south of Hawaii. He calls its residents 'Bushmen', he knows it has kangaroos, and the inhabitants speak a weird corruption of English when they are not drinking beer. Further the deponent sayeth not, but holdeth his own counsel.

The Americans have not convinced the rest of the world they are as wicked as they presume themselves to be, for all their killing of Indians and Communist children, for all their finding some pleasure in the sense and most pleasure in an aching conscience. Australian television producers are thoroughly fed up with the incessant exports from America of documentaries showing Americans squirting Chemical Mace into the faces of shaggy twenty-year-old children who are only asking to give cop-killing a chance.

Those who have visited Australia find at least two astonishing things that quite overcome the culture shock of finding boiled pumpkin on their dinner plates: that Americans are well liked and that being well liked is incomparably more satisfying to the normal soul than wallowing in guilt for sins their forefathers never committed. The American in Australia discovers that the bad conscience he has nourished all of his life is an operable nuisance.

The word is getting around. One hundred thousand Americans inquired about emigration to Australia in 1971. One in ten of them actually made the traumatic departure; perhaps two in ten will go in 1972. Many will come back, unable to attain separation speed. But that means nothing so far as the Australian land and Australian culture are concerned; half the number of Statesiders who emigrate to Hawaii come back again. The last frontier still holds its superiorities: jobs for everyone except university teachers (perhaps this deprivation is attributable to the Australians' understanding that most of the civil and social chaos in America can be laid at the door of the ivory tower), salaries high enough to offer a standard of living comparable to that of the United States with incomparably more opportunities for the enterprising and energetic, marvelous climate of any sort one fancies; bloody fine beer; and the world's best bushflies. And more than all these things, the chance to find America again.

Bibliography

ADAMS, James Truslow, *The Founding of New England*. Boston: The Atlantic Monthly Press, 1921

ALLEN, H. C., *Bush and Backwoods. A Comparison of the Frontier in Australia and the United States*. East Lansing: Michigan State University Press, 1959

ASBURY, Herbert, *The Barbary Coast*. New York: Alfred A. Knopf, 1933

AUSTRALIA: Commonwealth Bureau of Census and Statistics. *Official Yearbook of the Commonwealth of Australia*. Canberra: Commonwealth Government Printer, 1968. No. 54

AUSTRALIA: Ministry of the Interior. *Handbook – Australia 1969* Sydney: Halstead Press, 1969

AUSTRALIA: Australian News and Information Bureau. *Australian Weekly News*. San Francisco: Australian Consulate General

BACON, Sir Francis. *Essays or Counsels, Civil and Moral*. 1625 (Edition of Ellis, Spedding, and Heath, 1857-1859)

BAKER, Sidney J. *The Pacific Book of Australiana*. Sydney: Angus and Robertson, 1967

BARKER, H. M. *Camels and the Outback*. Sydney: Angus and Robertson, 1964

BARNARD, Marjorie. *A History of Australia*. Sydney: Angus and Robertson, 1963

BEADELL, Len. *Too Long in the Bush*. Adelaide: Rigby, Ltd. 1965

BEEBE, Lucius and Charles Clegg. *The American West: The Pictorial Epic of a Continent.* New York: E. P. Dutton, 1955

BILLINGTON, Ray Allen. *America's Frontier Heritage.* New York: Holt, Rinehart and Winston, 1966

BLAINEY, William. *The Rush that Never Ended.* Melbourne: Melbourne University Press, 1963

BOYD, Robin. 'American Culture in Australia: Mass Communications'. *In* Harper, *Pacific Orbit,* 144-154

BRADFORD, William. *History of Plimmoth Plantation.* First printing: Boston Historical Society, 1856

BRASH, Donald T. *American Investment in Australian Industry.* Canberra: Australian National University Press, 1966

BULL, John Wrathall, *Early Experiences of Colonial Life in South Australia.* Adelaide: *Advertiser,* 1878

BURT, A. L. 'If Turner Had Looked at Canada, Australia, and New Zealand When He Wrote about the West'. *In* Wyman-Kroeber, 79-94

BURT, Olive Woolley. *American Murder Ballads and Their Stories.* New York: Oxford University Press, 1958

CARNEGIE, David W. *Spinifex and Sand: A Narrative of Five Years' Pioneering and Exploration in Western Australia.* New York: M. F. Mansfield and Company, 1898

CARTER, H. B. *His Majesty's Spanish Flock.* Sydney: Angus and Robertson, 1964

CASEY, Gavin, and Ted Mayman. *The Mile that Midas Touched.* Adelaide: Rigby, Ltd. 1964

CAUDILL, Harry. *Night Comes to the Cumberlands.* Boston: Little, Brown and Co., 1962

CHADWICK, R. 'New Extraction Processes for Metals'. *In* Singer, Holmyard, Hall, and Williams, V, 72-101

CHISHOLM, Alec H., gen. ed. *The Australian Encyclopaedia.* Sydney: Grolier Society, 1965 (actual date of publication: 1969)

CLARK, Manning. *A Short History of Australia.* New York: The New American Library (Mentor), 1963

CLARK, Manning, ed. *Sources of Australian History*. London: Oxford University Press, 1957

CLARK, Thomas D. *The Rampaging Frontier*. Bloomington: Indiana University Press, 1939

CLEMENS, Samuel L. [Mark Twain]. *Following the Equator*. Hartford, Connecticut: The American Publishing Co., 1897

COCHRAN, Thomas C. and William Miller. *The Age of Enterprise: A Social History of Industrial America*. New York: The Macmillan Company, 1942

COLE, G. D. H. and Raymond Postgate. *The British People*. New York: Alfred A. Knopf, 1947

COLLINS, Tom [Joseph Furphy]. *Such Is Life*. Sydney: The *Bulletin*, 1903

CRAWFORD, J. G. 'Partnership in Trade'. *In* Harper, Norman, 42-66

DAMPIER, William. *A New Voyage Around the World*. London: The Argonaut Press, 1927

DELORIA, Vine, Jr. *Custer Died for Your Sins*. London: The Macmillan Company, 1969

DE TOCQUEVILLE, Alexis. *Democracy in America*. Oxford: World Classics Edition, 1946

DODD, Alan P. 'The Biological Control of Prickly Pear in Australia'. *In* Keast, A., *Biogeography and Ecology in Australia*, 565-577

DOWNES, R. G. 'The Ecology and Prevention of Soil Erosion'. *In* Keast, A., *Biogeography and Ecology in Australia*, 473-486

DRAGO, Harry Sinclair. *Great American Cattle Trails*. New York; Dodd, Mead & Company, 1956

DROWER, M. S. 'Water-Supply, Irrigation, and Agriculture'. *In* Singer, Holmyard, and Hall, I, 520-557

DUGGER, Ronnie. 'Oil and Politics'. *In The Atlantic*, September, 1969, 66-90

DUTTON, Geoffrey. *The Hero as Murderer: The Life of Edward John Eyre Australian Explorer and Governor of Jamaica 1815-1901.* Sydney: William Collins Limited, 1967

EARP, G. Butler. *The Gold Colonies of Australia: Compromising Their History, Territorial Divisions, Produce, and Capabilities; Also, Ample Notices of the Gold Mines, and How to Get to Them: with Every Advice to Emigrants.* London: 1852

FERRIS, Robert G., ed. *Prospector, Cowhand, and Sodbuster. Historic Places Associated with the Mining, Ranching, and Farming Frontiers in the Trans-Mississippi West.* Washington, D.C.: U.S. Department of the Interior, 1967

FITZPATRICK, Brian. *A Short History of the Australian Labor Movement.* Melbourne: Rawson's Bookshop, 1944

FORBES, R. J. 'Extracting, Smelting, and Alloying'. *In* Singer, Holmyard, and Hall, I, 572-599

FOWLER, Harlan D. *Camels to California.* Stanford: Stanford University Press, 1950

GILES, Ernest. *Australia Twice Traversed.* London: Sampson Low, Marston, Searle & Rivington, 1889

GILLETT, James B. *Six Years with the Texas Rangers, 1875 to 1881.* Edited, with an Introduction, by M. M. Quaife. New Haven: Yale University Press, 1963 (first published 1921)

GLEASON, Henry A., and Arthur Cronquist. *The Natural Geography of Plants.* New York: Columbia University Press, 1964

GOULD, Peter R. 'Man Against His Environment: A Game Theoretic Framework'. *In* Andrew P. Vayda, ed., *Environment and Cultural Behavior.* Garden City, NY: The Natural History Press, 1969

GREENWAY, Joan Disher. Interview with Shorty O'Neill

GREENWAY, John. *American Folksongs of Protest.* Philadelphia: University of Pennsylvania Press, 1953

GREENWAY, John. 'Australian Cattle Lingo'. *In American Speech,* October, 1958, 163-169

GREENWAY, John. 'Australian Folksongs and Ballads'. 12" LP

phonograph record, with background notes. New York: Folkways Records and Service Corp., 1959

GREENWAY, John. 'The Austramerican West'. *In The American West*, V, 1 (January, 1968), 33-37, 75-79

GREENWAY, John. Foreword to George Korson, *Coal Dust on the Fiddle*. Hatboro, Pa.: Folklore Associates, 1965

GREENWAY, John. *The Inevitable Americans*. New York: Alfred A. Knopf, 1964

GREENWAY, John. 'The Songs and Stories of Aunt Molly Jackson'. 12" LP phonograph record, with background notes. New York: Folkways Records and Service Corp., 1961

HANCOCK, W. K. *Survey of British Commonwealth Affairs*. Vol. II: *Problems of Economic Policy, 1918-1939*. Part 1. London: Oxford University Press, 1942

HARPER, Norman. *Pacific Orbit: Australian-American Relations Since 1942*. New York: The Humanities Press, 1969

[HARRIS, Alexander] *Settlers and Convicts: or Recollections of Sixteen Years' Labour in the Australian Backwoods. By an Emigrant Mechanic*. London: 1847. Reprinted, London: Cambridge University Press, 1953

HARRIS, Marvin. *The Rise of Anthropological Theory*. New York: Crowell, 1968

HOFFER, Eric. *The True Believer*. New York: Harper and Brothers, 1951

HOFSTADER, Richard and Seymour Martin Lipset, eds., *Turner and the Sociology of the Frontier*. New York: Basic Books, 1968

HOLBROOK, Stewart H. *The Age of the Moguls*. New York: Doubleday & Co., 1953

HOOVER, Herbert. *Memoirs*. Volume One: *Years of Adventure, 1874-1920*. New York: Macmillan, 1951-1952

HORAN, James D. *The Great American West*. New York: Crown Publishers, Inc., 1959

HORNE, Donald. *The Lucky Country. Australia in the Sixties*. Adelaide: Penguin Books, rev. ed., 1964

HORNE, Donald, and David Beal. *Southern Exposure*. Sydney: Collins, 1967

HOUSEHOLD, Geoffrey. *Thing to Love*. London: Michael Joseph, 1963

INGLETON, Geoffrey Chapman, ed. *True Patriots All, or News from Early Australia as Told in a Collection of Broadsides*. Sydney: Angus & Robertson, 1952

JENKS, Leland Hamilton. *The Migration of British Capital to 1875*. London: Thomas Nelson and Sons Ltd., 1927

JONES, Kenneth L. *Botanical Essays for Humanists*. Ann Arbor, Mich.: George Wahr Publishing Co., 1968

KEAST, Allen. *Biogeography and Ecology in Australia*. Den Haag: Uitgeverij Dr W. Junk, 1959

KLOSE, Nelson. *A Concise Study Guide to the American Frontier*. Lincoln: University of Nebraska Press, 1964

LEARMONTH, A. T. A. and A. M. Learmonth. *Encyclopaedia of Australia*. London: Frederick Warne & Co. Ltd., 1968

LEET, L. Don, and Sheldon Judson. *Physical Geology*. Englewood Cliffs, N. J.: Prentice-Hall, Inc., 1965

LEWIS, Marvin. *The Mining Frontier. Contemporary Accounts from the American West in the Nineteenth Century*. Norman: University of Oklahoma Press, 1967

LINGENFELTER, Richard E., Richard A. Dwyer, and David Cohen, eds., *Songs of the American West*. Berkeley: University of California Press, 1968

LINTON, Ralph. *The Tree of Culture*. New York: Alfred A. Knopf, 1957

LONG, Luman H., ed. *1969 Edition the World Almanac and Book of Facts*. New York: Newspaper Enterprise Association , Inc., 1969

MACDOUGAL, Daniel Trembly. *Botanical Features of North American Deserts*. Washington: Carnegie Institution of Washington, 1908

MALORY, Sir Thomas. *Le Morte Darthur*. London: Macmillan and Co., 1893 (first published 1485 by William Caxton; MS concluded 1469)

MERRY, D. H. 'The American Impact on Australian Business'. *In* Harper, 108-122

MIKESELL, Marvin. 'Comparative Studies in Frontier History'. *In Annals* (Association of American Geographers), Vol. 50, 1960, 62-74

MIKESELL, Marvin W. 'Patterns and Imprints of Mankind'. *In* Forstall, Richard L. *et al., Rand McNally The International Atlas.* Chicago: Rand McNally & Company, 1969·

MONAGHAN, Jay. *Australians and the Gold Rush. California and Down Under 1849-1854.* Berkeley: University of California Press, 1966

MOORE, R. M. 'Ecological Observations on Plant Communities Grazed by Sheep in Australia'. *In* Keast, *Biogeography and Ecology in Australia,* 500-513

MOOREHEAD, Alan. *Cooper's Creek.* London: Hamish Hamilton, 1963

MUDIE, Ian. *Riverboats.* Melbourne: Sun Books, 1965

NEF, J. U. 'Coal Mining and Utilization'. *In* Singer, Holmyard, Hall, and Williams, III, 72-88

PARAMONOV, S. J. 'Zoogeographical Aspects of the Australian Dipterofauna'. *In* Keast, *Biography and Ecology in Australia,* 164-210

PARRINGTON, Vernon Louis. *Main Currents in American Thought.* New York: Harcourt, Brace and Company, 1930

PEARL, Irma and Cyril Pearl. *Our Yesterdays: Australian Life Since 1853 in Photographs.* Sydney: Angus and Robertson, 1954

PORTIS, Charles. *True Grit.* New York: Simon and Schuster, 1968

RAGGATT, H. G. *Mountains of Ore.* Melbourne: Lansdowne Press, 1968

RARICK, John R. 'Censorship of Free Speech'. *U.S. Congressional Record,* 23 January 1969

RATCLIFFE, F. N. 'The Rabbit in Australia'. *In* Keast, *Biogeography and Ecology in Australia,* 545-564

RITSON, J. A. S. 'Metal and Coal Mining, 1750-1875'. *In* Singer, Holmyard, and Hall, IV, 64-98

ROBBINS, Roy M. *Our Landed Heritage. The Public Domain, 1776-1936.* Princeton: Princeton University Press, 1942

ROBINSON, Ray, compiler. *The Wit of Sir Robert Menzies.* London: Leslie Frewin, 1966

RUDD, Steele [Arthur Hoey Davis]. *On Our Selection and Our New Selection.* Sydney: Angus and Robertson, 1955 (first published in 1899)

SAGAN, Carl, Jonathan Norton Leonard, and the editors of *Life. Planets.* New York: Time Incorporated, 1966

SAN Jacinto Museum of History Association. *Camels in Texas.* San Jacinto, Texas: n.d.

SAUER, Carl O. 'Historical Geography and the Western Frontier'. *In* Willard, James F. and Colin B. Goodykoontz, eds., *Trans-Mississippi West.* Boulder, Colo.: University of Colorado Press, 1930

SCHANTZ, H. L. and Raphael Zon. *Atlas of American Agriculture.* Washington: Bureau of Agricultural Economics, 1924

SCHULTZ, William J. *Financial Development of the United States.* New York: Prentice-Hall, Inc., 1937

SHIRLEY, Glenn. *Law West of Fort Smith. A History of Frontier Justice in the Indian Territory, 1834-1896.* Lincoln: University of Nebraska Press, 1957

SIDNEY, Samuel. *The Three Colonies of Australia.* London: Ingram, Cooke, and Co., 1853

SIMON, André. *The Wines, Vineyards, and Vignerons of Australia.* London: Paul Hamlyn, 1967

SINGER, Charles, E. J. Holmyard, A. R. Hall, and Trevor I. Williams, eds. *A History of Technology.* New York: Oxford University Press, 5 volumes, 1954-1958

SMITH, Eleanor. *The Beckoning West. The Story of H. S. Trotman and the Canning Stock Route.* Sydney: Angus and Robertson, 1966

SMITH, Henry Nash. *Virgin Land. The American West as*

Symbol and Myth. Cambridge: Harvard University Press, 1950

STEFFENS, Lincoln. *The Autobiography of Lincoln Steffens*. New York: Harcourt, Brace and Company, 1931

ST John, J. Hector [St Jean de Crevecoeur] *Letters from an American Farmer*. London, 1782

STURT, Charles. *Narrative of an Expedition into Central Australia . . . During the Years 1844, 5, and 6*. London: T. and W. Boone, 1849. Two volumes

[THATCHER, Charles] *Thatcher's Colonial Songs. Forming a Complete Comic History of the Early Diggings*. Melbourne: Charlwood and Son, 1864

TRAIN, George Francis. *My Life in Many States and in Foreign Lands*. New York: D. Appleton and Company, 1902

TROLLOPE, Mrs Frances. *Domestic Manners of the Americans*. New York: Alfred A. Knopf, 1949 (first published in London, 1832)

TROUGHTON, E. le G. 'The Marsupial Fauna: Its Origin and Radiation'. *In* Keast, *Biogeography and Ecology in Australia*, 69-88

UPFIELD, Arthur. *Death of a Lake*. Garden City, N.Y.: Doubleday, 1954

U.S. Bureau of the Census. *Historical Statistics of the United States*, Colonial Times to 1957. Washington, D.C.: 1960

U.S. Bureau of the Census. *Statistical Abstract of the United States: 1969* (90th edition). Washington, D.C.: 1969

U.S. Department of Labor. *Labor Law and Practise in Australia*. Washington, D.C. Superintendent of Documents, BLS Report No. 328, 1967

VOGT, William. *Road to Survival*. New York: William Sloane Associates, Inc. 1948

WALLACE, Christopher M. *Water Out of the Desert*. El Paso: Texas Western Press (Southwestern Studies, Monograph No. 22), 1969

WANNAN, Bill. *The Australian. Yarns, Ballads, Legends and*

Traditions of the Australian People. Melbourne: Australasian Book Society, 1954

WANNAN, Bill, ed. *A Treasury of Australian Frontier Tales*. Melbourne: Lansdowne Press, 1961

WARD, Russel. 'American Roles in Australian Folk Ballads'. Broadcast lecture recorded for the Australian Broadcasting Commission 20 October 1954

WARD, Russel. *The Australian Legend*. Melbourne: Oxford University Press, 1958

WEBB, Walter Prescott. *The Great Frontier*. Boston: Houghton Mifflin Company, 1951-1952

WEBB, Walter Prescott. *The Great Plains*. Boston: Ginn and Company, 1931

WHITE, Osmar. *Guide to Australia*. Melbourne: Heinemann, 1968

WINTHROP, John. *Winthrop's Journal: 'History of New England', 1630-1649*. Edited by James Kendall Hosmer. New York: Charles Scribner's Sons, 1908

WOODHAM-SMITH, Cecil. *The Great Hunger: Ireland 1845-1849*. New York: Harper & Row, Publishers, Inc., 1964

WYMAN, Walker D., and Clifton B. Kroeber. *The Frontier in Perspective*. Madison: *University of Wisconsin Press*, 1957

Index

Index

VERMONT COLLEGE
MONTPELIER, VERMONT